SCIENCE AND CULTURE PRESS INC.

HANDBOOK PLUS

THE HANDBOOK FOR TODAY'S DRIVER

EFFICIENT DRIVING

INTELLIGENT DRIVING

DEFENSIVE DRIVING

Student's name : Aaron Sutton

PROPULSION INTERNATIONAL INC.

Preface

You are soon going to find yourself behind the wheel of a motorized vehicle assuming some very serious responsibilities. Your goal will be to share the roadway with all the other vehicles, cyclists, and pedestrians in such a manner as to acquit yourself both DEFENSIVELY, INTELLIGENTLY and COOPERATIVELY.

This text, presented in a concise, informative and instructional format, synthesizes the improvements that both science and research have made in the strategies needed to safely and intelligently operate a vehicle in this day and age on our modern highways.

Your best teacher will be experience, but it must be based on the professional training you received from a traffic safety education program. Building on this training, you have a solid foundation on which you can continue developing your skills. Your driving will then be a safe, pleasant and rewarding experience.

Charles D. Torreiro

Charles D. Torreiro
Editor

William M. Cole, Ph.D.
Dan Com
Jean Pierre Plouffe
Peter Ross-Easton
Consultants

PIX•IMAGE
Eric Beaulieu
Illustrator

CINTOR
PRODUCTIONS
Page Setting

PROPULSION INTERNATIONAL WISHES TO THANK ALL THE TRAFFIC SAFETY EDUCATORS, DRIVING INSTRUCTORS, RESEARCHERS, ETC. WHO CONTRIBUTED TO THIS MANUAL!

EXCLUSIVE DISTRIBUTOR

Calgary / Los Angeles / Moncton
Montréal / Seattle / Toronto
3500 Boul. Matte, Suite 214
Brossard, Québec
J4Y 2Z2

Tel.: (450) 444-7000   Toll free: 888 444-7001
Fax: (450) 444-1625   Web site: Prop-Drivers-Ed.com

Table of Contents

CHAPTER 1 - HIGHWAY TRANSPORTATION SYSTEM

1 - A   Understanding the H.T.S. 1.2
1 - B   Sharing the Road 1.2
1 - C   Responsibilities of Road Users 1.5
1 - D   Review 1.6

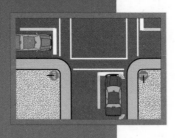

CHAPTER 2 - TRAFFIC CONTROL DEVICES

2 - A   Traffic Signs 2.2
2 - B   International Signs 2.16
2 - C   Pavement Marking 2.20
2 - D   Traffic Signals 2.22
2 - E   Traffic Control Persons 2.25
2 - F   Hand Signals 2.26
2 - G   Review 2.27

CHAPTER 3 - ADMINISTRATIVE LAWS

3 - A   General Information 3.2
3 - B   Driver's Licenses 3.2
3 - C   Certificate of Title/Registration 3.3
3 - D   License Control Measures 3.4
3 - E   Rules of the Road 3.6
3 - F   In Case of a Collision 3.9
3 - G   Review 3.10

CHAPTER 4 - PHYSICAL AND MENTAL HEALTH

4 - A   Physical Health 4.2
4 - B   Mental Health 4.4
4 - C   Vision 4.9
4 - D   Carbon Monoxide 4.11
4 - E   Review 4.12

CHAPTER 5 - KNOWING YOUR VEHICLE

5 - A   The Cockpit Drill 5.2
5 - B   The Instrument Panel 5.2
5 - C   The Vehicle Controls 5.4
5 - D   Comfort and Convenience Devices 5.10
5 - E   Review 5.11

CHAPTER 6 - PRELIMINARIES

6 - A   Approach to the Vehicle 6.2
6 - B   Pre-Driving Protocol 6.3
6 - C   Blind spots 6.5
6 - D   Pre-Drive Inspection and Maintenenace 6.7
6 - E   Review 6.9

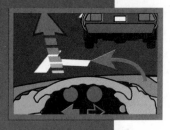

CHAPTER 7 - BASIC MANEUVERS

7 - A   Starting the Engine 7.2
7 - B   Steering and Visual Tracking 7.4
7 - C   Entering Traffic 7.5
7 - D   Acceleration and Braking 7.7
7 - E   Reversing 7.12
7 - F   Leaving Traffic 7.13
7 - G   Visual Referencing 7.17
7 - H   Review 7.18

SCAN
IDENTIFY
PREDICT
DECIDE
EXECUTE

CHAPTER 8 - DEFENSIVE DRIVING

8 - A   The Attitude 8.2
8 - B   The SIPDE System 8.2
8 - C   Managing Time and Space 8.4
8 - D   Adapting to the H.T.S. 8.8
8 - E   Review 8.9

CHAPTER 9 - LAWS OF PHYSICS

9 - A   Friction 9.2
9 - B   Gravity 9.3
9 - C   Kinetic Energy 9.5
9 - D   Inertia 9.6
9 - E   Force of Impact 9.8
9 - F   Review 9.9

CHAPTER 10 - STOPPING DISTANCES

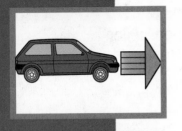

10 - A Time and Distances 10.2
10 - B Danger Zone 10.4
10 - C Braking Techniques 10.5
10 - D ABS Brakes 10.6
10 - E Review 10.7

CHAPTER 11 - RESTRAINT SYSTEMS

11 - A Safety Belts 11.2
11 - B Air Bags 11.4
11 - C Child Restraints 11.4
11 - D A Few Facts 11.6
11 - E Review 11.7

CHAPTER 12 - DRIVING TECHNIQUES

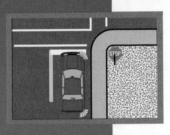

12 - A Basic Rules 12.2
12 - B Intersections 12.5
12 - C The Urban Environment 12.9
12 - D The Rural Environment 12.10
12 - E The Expressway Environment 12.12
12 - F Turning About 12.15
12 - G Parking 12.19
12 - H Review 12.26

CHAPTER 13 - ADVERSE CONDITIONS

13 - A Road Conditions 13.2
13 - B Visual Conditions 13.9
13 - C Winter Conditions 13.15
13 - D Review 13.21

CHAPTER 14 - EMERGENCY SITUATIONS

14 - A Vehicle Failures 14.2
14 - B Driver Error 14.9
14 - C Road Sharing Errors 14.12
14 - D Emergency Vehicles 14.13
14 - E Unusual Occurrences 14.14
14 - F Review 14.15

CHAPTER 15 - **THE ENGINE AND POWER TRAIN**

15 - A Internal Combustion Engine 15.2
15 - B The Cooling System 15.4
15 - C The Lubrication System 15.5
15 - D The Electrical System 15.7
15 - E The Fuel System 15.8
15 - F The Exhaust System 15.10
15 - G Power Train 15.11
15 - H Boosting a Vehicle 15.12
15 - I   Review 15.13

CHAPTER 16 - **THE CHASSIS**

16 - A Tires 16.2
16 - B The Suspension System 16.5
16 - C The Steering System 16.6
16 - D The Brake System 16.7
16 - E The Body 16.8
16 - F Review 16.9

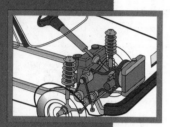

CHAPTER 17 - **BUYING A VEHICLE**

17 - A Deciding to buy 17.2
17 - B Choosing a Vehicle 17.2
17 - C Financing your Purchase 17.7
17 - D Insuring your Vehicle 17.8
17 - E Review 17.10

CHAPTER 18 - **PLANNING A TRIP**

18 - A Choosing a Safe Route 18.2
18 - B Preparing the Vehicle 18.3
18 - C Preparing Yourself 18.4
18 - D Planning the Route 18.5
18 - E Review 18.6

GLOSSARY

INDEX

ANSWER KEY

I - A
Understanding the HTS

I - B
Sharing the Road

I - C
Responsibilities of Road Users

I - D
Review

The Highway Transportation System

The United States is one of the most mobile societies in the world. A vast network of highways has been built to accommodate the public and private vehicles that provide this mobility. From pedestrians to the largest transport trucks, they all share this system.

Each individual person, whether walking, riding a bicycle or operating a motorized vehicle, is the nucleus of the safe and efficient operation of the Highway Transportation System or HTS.

The responsibility of each individual is to respect the rules of the system as they apply to him or her and cooperate with other road users. You are already familiar with the HTS as it applies to pedestrians and, perhaps, cyclists. Now that you are becoming a driver, you must become more familiar with this role and its responsibilities.

AFTER COMPLETING THIS CHAPTER, THE STUDENT MUST BE ABLE TO UNDERSTAND, IDENTIFY AND RESPOND TO:

- **the concept of the Highway Transportation System.**
- **sharing the HTS with other road users.**
- **the individual role and responsibilities of road users.**

Understanding the HTS

As a passenger, you have more than likely experienced some of the freedom that an automobile provides. Many millions of Americans drive countless miles every day in their automobiles for a wide variety of reasons. Meanwhile, others ride bicycles or motorcycles, drive trucks, vans, or buses to earn their livelihood, or operate emergency or other vehicles to supply essential public services. All of these people (and others) must share the same streets, roads, and highways. This inevitably leads to conflicts.

A multitude of professionals are involved in the proper planning or improvement of this complex system of roadways. From the planning, the design, to the placement of traffic control devices, engineers labor to provide a safe environment. Municipal, state and federal regulations govern all aspects of the use of the HTS. Yet, despite all of these efforts, the safe operation of the HTS depends on the attitude and behavior of each of its users.

With the freedom and mobility that the ability to drive will grant you, you must be prepared to accept the responsibilities as well. It is your duty to know the rules, to abide by them and, further, to be courteous and communicate with other road users. You are responsible for your safety, the safety of your passengers, as well as the safety of other users who share the HTS.

If your vehicle was alone on the road, driving would be a simple task. The fact is that the HTS is becoming more and more crowded every day.

Sharing the Road

In order to be able to anticipate potential hazards, it is important to understand the special needs and characteristics of the others who will be sharing the roadway.

To share the road safely and effectively, you must observe, anticipate the movements of others, and communicate your intentions. Proper management of visibility, time and space (Chapter 8) will minimize the risks that are inherent in driving a vehicle in the HTS.

PEDESTRIANS

Pedestrians are the most vulnerable and least trained of roadway users. Many do not drive and do not understand the characteristics of motorized vehicles. They may not know or obey the traffic rules and signals; nor understand the problems of visibility when driving, especially at night.

Children are unpredictable. They are smaller and more difficult to see. Their poor judgement and understanding of the consequences may lead them to run into the roadway. Watch for them near playgrounds, schools, at the side of the road and, in many areas where they may use the street as their playground.

The elderly and the physically or visually impaired are slower to decide and then to cross the roadway. Be patient, give them the extra time required.

Adults, who should know better, often jaywalk or dart into the roadway without looking especially in bad weather, when jogging, or when hurrying.

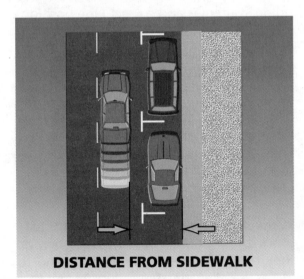

DISTANCE FROM SIDEWALK

Always yield to pedestrians, even when they do not have the right-of-way.

Cooperate and stop when other drivers stop to yield to pedestrians crossing. Reduce your speed and increase your space from the curb in areas where they are present. Communicate, tap your horn from a distance to attract their attention. Make sure they see you. At intersections, always check for pedestrian movement before entering, whether turning or proceeding straight ahead.

ANIMALS

Small animals, whether a dog in the city or a raccoon in the country, may dart into your path. Swerve or brake sharply if either can be done safely; never risk a collision or put someone's life in jeopardy to avoid a small animal.

Large animals, like deer, horses, etc., can cause considerable damage to your vehicle and its occupants. Swerve or brake sharply and, if a collision is inevitable, choose the less critical option.

In either situation, you can minimize the hazard by watching for animals, reducing your speed and leaving as wide a margin of safety as possible. Be especially vigilant at dusk, at night, in fog, and when signs are posted to warn of animal crossings or "Open Range".

BICYCLES

Cyclists are using the HTS in ever increasing numbers for pleasure, to work, or to commute. They swerve to avoid storm drains, puddles, potholes, and debris on the roadway and may move into your path. Many disregard traffic signs, signals, and rules of right-of-way. Often they ride at excessive speeds for the driving conditions.

Check for cyclists before turning, changing lanes, or opening your door when parked. Make cyclists aware of your position and your intentions. Tap the horn (from a distance) to communicate. Be sure to give them plenty of space when passing in the city and even more when passing in the country where the higher speed may cause cyclists problems because of air turbulence.

If you ride a bicycle, obey the rules, signs and signals. Ride with the flow of traffic and use hand signals to communicate your intentions. Wear light colored clothing and make sure your bicycle is properly equipped with a headlight and reflectors if you ride at night.

MOTORCYCLES

Motorcyclists are usually better trained and more observant of the HTS rules, signs and signals than cyclists and pedestrians. When properly trained, they are more mobile and can stop more

quickly. If inexperienced, they may have problems swerving, braking and handling curves. Often, they may exceed the limits of their experience.

Because of their size, motorcycles are less visible. Watch for them when changing lanes, turning (especially when turning left across their path), or when opening your door after parking. Increase your following distance when a motorcycle precedes you. Always leave them a full lane of traffic, especially when passing, even though they may only occupy the right or left third of the lane.

If you ride a motorcycle, learn to ride properly and practice avoidance and emergency braking techniques. Dress properly, including a helmet. Enroll yourself in a Motorcycle Safety Foundation approved program and learn the riding strategies and correct lane positions in traffic that will keep you out of trouble.

HEAVY VEHICLES

Vans, trucks, trailer trucks, and buses are usually operated by professionals. They have an excellent view of the road, but this is offset by their lack of maneuverability, longer braking distances, and much slower acceleration.

In the city, they stop frequently and may block the flow of traffic. On highways, they climb hills more slowly and tend to increase speed on downhills. Because of their size, they block your field of vision. Increase your following distance to diminish this effect if it is not possible to pass the obstructing vehicle. When passing, realize the maneuver will take longer. Beware of the air turbulence they produce; leave extra space by moving to the side of your lane away from them. If a heavy vehicle approaches from the rear and follows your vehicle too closely (tailgates), ease off the accelerator or change lanes to encourage it to pass. Cooperate with these vehicles as they have difficulty moving in the HTS.

OTHER VEHICLES

Emergency vehicles - they are responding to emergencies when lights and/or sirens are operating. The law obliges you to cooperate and clear the way within the limits of safety.

Slow-moving vehicles - be patient. Follow at a safe distance. Look for a safe opportunity to pass.

Recreational vehicles - RVs - they are heavy and usually have poor road handling capabilities. Allow extra space around them and increase your following distance.

All-terrain vehicles and snowmobiles - watch for them at the sides of the road, when approaching and when crossing the road.

Responsibilities of Road Users

Each and every individual who shares the HTS is responsible for knowing the rules and regulations that govern its operation. **IGNORANCE IS NO EXCUSE.** As you progressed from pedestrian to cyclist and now, becoming a driver, your awareness and responsibilities must increase accordingly.

As a driver, you have four basic legal responsibilities: your physical condition, the condition of your vehicle, you must possess a valid driver's license for the class of vehicle that you are driving, and you must be able to satisfy the demands of state financial responsibility laws.

Throughout this text, you will learn how to utilize the HTS properly and safely as the driver of a motorized vehicle. Your legal responsibilities will be discussed in detail. Moreover, you will learn a system to prepare yourself to drive defensively, never taking it for granted that other road users will conduct themselves correctly. **EXPECT THE UNEXPECTED.** You must learn to manage your time, space, and visibility to reduce the element of risk that is inherent in the use of the HTS. Your safety, your passengers' safety, and the safety of the other road users with whom you share the roadway is **YOUR RESPONSIBILITY**.

 # Review

TERMS TO REMEMBER - WRITE A SHORT DEFINITION FOR THE FOLLOWING :

- HTS
- Pedestrians
- Jaywalk
- Cyclists

- Motorcyclists
- Following distance
- Tailgater
- Emergency vehicles

- Slow-moving vehicles
- Recreational vehicles
- All terrain vehicles
- Driver's responsibilities

SUMMARY

The main goal of the HTS is to facilitate the safe and efficient movement of all road users from place to place. Sharing the road requires every participant to abide by his/her responsibilities. The driver of a motorized vehicle must be aware of all the characteristics of the different individuals who may share the HTS in order to minimize the risks that they may present.

TEST A - COMPLETE THE SENTENCES BY FILLING IN THE BLANKS

1. The goal of the _____ is to enable the safe and efficient movement of all road users.

2. _____, _____ and _____ regulations govern all aspects of the use of the HTS.

3. It is your duty to know the rules, to abide by them and, further, to be _____ and _____ with other road users.

4. Pedestrians are the most _____ of roadway users.

5. Always yield to _____, even when they do not have the right-of-way.

6. _____ are less visible than other road vehicles.

7. When following a motorcycle, you should _____ your following distance.

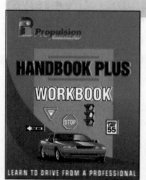

HANDBOOK PLUS WORKBOOK

*Check your comprehension and mastery of the contents of this chapter by completing the corresponding exercise that is found in the complement to the **HANDBOOK PLUS**:*

HANDBOOK PLUS WORKBOOK

Complete the exercise on Pages 2 and 3 then check your responses by referring to the answer key on Page 107.
If necessary, review the chapter for each error and refer to your instructor for further guidance.

Traffic Control Devices

2

2 - A
Traffic Signs

2 - B
International Signs

2 - C
Pavement Markings

2 - D
Traffic Signals

2 - E
Traffic Control Persons

2 - F
Hand Signals

2 - G
Review

Could you imagine using the Highway Transportation System (HTS.) if there were no traffic control devices at all? No lines on the pavement! No signs! No traffic signals!

Road signs and traffic signals are the visual vocabulary of all road users that facilitate the use of the H.T.S. for everyone. It is an evolving language that all road users are required to know. Fortunately, the vocabulary is based on shapes, colors, and symbols and once-learned, permits the understanding of new signs that may not have previously been seen.

Attempts are in progress to achieve world-wide standardization of this vocabulary in our ever-shrinking global community. Until such time, we are responsible for interpreting these traffic control devices correctly, wherever you may drive a motorized vehicle or use the HTS.

AFTER COMPLETING THIS CHAPTER, THE STUDENT MUST BE ABLE TO UNDERSTAND, IDENTIFY AND RESPOND TO:

- **traffic signs, signals and pavement markings.**
- **traffic control persons.**
- **hand signals.**

Traffic Signs

National standards for road signs have been set up by the National Joint Committee on Uniform Traffic Control Devices. Using shapes, colors, and symbols, as the basis of a clear and accurate language which is easily understood. It is a universal language that even the non-reader can decipher.

Before studying these signs individually, some basic principles are:

• Sign symbols are generally read from the bottom towards the top
• Arrows indicate the direction of the flow of traffic
• A black shield indicates a fixed obstacle.

THERE ARE FOUR CATEGORIES OF ROAD SIGNS

1- REGULATORY SIGNS
• Remind road users of specific rules (obligations, prohibitions, etc.) that apply in each traffic situation where they are posted.
• The background colors are red, white and black.

2- WARNING SIGNS
• Draw the attention to imminent danger or upcoming regulatory signs.
• The background color is yellow.
• The diamond shape indicates the danger is up ahead.

3- GUIDE SIGNS
• Provide information. - route markers, directions, destinations, services, points of interest or recreation, etc.
• The background colors are: BLUE + RED, WHITE + BLACK, GREEN, BLUE, & BROWN.

4- CONSTRUCTION SIGNS
• Draw the attention of road users to road repairs, detours, special road closing for sports events, etc.
• The background color is orange.
• The diamond shape indicates the danger is up ahead.

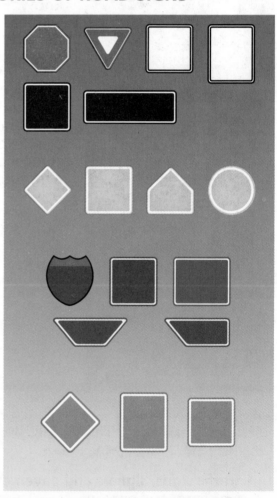

1 - REGULATORY SIGNS

Regulatory signs tell road users what they may or may not do in any specific area of the HTS. These signs are usually square or rectangular with black lettering or symbols on a white background, white lettering or symbols on a black background, or white lettering or symbols on a red background. Some regulatory signs are exceptions; they are :

UNIQUE PURPOSE REGULATORY SIGNS

The **STOP SIGN** is a red octagon with white markings. It requires a mandatory stop at the white line or before the crosswalk if there is no stop line. If there is neither a line or a crosswalk, stop before your vehicle reaches the cross street.
Check that you may proceed safely after yielding to all road users that do not have to stop.

The **YIELD SIGN** - a red and white triangle pointing downward - requires that you slow (stop if necessary) and give the right of way to the other traffic. Proceed when you can do so without interfering with the flow of traffic.

The **WRONG WAY SIGN** indicates that traffic is moving in an oncoming direction on this roadway. It prohibits you from entering the roadway. If you are already on the roadway, steer off the travelled portion of the road and change direction as soon as you safely can.

The **DO NOT ENTER SIGN** prohibits you from entering the roadway. Traffic is moving in an oncoming direction on the roadway; it is either a one-way road or an exit ramp for an expressway.

A white rectangle with black lettering - **DO NOT PASS** - posted on the right side of the road indicates a no passing zone. A yellow pennant with similar lettering posted on the left is a highly visible warning of the same regulation. A white rectangle with black lettering - PASS WITH CARE - indicates the end of the no passing zone.

The **RAILROAD CROSSBUCK** posted a few feet from the railroad tracks is a white X with railroad crossing in black lettering. This sign obliges some road users to make a complete stop whether a train is coming or not. Passenger vehicles should slow down and check both ways carefully. Be prepared to stop in case a train is approaching or you are following a vehicle that is required to stop.

SPEED LIMIT SIGNS

The ABSOLUTE or POSTED SPEED LIMIT is the maximum or minimum speed at which you can legally drive in this particular zone based on road and normal traffic conditions. These speeds are intended for ideal driving conditions.

When road, weather, visibility, or traffic conditions are not ideal, the driver must determine the BASIC SPEED LIMIT; the speed that will be safe for the existing conditions. Normally, minimum speed limits will no longer apply in poor driving conditions.

Many states post NIGHT SPEED LIMIT SIGNS - white lettering on a black square background - because of reduced visibility at night. Like all speed limits, the night speed limit is based on ideal road conditions.

REDUCED SPEED SIGNS inform the driver that a lower speed is posted ahead; the driver should begin to slow in order to be able to comply with the reduced speed when he reaches the zone.

ONE WAY SIGNS

The ONE-WAY SIGN designates the direction of the flow of traffic. Signs at intersections, are posted on the near right and the far left corners or above the roadway where they are most visible to traffic from both directions.

LANE-USE CONTROL SIGNS

LANE-USE CONTROL SIGNS mounted at the side of the roadway - white rectangles with black arrows and lettering oblige the driver in the lane indicated to travel in the direction shown, or restrict the use of the lane to certain vehicles.

Drivers must plan ahead and place their vehicles in the correct lane to maneuver in the intended direction. Do not occupy the restricted lane unless permitted

LANE-USE CONTROL SIGNS

LANE-USE CONTROL SIGNS mounted overhead designate the lane below the sign for a specific purpose. They have similar shapes and colors. They also inform the driver of the same regulations and restrictions as the signs posted at the side of the roadway. Both of these types of signs are usually accompanied by arrows and/or symbols painted on the pavement in the applicable lanes.

TRAFFIC DIRECTION SIGNS

Black lettering or symbols on a white background, these signs oblige drivers to pass on the indicated side of an obstacle or median in the roadway.

PROHIBITORY SIGNS

New signs using a red circle and bar with a black symbol on a white square background are gradually replacing white rectangles with black lettering. The red circle and bar means NO.

TURN PROHIBITION SIGNS
When used in conjunction with black arrows it prohibits a left turn, right turn, or U turn.

EXCLUSION SIGNS
When used with a black symbol, it prohibits the vehicle represented from using this roadway.

PEDESTRIAN CONTROL SIGNS

PEDESTRIAN CONTROL SIGNS remind pedestrians of the need to walk facing the traffic on rural roads where no sidewalks are provided; limit pedestrian crossing to safe places; and instruct pedestrians on the use of the traffic control lights.

PARKING + STOPPING CONTROL SIGNS

These signs regulate the zones, times and days where parking or stopping is permitted or prohibited - variations occur from one municipality to another.
- Red - No parking, standing or stopping
- Green - Time limited parking.

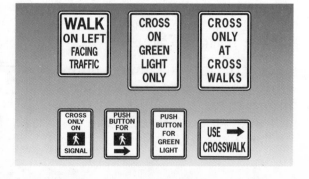

OTHER REGULATORY SIGNS

The DIVIDED HIGHWAY SIGNS advise the driver of an upcoming intersection where the roadway is divided by a median or a separation. If the roadway does not continue, the driver must turn onto the highway.

The STOP HERE ON RED sign is posted near some intersections with traffic lights. When the stop is abnormally far from the corner for whatever reason, it indicates where you must stop your vehicle when the light is red.

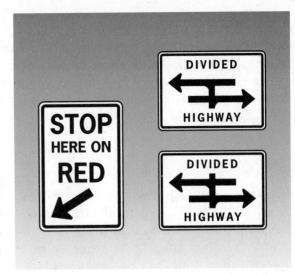

HEAVY VEHICLE SIGNS

Where an extra lane has been provided on an upgrade for slow-moving traffic, these signs direct heavy vehicles to use this lane.

Due to severe weakening of the road surface, condition of the pavement, or bridges, the limiting of vehicle loads is often necessary.

This black rectangle with white lettering indicates a weigh station for heavy vehicles, it requires these vehicles to exit and have their load limits verified.

TRUCK ROUTE and HAZARDOUS CARGO signs oblige such vehicles to follow the designated roadways.

2 - WARNING SIGNS

WARNING SIGNS draw the attention of road users to imminent or upcoming danger or, on occasion, upcoming regulatory signs.

- The background color is yellow with black lettering or symbols.
- The diamond shape is the most common and warns of upcoming danger. The pentagon, circle, and rectangle are also used in specific circumstances.

SCHOOL SIGNS

The yellow pentagon with black symbols of school children warns the driver of the beginning of a SCHOOL ZONE or a school crossing ahead. Whether or not special speed limits are present, prudent drivers will slow down and be extra vigilant for the possible presence of children. The addition of crossing lines on the pentagon indicates the location of the SCHOOL CROSSING. The possible presence of crossing guards or school patrols will help control the traffic.

ADVANCE REGULATORY SIGNS

The STOP AHEAD, YIELD AHEAD and SIGNAL AHEAD warning signs (whether using the symbols or the word messages) are intended for use on approaches to these regulatory signs. They are posted when the regulatory signs are not clearly visible for a sufficient distance to permit drivers to bring their vehicles to a stop in time under normal driving conditions. The problem may be a curve in the roadway or an overpass that obstructs the approaching driver's view.

A TAB indicating the distance to the regulatory sign may be installed below the warning sign.

Drivers should slow and prepare to stop.

ADVANCE TURN OR CURVE SIGNS

These warning signs, posted before turns and curves, are primarily for the benefit of drivers unfamiliar with the road. They do, however, by the symbol inform all drivers what to expect.

The ADVISORY SPEED PLATE may accompany a curve sign and recommend the maximum safe speed in ideal conditions.

The CHEVRON ALIGNMENT may replace delineators on a curve.

The LARGE ARROW (on a yellow rectangle) when posted in a curve warns of an especially dangerous point in the curve.

ADVANCE CROSSING SIGNS

ADVANCE CROSSING SIGNS alert drivers to unexpected entries into the roadway. The type of possible entry is symbolized on the sign.

If such crossings occur at a particular location , a tab or auxiliary distance sign may supplement these signs to indicate the distance to the exact location.

At the particular location a CROSSING SIGN may be posted. (The addition of crossing lines to the same sign).

Drivers should reduce their speed in order to be able to stop if necessary.

ADVANCE INTERSECTION SIGNS

ADVANCE INTERSECTION SIGNS indicate the presence of obscured junctions ahead. The symbol represents the situation graphically and the relative widths of the lines demonstrate the importance of the intersecting roads. These signs are not usually posted where junction or directional signing is already present.

Drivers should verify the situation ahead, be prepared for unexpected entries into the roadway, and remember that passing maneuvers are illegal when approaching intersections.

LANE REDUCTION SIGNS

LANE REDUCTION signs warn drivers of the loss of one or more traffic lanes on a multi-lane roadway. Drivers should safely enter the continuing lane as soon as possible, and/or facilitate the lane change maneuver for other drivers.

The NARROW BRIDGE sign warns the driver to adjust his speed so that he will reach the bridge before or after the oncoming traffic.

DIVIDED HIGHWAY SIGNS

DIVIDED HIGHWAY ENDS warns the driver that the highway ahead will no longer be divided by a physical barrier.

DIVIDED HIGHWAY AHEAD is posted on the approaches to a section of roadway where the traffic will be separated by a physical barrier.

The TWO WAY TRAFFIC sign supplements the message (divided highway ends) and may be posted at intervals to remind drivers that they are no longer on a divided highway.

RAILROAD SIGNS

The round, yellow sign, with a black X and two R's, is a warning of a RAILROAD CROSSING AHEAD. Slow down, be prepared to stop, and check both ways carefully.

The tab EXEMPT under, this sign indicates that drivers normally required to stop, are free from that obligation in this case, UNLESS A TRAIN IS COMING.

CONVERGING ROADWAYS

This MERGE SIGN warns motorists that possible vehicles on an entrance ahead will attempt to join the flow of traffic. Drivers should be prepared to facilitate the merging maneuvers; if possible, a lane change to the left.

The ADDED LANE SIGN is posted in advance of a point where two roadways converge and merging maneuvers are not required - a parallel lane exists for the entering traffic. Drivers should still exercise caution as some vehicles might try to enter their lane.

WARNING - NO PASSING ZONE - SIGN

The yellow pennant posted on the left side of the roadway indicates the beginning of the no passing zone. The high visibility of this sign in passing maneuvers warns drivers from an adequate distance of the no-passing zone.

OBSTACLES IN THE ROADWAY

Signs posted on obstacles within or at the side of the road to warn drivers.

The DOUBLE ARROW indicates traffic may pass on either side of the obstacle.
The HAZARD MARKERS channel traffic to the lower end of the stripes: to the right or to the left.

HILL SIGNS

The HILL sign is posted in advance of a downgrade that requires some special precautions. Supplemental plaques with respect to the grade and the length may also be installed.

Drivers should check their brakes by applying the brake pedal and also prepare to downshift to an appropriate gear to take advantage of engine compression on the slope.

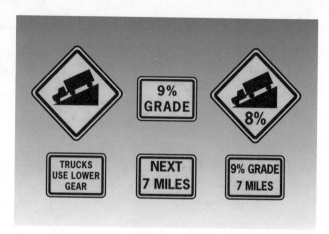

HAZARDOUS ROAD SIGNS

BUMP or DIP signs warn of a sharp rise or depression that creates discomfort for passengers or may deflect a vehicle from its true course. Drivers should reduce speed to minimize any possible effect on their vehicle.

PAVEMENT ENDS warns of a change in the road surface ahead. Drivers should slow down prior to the change as road traction will decrease and the danger exists of potholes at the end of the pavement.

The SOFT SHOULDER advises that the shoulder cannot safely support the weight of a vehicle. Drivers should avoid using the shoulder and proceed to a paved area if they must leave the roadway.

The SLIPPERY WHEN WET sign warns of a section of roadway where traction is severely reduced when wet. Drivers should reduce speed when wet.

SAFETY TIPS

?

WARNING SIGNS ALERT YOU TO SITUATIONS ON OR NEAR THE ROADWAY AHEAD.
- *you should reduce your speed and proceed cautiously.*
- *you should increase your visual search pattern to locate the hazards.*
- *you should manage your speed, time, and space to reduce the level of danger.*

3 - GUIDE SIGNS

GUIDE SIGNS are essential to direct drivers along roadways; to inform them of interesting routes; to guide them to cities, towns or villages; to identify nearby rivers, streams, parks, or historical sites; and to inform them of available roadside services. These signs are usually square or rectangular and color-coded as to their purpose.

ROUTE MARKERS

ROUTE MARKERS are used to identify and mark all numbered highways. The markers for each system, which are distinctive in shape and color, are used only on that respective system and the approaches thereto.

Auxiliary tabs such as TO, arrows, cardinal directions, or distances are often added to form trailblazers. The use of the tab with the word TO indicates that where the marker is posted is not a part of the indicated route, merely a progressive direction to the route in question.

These trailblazers inform road users and guide them to the nearest access point of the designated facility.

DESTINATION SIGNS

DESTINATION SIGNS are green horizontal rectangles of varying sizes with white lettering, symbols, and numbers. They are posted to assist travellers to their destinations. Arrows to indicate the direction to travel as well as distances to the indicated destination. The number of the roadway to be used may also be included. On major highways, there are at least 3 signs posted prior to the exit that is identified.

Drivers should have plenty of time to prepare to exit.

RECREATION SIGNS

A brown background (square, rectangle or trapezoid in shape) with white lettering or symbols is reserved for recreational and cultural interest signs.

They may be posted on any conventional roadway or expressway to direct motorists to facilities; to identify recreational areas and services; and to inform of cultural interest structures and places.

The concept is to guide motorists to a general area and then to specific amenities within the area without confusing these signs with other traffic control signs.

ROADSIDE SERVICES

On conventional highways services are generally within sight and available to the traveller at reasonably frequent intervals along the route. The blue square or rectangular SERVICE signs are not posted on these roadways.

When such services are infrequent and are found on intersecting highways and at crossroads, these signs will be posted to advise travellers as to the location, distance, and direction.

The service legends may be either symbols or word messages - they should not be mixed.

4 - CONSTRUCTION SIGNS

Signs with an orange background and black symbols or lettering are used when traffic must be moved through or around road construction work, maintenance operations, utility work, and special sporting events on or adjacent to the roadway. These signs (both construction and temporary signs) have to control a wide variety of situations and conditions and as such they present a wide assortment of messages.

SPEED

A flag person ahead may slow or stop the traffic (see 2-E Traffic Control Persons) as the situation requires.

The driver is well advised to reduce speed to the posted speed limit, suggested speed, or to a speed in keeping with the abnormal driving conditions.

WORK SITE LIMITS

These signs indicate the distance to the work area, the length of the work site and the end of the zone.

A DETOUR sign indicates that traffic must deviate around the work in progress up ahead. Square detour signs are posted to delineate the route to be followed.

CONDITIONS IN THE WORK SITE

These signs inform of the type of activity in the area, the conditions, changes in the number or position of lanes, etc.

A reduced speed and increased visual scanning will permit the driver to adapt. This will produce extra time to judge, decide and react to these conditions.

International Signs

As more people travel internationally, the need to recognize international signs increases every year. Local auto clubs should be consulted prior to road excursions in foreign lands; they can supply pertinent information with respect to signs and laws for the country where you intend to travel. INTERNATIONAL signs convey their message with symbols, colors, numbers, and shapes rather than words.

SPEED LIMIT SIGNS

White numbers on a blue circle indicate the minimum speed. Black on a white circle with a red border indicate maximum speed.

In some cases, the words maximum replace the words speed limit. Remember the speed limit is posted in kilometers per hour.

REGULATORY SIGNS

PROHIBITION SIGNS- a white circular sign with a red border and slash means NO. The black symbol indicates what is prohibited.

OBLIGATION SIGNS, white squares with green circles and black symbols oblige all of the traffic to proceed in the indicated direction.

WARNING AND GUIDE SIGNS

WARNING SIGNS- white triangles with red borders warn of hazards. The black symbol illustrates the upcoming danger.

GUIDE SIGNS- white squares on blue rectangular backgrounds provide information about services that are adjacent to the roadway. The symbols indicate the services.

Pavement Markings

Lines, lettering, symbols and occasionally shading painted directly on the road surface make up PAVEMENT MARKINGS. Sometimes special markings may also be painted on curbs and other surfaces. They are normally white or yellow in color and are used to assist in regulating the flow of traffic. These markings define lanes, delineate roadways, reinforce information given by signs or signals, and sometimes warn of possible dangers.

The most common pavement markings are lines. They are painted in two colors: **yellow lines** that separate traffic travelling in opposite directions and **white lines** that separate lanes of traffic travelling in the same direction.

YELLOW LINES

A CENTER LINE, yellow in color, need not be at the geometric center of the roadway. It may be a single BROKEN LINE which permits passing if the way is clear; or a SOLID YELLOW LINE which prohibits passing (except in special cases: slow-moving vehicles, bicycles, etc.).

Center lines composed of double lines with one broken line and one solid line permit passing for drivers travelling beside the broken line and prohibit passing for drivers beside the solid line.

While driving on a two-lane roadway, you are required to use the right lane. You may use the left lane to pass another vehicle or in the event that your lane is obstructed or closed to traffic.

Before entering the left lane, you must yield the right-of-way to any oncoming traffic. The complete procedures for all passing maneuvers will be discussed later in the text in Chapter 12.

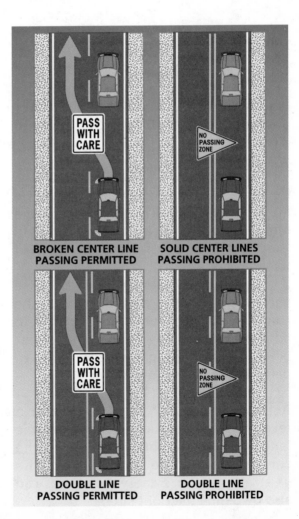

BROKEN CENTER LINE
PASSING PERMITTED

SOLID CENTER LINES
PASSING PROHIBITED

DOUBLE LINE
PASSING PERMITTED

DOUBLE LINE
PASSING PROHIBITED

THREE LANE ROADWAYS

On a 3- lane roadway, a DOUBLE BROKEN YELLOW LINE on either side of the center lane indicates this lane is reserved for passing and turning left in both directions.

THEREIN LIES THE DANGER.

Extreme caution should always be maintained when driving on three lane highways. As much as possible, drive in the right lane and follow the flow of traffic.

If a passing situation should become necessary, take extra care in checking the roadway and the oncoming traffic in both the center lane as well as the far left lane before entering the center lane to perform the passing maneuver.

Attempts to reduce the hazard of a reversible lane have led to many variable lane markings to control access to the center lane (some examples in the illustration, realize the yellow lines can also be beside the right lane).

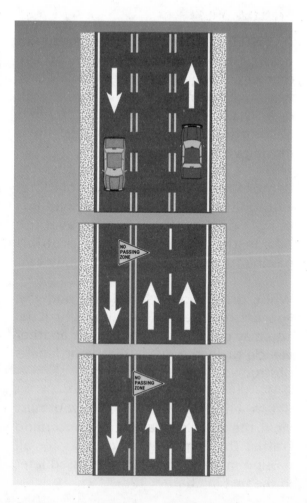

FOUR LANE ROADWAYS

On 4-lane roadways, two lanes are used in each direction - a double yellow median line should not be crossed in either direction. If a divider or median separates the roadways, a solid yellow line will border the median on either side.

You should drive in the right lane and follow the traffic flow. The left lane should be used when passing or to avoid potential dangers on the shoulder as well as when you approach hidden entrance ramps or entrance ramps where vehicles are entering the roadway.

FIVE LANE ROADWAYS

On a 5-lane roadway, the center lane is delineated by double yellow lines (one solid and one broken) on either side. This lane is reserved for vehicles turning left driving in both directions. At major intersections, the lane markings will change to highlight the left turn lanes in both directions.

You should drive in the right lane; however, to make a left turn, you must position your vehicle in the 2nd lane in time to enter the marked left turn lane at the major intersection. If you want to turn left at any other location, you may cross the solid yellow line to enter this reserved lane after checking carefully that no other oncoming vehicle and/or vehicle following is entering the lane.

DO NOT DRIVE IN THIS LANE!

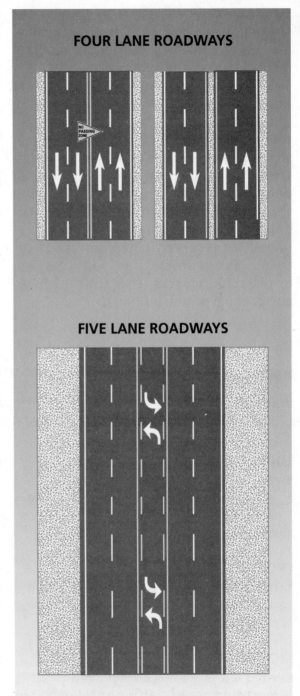

FOUR LANE ROADWAYS

FIVE LANE ROADWAYS

SIX LANE HIGHWAYS

On multi-lane highways, the center line may be a double-yellow, though usually a median strip or concrete divider.

You should drive in the right lane in order to turn, exit or to drive at less than the posted speed limit. The second lane should be used when driving at the speed limit as well as to pass or avoid dangers from the right. The left lane should be reserved for passing or preparing to turn left.

Check for reserved lanes, left exits or turns and vehicles at high speed approaching from the rear before encroaching on the left lane.

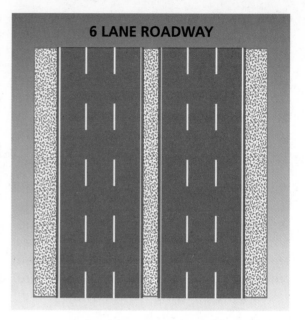

6 LANE ROADWAY

WHITE LINES ON THE PAVEMENT

White lines separate traffic moving in the same direction. They channel traffic into orderly lanes and assist drivers to control their path of travel. Lines are also used as:

EDGE LINES:
- mark the right edge of the roadway
- on one-way streets, the left edge line should be painted yellow but is often white in color,

CROSSWALKS:
- horizontal or perpendicular wide lines delineate walkways to guide pedestrians and warn drivers

STOP LINES:
- wide lines that mark where vehicles must stop at red traffic signal lights and stop signs.

OBSTRUCTION MARKINGS:
- guide traffic around fixed obstructions
- slanted stripes indicate where vehicles should not pass.

PARKING SPACES:
- controlled by white lines on the pavement. They encourage an orderly and efficient use of space while preventing encroachment on bus stop zones, fire hydrant zones, etc.

CURB MARKINGS:
- white, yellow, blue, green and red may be used to control parking.

WHITE LETTERING AND SYMBOLS ON THE PAVEMENT

White lettering or symbols painted on the pavement may supplement signs posted overhead or at the side of the roadway. They may designate lanes, warn of hazards, provide information, etc. Some examples are:

LANE DESIGNATION:
- arrows indicate to drivers in a given lane, the direction that they must travel.
- the word ONLY indicates one direction of travel is permitted.

RAILROAD CROSSINGS:
- are delineated by a white crossbuck and double R.

SCHOOL ZONES:
- indicated by the word SCHOOL .
- SCHOOL X ing indicates where students cross.

WARNINGS:
- stops and signal lights may be lettered on the pavement.

INFORMATION:
- speed limits, route numbers, and other information may be painted on the roadway.

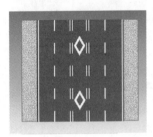

RESERVED LANES:
- white diamonds painted on the lane as well as signs above the lane or at the side of the road identify lanes reserved for special vehicles.

RESERVED PARKING:
- handicapped symbol or other in a parking space reserves that space.
- blue curb markings also identify spaces reserved for disabled persons or veterans.

Traffic Signals

Traffic control signals are valuable devices for the regulation and orderly movement of vehicular and pedestrian traffic. They control traffic at one location and are clearly visible, mounted on posts at the corners of intersections or hung over the roadway. The position and colors of the signals are standardized. **When lights are not operating, drivers should stop (proceed as if it were a four-way stop intersection).**

RED SIGNAL LIGHT

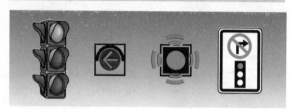

The **RED** signal light is located at the top when mounted vertically or on the left when horizontal. If the **RED LENS IS LIT**, drivers must stop their vehicles at the indicated stop line; if none is marked, before reaching the crosswalk on the near side of the intersection.

Unless a sign indicates otherwise, the driver may then cautiously enter the intersection in order to turn right. (Also to turn left from a one-way street to another one-way street.)

WARNING: turns on red lights are not universal; check with local authorities when driving in other countries.

If the driver intends to proceed straight ahead, he must wait for the signal to change before continuing.

RED ARROW:
• stop. Turns prohibited in the direction of the arrow.

FLASHING RED LIGHT:
• stop, then proceed only when it is safe to do so. (Similar to a stop sign)

YELLOW (AMBER) SIGNAL LIGHT

The **AMBER** signal light is located in the middle whether mounted vertically or horizontally. If the **YELLOW LENS IS LIT**, the green signal has ended and the signal is about to change to red. Drivers are required to stop. However, if the light changes to yellow and you cannot stop safely, you may continue.

Crossing an intersection on a yellow amber signal is a hazardous maneuver, it is highly recommended to stop. In order to do this, good drivers are continually aware of the traffic situation, the signals ahead as well as the traffic ahead and behind. Approaching intersections, you should "cover the brake" ready to stop.

How long has the signal been green? Will the traffic behind be able to stop? How much space will you need to stop? These questions should be considered while nearing any green signal.

The basic concept is, when a signal light changes to yellow, **you should stop!**

YELLOW ARROW:
- if you were intending to turn, you should stop.

FLASHING YELLOW:
- slow down, proceed with caution, check before crossing the intersection. (Similar to a yield sign)

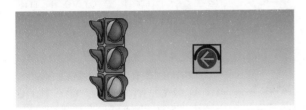

The **GREEN** signal light is at the bottom when mounted vertically and on the right when horizontal. When the **GREEN LENS IS LIT**, the driver is authorized to proceed into the intersection. This does not guarantee that the way is clear.

When a red light changes to green, you should yield to any other vehicles or pedestrians that have not cleared the intersection. There is also a possibility of late arrivals who tried to "run the yellow". **Check the traffic to the left, center and right before entering.** Do not enter if other road users do not appear to be stopping or are still engaged.

When approaching a green signal light, is it a "stale green"? (A light that has been green for some time, since you first noticed it. It might be ready to change to yellow any second.) "Cover the brake" and check traffic to the rear, be prepared to stop safely prior to entering the intersection.

If the light is still green as you pass the "point of no return" (the last chance to stop safely prior to the intersection), check the cross traffic and then proceed to cross the intersection while returning to your normal cruising speed.

GREEN ARROW:
- you may turn in the direction of the arrow after checking and yielding to pedestrians.
- this light may accompany a red signal. You may move in the direction of the arrow.

PEDESTRIAN SIGNALS are used at

The concept is to regulate the flow of traffic in order to allow pedestrians time to cross while minimizing the possibility of conflicts. Pedestrians are still required to check traffic with due care before crossing and to avoid causing untoward delays for traffic.

Drivers must yield to pedestrians and pay special attention to those who are visually (white cane) or hearing impaired.

- The illuminated **WALK** or a walking person symbol indicates pedestrians may enter the crosswalk.
- When flashing hurry to safety.

- The illuminated **DON'T WALK** or orange hand symbol prohibits entering the crosswalk.
- When flashing hurry to safety.

In some areas, an audio signal assists the visually impaired - continuous sound to cross; intermittent sound when the lights flash; and no sound at all when they should not cross.

LANE-USE SIGNALS

Special overhead signals control the use of lanes on bridges, in tunnels, reversible lanes, etc. They inform road users of the availability of the lanes ahead.

 A STEADY RED X identifies the lane below the signal as a lane that you may not use.

 A STEADY DOWNWARD GREEN ARROW, indicates you are permitted to drive in the lane under this signal.

 A STEADY YELLOW X means you should prepare to vacate, in a safe manner, the lane under the signal.

 A FLASHING YELLOW X identifies a lane reserved for left turns in both directions.

 A FLASHING HORIZONTAL YELLOW OR GREEN ARROW indicates the direction in which you should direct your vehicle to change lanes in complete safety.

Traffic Control Persons

Traffic control persons are authorized to direct and control the traffic flow for a specific purpose. Failure to obey them is hazardous, as well as entailing penalties similar in most states to passing a traffic signal. Some examples:

FLAG PERSONS:
- using a flag or a standard, they control traffic at construction sites, etc.

CROSSING GUARDS:
- using a hand-held stop sign symbol, they control traffic to protect school children while crossing.

POLICE OFFICERS:
- using hand signals and/or a whistle, they direct traffic.

- in any situation where there is a traffic signal or sign, as well as a peace officer or other traffic control person, you must obey the directions given.

FLAG PERSONS — STOP, SLOW, PROCEED

CROSSING GUARD — STOP

POLICE OFFICERS — STOP, SLOW, PROCEED

Hand Signals

Hand signals must be used to com-municate road users intentions on vehicles that are not equip-ped with electronical signals or when the signals may not be operative for any reason.

Road users may supplement their mechanical signals with a manual signal. This adds a personal aspect to the com-munication and can be more effective. Positive results from other drivers and road users are much more likely.

You must signal your intentions (by law) with respect to any maneuvers - turns or lane changes - by signalling steadily for a sufficient distance (usually one hundred feet), in order to permit other drivers to react and be able to take appropriate action should it be necessary.

LEFT TURN

RIGHT TURN

SLOW OR STOP

SAFETY TIPS

COMMUNICATION IS ONE OF THE ESSENTIALS TO SHARING THE HTS SAFELY.

Hand signals can be used in conjunction with the electric turn signals. They often result in a more positive response from other road users. Other hand signals can be used as well - a gesture to proceed at a four-way stop intersection, for example.

TRAFFIC CONTROL DEVICES

Review

WORDS TO REMEMBER - WRITE A SHORT DEFINITION FOR THE FOLLOWING :

- Yield
- Basic speed limit
- Absolute speed limit
- Hazardous cargo

- Trailblazer
- Reversible lane
- Reserved lane
- Flagperson

- Regulatory sign
- Warning sign
- Construction sign
- Guide sign

SUMMARY

TRAFFIC SIGNS:
inform of rules, warn of hazards and provide information to assist drivers. Colors, shapes, and symbols provide a language that is easier to interpret.

PAVEMENT MARKINGS:
define lanes, delineate roadways, reinforce information provided by signs and signals, and sometimes warn of possible hazards.

TRAFFIC SIGNALS:
regulate movement of traffic at a specific location to facilitate the use of the HTS. When lights are not operating, all drivers must stop (proceed as if it were a four-way stop intersection).

TRAFFIC CONTROL PERSONS:
direct and control traffic movement for a specific reason. They override other traffic control devices.

TEST A - COMPLETE THE SENTENCES BY FILLING IN THE BLANKS.

1. _____ signs remind road users of specific rules (obligations, prohibitions, etc.) that apply in a traffic situation.

2. _____ signs draw attention to imminent danger or upcoming regulatory signs.

3. _____ signs provide information - route markers, directions, destinations, services, points of interest, recreation, etc.

4. _____ signs draw the attention of road users to road repairs and detours.

5. The _____ sign is a red octagon with white lettering.

6. The _____ sign designates the direction of the flow of traffic and is usually posted at the near right and far left corners where they are most visible.

7. Signs, using a red circle and bar on a white square background in conjunction with black arrows or symbols are called _____ maneuver signs.

8. _____ are posted on obstacles using black and yellow bands slanted at a 45° angle to channel traffic toward the lower end of the stripes.

9. _____ lines separate traffic moving in the same direction. They channel traffic into orderly lanes and assist drivers to control their path of travel.

10. _____ lines separate traffic moving in opposite directions.

Student notes

_____
_____
_____
_____
_____
_____
_____
_____
_____
_____
_____
_____
_____
_____
_____
_____
_____
_____

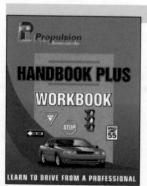

HANDBOOK PLUS WORKBOOK

*Check your comprehension and mastery of the contents of this chapter by completing the corresponding exercises that are found in the complement to the **HANDBOOK PLUS**:*

HANDBOOK PLUS WORKBOOK

Complete the exercises on Pages 4 to 19 then check your responses by referring to the answer key on Page 107.
If necessary, review the chapter for each error and refer to your instructor for further guidance.

Administrative Laws

3 - A
General Information

3 - B
Driver's Licenses

3 - C
Certificate of Title/Registration

3 - D
License Control Measures

3 - E
Rules of the Road

3 - F
In Case of a Collision

3 - G
Review

The adoption, promulgation, and enforcement of new laws is an important step towards road safety. These laws, whether federal, state, or municipal, are compiled under a variety of names. For simplicity, the title, "THE HIGHWAY CODE" refers to all the laws that govern the operation of the HTS.

This highway code establishes norms for all motorized vehicles and their manufacturers. Rules for road sharing and safety, from professional truckers to pedestrians, are specified in these laws.

Law enforcement is the responsibility of the police agencies who patrol the HTS. Judges and the court systems will apply the penalties. Failure to obey the norms will result in fines, demerit points, possible jail terms, and/or the loss of the driving privilege.

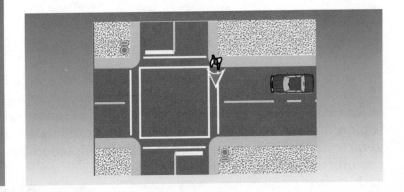

AFTER COMPLETING THIS CHAPTER, THE STUDENT MUST DEMONSTRATE KNOWLEDGE OF AND WILLINGNESS TO ACCEPT PERSONAL RESPONSIBILITY FOR:

- the licensing procedures and vehicle registration requirements.
- the rules of the road and license control measures.
- required duties in case of a collision.

General Information

Federal, state, and local governments cooperate to enact legislation that governs the use of the HTS.

THE FEDERAL GOVERNMENT passes laws that set general standards for the operation of the HTS. Some examples are:

- THE NATIONAL TRAFFIC AND MOTOR VEHICLE SAFETY ACT- legislating regulations for vehicle manufacturers; such as safety features, vehicle emissions and recall of defects.
- THE NATIONAL HIGHWAY SAFETY ACT- establishing general guidelines for state regulations concerning vehicle registration and inspection, driver licensing and traffic laws.
- THE UNIFORM TRAFFIC CONTROL DEVICES ACT- regulating the shape, color, and location of road signs.

STATE GOVERNMENTS, following the guidelines set by federal laws, enact statutes that regulate all aspects of the HTS: the ownership, registration and inspection of vehicles; the licensing of drivers; traffic laws and courts; and highway construction/maintenance.

LOCAL GOVERNMENTS, cities and towns, pass by-laws that regulate the use of the HTS within their regions. They govern the speed limit, one-ways, particular rules at intersections, parking rules, etc.

It is your responsibility to know the rules. Your state Department of Motor Vehicles issues a handbook on the specific rules and regulations that apply in your state. **IGNORANCE IS NO EXCUSE!**

Driver's Licenses

The state authority, the Department of Motor Vehicles (DMV), authorizes individuals to operate motor vehicles by issuing licenses according to the class of vehicle that will be operated. Certain requirements must be met to apply for each class of license. Rules vary from one state to another. Most are considering or preparing legislation, that will be called **graduated licensing**, for new drivers.
The new driver may be prohibited from driving on freeways or at night, must

have a zero BAC and be accompanied by an adult/parent. **The main concept is to increase driving privileges as the candidate demonstrates responsible and violation-free driving behavior.**

YOUR FIRST DRIVER'S LICENSE

All states have minimum age requirements (parental consent for minors) to apply for a driver's license. You must fill out an application, pass a vision screening test, a general health questionnaire, and a knowledge test (traffic signs, signals, laws, and safe driving practices) evaluated either in a written or computerized format. If you satisfy requirements and pay the necessary fees, an instruction permit will be issued.

You may then practice driving, with this permit in your possession, while accompanied by a qualified instructor or other licensed adult (in some states you may not drive at night). Once you have mastered the necessary vehicle control skills, you may book an appointment at the motor vehicle bureau (DMV office) for the road test (provided you meet the legal age requirements in your state).

If you pass the in-vehicle exam, you must pay the required fees and you will receive your driver's license.

When you drive, this license must be in your possession and you must present it when requested by any police officer.

Certificate of Title/Registration

States issue a certificate of title when you purchase an automobile. It lists the owner, make, model, vehicle identification number (VIN), and engine number of your vehicle. The state retains a copy. Whenever you sell your vehicle, you must supply the new owner with this certificate.

When you purchase a vehicle, you must apply for a registration certificate from the DMV. The state will issue a registration card along with the license plates for your vehicle. This is renewable according to the procedures required by your state government.

In most states, you will be required to show proof of financial responsibility in order to receive the registration card. Proof is usually a certificate from your insurance company (Chapter 18). When you drive, you must have the registration card, insurance certificate and your license in your possession and be prepared to present it if requested or if you are involved in a collision.

License Control Measures

A driver's license is a privilege, not a right, that is granted by the state. This also means that the DMV may refuse to issue or renew a license to individuals who don't meet the necessary standards.

Those persons who will be refused are :
- not of legal age
- unable to show, by examination, reasonable knowledge of the vehicle code, signs and signals (and simple English used in traffic control signs)
- unable to show minimum competence in operating a motor vehicle
- who are chronic and excessive alcohol and/or drug abusers (alcoholics/addicts unless participating in treatment)
- who are subject to a physical/mental disability that may cause lapses of consciousness, confusion, disorientation, etc. unless under medical control
- whose license from another state or legal jurisdiction is under suspension or revocation
- who refuse to surrender a valid license issued by a foreign jurisdiction.

The state also has the power to take away licenses from any drivers who have demonstrated a disregard for the rules and regulations. Because of this and the devastating toll of carnage on American highways, most state legislatures have enacted laws empowering the DMV to regulate drivers with a track record of improper use of the HTS.

The two most common methods are a system based on demerit points with prescribed penalties and a system based on automatic penalties for certain infractions over and above court imposed sanctions, usually entitled Admin Per Se.

DEMERIT POINT SYSTEM

The DMV is required to maintain a record of every individual who operates a motorized vehicle in the HTS. The system inscribes points on the driver's record for moving-vehicle violation as well as, in some states, for collisions in which the driver is held responsible by the DMV.

Upon conviction by the court or payment of the fine, a report is forwarded to the DMV and the demerit points are added to the driver's record. These points remain on record for a specified period of time or, in some states, a specified number of points can be removed for each year of point-free driving and/or a court approved Violator's Program.

The intention of this system is to identify negligent drivers by the accumulation of points. Once identified by records that have a specified number of points, they are warned by a form letter of their status and of the possible penalties that may be imposed on them. The purpose is to encourage modification of the drivers' attitudes and behavior and thereby allow them to retain the driving privilege.

Any addition of points after the warning letter will cause the DMV to send another letter announcing the intention to suspend the driving privilege if any further infractions are committed.

If a driver does not change and more points are accumulated to reach the specified level, the license will be suspended for a period of time (usually 30 to 90 days) and an administrative fee will be charged to reinstate the license once the suspension has ended. If the driver continues to commit infractions after the license is reinstated, the driving privilege can be suspended a second time for a longer period or it may be revoked for a year or more. The person will then have to apply for another license.

The revocation can be made permanent for offenders whose record demonstrates repeated serious traffic violations.

ADMIN PER SE

Many states have passed legislation that has created an administrative license suspension law (commonly called Admin Per Se) over and above any sanctions that the court may impose.

This law applies to any driver who:

a) refuses to submit to or complete the required impairment test
b) takes a breath test that shows a BAC exceeding the legal limit
c) takes a urine or blood test and the officer believes the results will show impairment

d) is driving while under suspension
e) fails to show proof of financial responsibility when requested.

The Admin Per Se law specifies that:

- the officer arrest the driver
- the driver's license is confiscated and/or the vehicle is impounded
- a suspension form is completed and served on the driver (suspension to begin 30 days later)
- the officer forward a sworn statement of the facts as well as all required documentation to the DMV.

The DMV will review the documentation and may set aside the action against the driver if all conditions have not been met. If not set aside, the driver may request a hearing or a court review. Needless to say, if all conditions are met by the police officer, it is highly unlikely that these reviews will alter the situation.

IMPLIED CONSENT

Most states, have also enacted legislation which stipulates that any person who drives a motor vehicle is deemed to have given his/her consent to be tested for the purpose of determining the alcohol/drug content of his/her blood.

Usually, the person may choose the type of test if available; the officer may also request a blood test if evidence suggests drug usage. The person does not have the right to consult an attorney prior to deciding nor to have counsel present during the testing procedure.

FINES AND PENALTIES - DUI

Due to statistical data and the actions of many interest groups, society has become much less tolerant toward driving while impaired and legislation has been enacted that reflects this attitude. As a result, stiffer fines, jail terms and other penalties are imposed on any driver convicted of this infraction besides the Admin Per Se procedures.

FIRST OFFENSE

- a fine from $300 to $1,000
- possible jail term - 48 hrs. to 6 mos.
- suspension of license - up to 6 mos.

The vehicle may be impounded and the driver will be billed for storage. An alcohol rehabilitation program may be imposed. An ignition interlock device, that prevents operation of the vehicle when alcohol is detected in the driver's breath, may be required. A fee when the suspension is completed is required.

SECOND OFFENSE (within 7 years)

- a fine from $500 to $1,000
- mandatory jail term - up to one year
- suspension of license - up to 18 months
- probation - up to 5 years

The vehicle may be impounded for up to 90 days. An ignition interlock device will be required. The driver must file proof of financial responsibility with the DMV and pay the re-instatement fee before the license will be re-issued.

ADDITIONAL PENALTIES ARE ADDED IF CONVICTED OF FAILURE TO SUBMIT TO OR COMPLETE A TEST.

MISDEMEANOR VS. FELONY

DUI is usually a misdemeanor; however, if anyone were injured as a result of a collision while a driver is impaired, the charge becomes a felony. A felony is punishable by a heavy fine, an automatic jail term, an extended probationary period and a permanent criminal record (just like bank robbers, murderers, etc.).

Rules of the Road

Traffic laws are important because they promote the orderly operation of the HTS. They govern the behavior of all road users and assist in predicting what others will do. They include basic driving rules, rules of right-of-way, and speed laws.

BASIC DRIVING RULES:

- always drive to the right of the center on a two-way roadway
- obey all posted signs and signals
- when traffic signal lights are defective, all drivers must stop (four-way stop)
- pass other vehicles on the left only when the way is clear (on multilane one-ways, passing or overtaking on the right is permitted)
- always communicate your intention to turn or change lanes by using your turn signals over a sufficient distance
- make sure that maneuvers can be performed safely before executing them
- drive at speeds that are safe for the road, weather and traffic conditions.

RIGHT-OF-WAY

The right-of-way rules are designed to determine who should go first when two road users want to occupy the same space. The primary concept is- YOU SHOULD ALWAYS YIELD THE RIGHT-OF-WAY IN ORDER TO AVOID A COLLISION! The rules specify who shall yield to whom. They never specify who has the right-of-way. This distinction is important. **You never have the right-of-way; SOMEONE ELSE MUST GIVE IT TO YOU.**

Drivers must yield to emergency vehicles when these vehicles have their sirens activated and/or lights flashing.

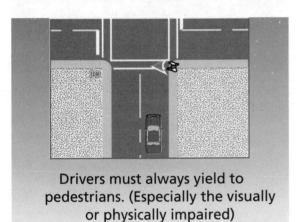

Drivers must always yield to pedestrians. (Especially the visually or physically impaired)

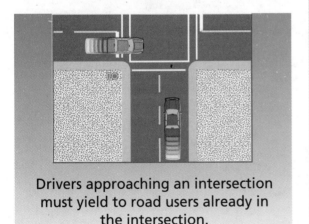

Drivers approaching an intersection must yield to road users already in the intersection.

AT A FOUR-WAY STOP INTERSECTION

1. The vehicle that stops first, should go first.
2. The vehicle that enters the intersection first, should go first.
3. If two or more vehicles stop simultaneously, the vehicle on the left should yield to the vehicle on the right.

AFTER STOPPING, ROLL SLOWLY FORWARD. OTHER DRIVERS CANNOT READ YOUR MIND. ANNOUNCE YOUR INTENT TO PROCEED WHEN IT IS YOUR TURN.

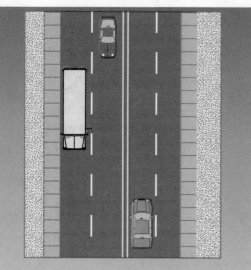

Drivers must stop in both directions when a school bus is stopped with its red signal lights flashing.
(If the roadway is separated by a median or physical divider, oncoming vehicles are not obliged to stop.)

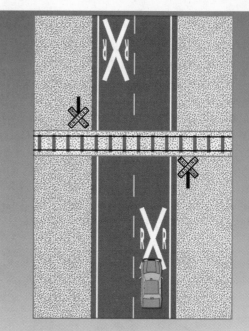

Drivers must stop when facing a railroad crossing with the lights flashing, gates down, or a train is approaching.

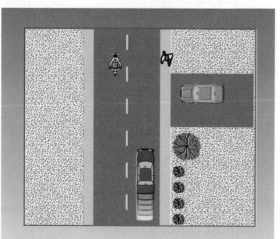

Drivers exiting private property must yield to road users on the roadway.

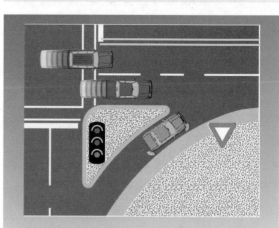

Drivers facing a stop or yield sign must let traffic on the crossroad go first.

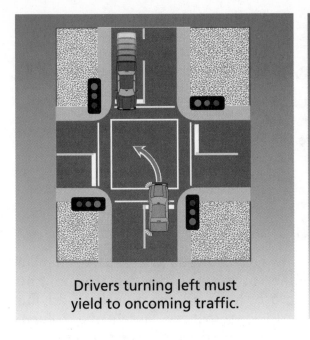

Drivers turning left must
yield to oncoming traffic.

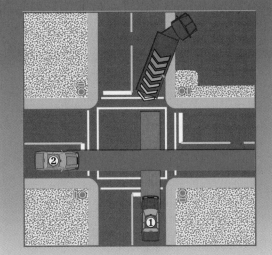

Drivers must not enter until they can
cross and exit the intersection in safety.

3 - F

In Case of a Collision

Despite your best intentions, you may be involved in a collision. Loss of time, human suffering, damage to your vehicle, and legal problems resulting in great expense can be the result. Remain calm.

- Stop immediately.
- Warn others if possible.
- Enlist the assistance of others to warn and/or direct traffic.
- Give aid to the injured within your abilities.
- Call for the police and medical aid.
- Exchange information.
- Write down the names and addresses of witnesses.

- Remain at the scene.
- Make an accident report.
- Do not admit fault or sign any documents other than those requested by the police.
- Have a medical check-up.
- Report the collision to your insurance.

If you are the first to arrive at the scene of a collision, be prepared to stop and render any assistance possible. When emergency vehicles are already at the scene, reduce speed and be prepared to stop if necessary.

State law may require further reporting of the collision: DMV report showing proof of financial responsibility (insurance).

Review

TERMS TO REMEMBER - WRITE A SHORT DEFINITION FOR THE FOLLOWING :

- Vision screening test
- Knowledge test
- Instruction permit
- Road test

- Certificate of title
- Registration card
- Insurance certificate
- Point system

- Suspension
- Revocation
- Yield
- Right-of-way

SUMMARY

The highway code is a body of rules that govern the operation of the HTS. A valid driver's license, proper registration and proof of insurance are necessary to operate a vehicle. The rules of the road assist all road users to anticipate and share the roadway. Traffic violators will be prosecuted and may find their driving privilege suspended. In case of a collision, proper procedures must be followed.

TEST A - WRITE "T" BESIDE STATEMENTS THAT ARE TRUE AND "F" BESIDE THOSE THAT ARE FALSE.

_____ **1.** With a learner's license, you must be accompanied by an instructor.

_____ **2.** Loaning your driver's license to someone else is permitted.

_____ **3.** You must inform the DMV of any change of address.

_____ **4.** It is illegal to drive while impaired by drugs or alcohol.

_____ **5.** Criminal code traffic infractions entail a minimum one year revocation.

_____ **6.** When a license is suspended for demerit points, all points are erased.

_____ **7.** Right-of-way is always given to the vehicle on the right.

_____ **8.** Using turn signals before a maneuver is always required by law.

_____ **9.** At a railway crossing, all vehicles are always required to stop.

_____ **10.** After a collision, you are always required to call for a peace officer.

TEST B - MATCH THE ITEMS IN COLUMN B TO THE ITEMS IN COLUMN A BY WRITING THE CORRECT NUMBER IN THE SPACE PROVIDED.

COLUMN A

_____ A) Graduated license

_____ B) Instruction permit

_____ C) Registration

_____ D) Demerit system

_____ E) Admin Per Se

_____ F) Implied consent

_____ G) Right-of-way

_____ H) Four-way stop

_____ I) Yield

_____ J) Witness

COLUMN B

1) An administrative license suspension law over and above court imposed sanctions.

2) Card identifying ownership of a vehicle.

3) New driver license with some limitations, such as zero BAC.

4) The immediate use of a portion of the HTS.

5) An individual who is willing to provide details or information as to what he/she has seen.

6) To give another road user the immediate use of the roadway.

7) A license control measure used to identify and correct negligent drivers.

8) An intersection with stop signs controlling the flow of traffic in all directions.

9) Legislation requiring every driver to submit to an alcohol/drug test upon request.

10) A learning license permitting a beginner to drive accompanied by a licensed adult.

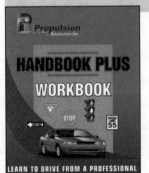

HANDBOOK PLUS WORKBOOK

*Check your comprehension and mastery of the contents of this chapter by completing the corresponding exercises that are found in the complement to the **HANDBOOK PLUS**:*

HANDBOOK PLUS WORKBOOK

Complete the exercises on Pages 20 to 32 then check your responses by referring to the answer key on Page 107.
If necessary, review the chapter for each error and refer to your instructor for further guidance.

Student notes

Physical & Mental Health

**4 - A
Physical Health**

**4 - B
Mental Health**

**4 - C
Vision**

**4 - D
Carbon
Monoxide**

**4 - E
Review**

Road conditions, the driver, and the vehicle are all elements in the safe and proper operation of the Highway Transportation System.

Despite administrative rules and controls, the cornerstone of traffic safety is the driver. The physical and mental fitness of the human being who will sit behind the steering wheel will be the final determination of the efficient use of the Highway Transportation System.

Medication, physical impairments, alcohol, drugs, fatigue, vision, and visual skills are some of the factors that can affect the driver's degree of attention, alertness, and ability to drive. In this chapter, we will examine these factors, and others, in detail.

AFTER COMPLETING THIS CHAPTER, THE STUDENT MUST BE ABLE TO DEMONSTRATE COMPETENCE IN THEIR KNOWLEDGE OF AND RESPONSIBILITY IN DECISION-MAKING WITH RESPECT TO:

- physical and mental health factors affecting driving skills.
- the laws, the effects and consequences of driving while impaired.
- vision and driving as well as the danger of carbon monoxide.

Physical Health

The driving task is not simply a robotic execution of maneuvers. Though not seemingly physically demanding, driving requires attention, decision making, coordination, and proper action. Many factors may have a profound influence on a driver's ability to perform.

Your nervous and muscular systems combine to provide the coordination necessary to drive. Different people have different levels of ability. The key is to adapt your driving to the level of your personal skills. As well, it is important to drive when your condition is at its best and to refrain from driving whenever they are not. To know your own limits.

AGE affects coordination and vision. Young drivers have the advantage; and yet, statistics demonstrate that younger drivers have more accidents. Older drivers, having slower reflexes and reduced hearing and vision, have less accidents because they adapt by driving more slowly. They depend on their experience to avoid critical situations.

YOUNG NOVICE DRIVERS with quick reflexes and excellent vision have to learn to control their impulsiveness, develop their judgement and build up their experience, thus avoiding the pitfalls that produce accidents.

Some physical disabilities are temporary in nature though they require the same vigilance and adaptation.
SOMETIMES THE DECISION NOT TO DRIVE IS THE ONLY INTELLIGENT CHOICE.

FATIGUE

Mental or physical work, emotional stress, lack of sleep or even a heavy meal can cause fatigue or drowsiness. These lessen your ability to drive. They can cause blurred vision, seeing double, loss of depth perception, and falling asleep at the wheel.

COMMON SYMPTOMS:
- Yawning
- Lack of co-ordination
- Tendency to stare
- Aggressiveness
- Itchy eyes
- Irritability
- Optical illusions.

If you must drive when fatigued - after a long day at work or school - here are some precautions to help compensate:

- Ventilate your vehicle (set the air conditioner at a lower temperature)
- Rest prior to starting out and at regular intervals
- Force your eyes to scan and move your eyes and head more than normally.
- Change your seating position slightly from time to time.
- Converse with passengers (try not to drive alone)
- Keep yourself mentally alert.

The only real solution is to STOP AND REST as long as is necessary or CHANGE DRIVERS for someone who is more alert.

On long trips, never start out at a time close to the hour when you would normally go to sleep. We are creatures of habit and our alertness is at its lowest at this time. If fatigue overtakes you, **STOP AND REST;** even if it means parking in a rest area and sleeping in the car. There is no fixed rule on how many hours to drive at any one time. **PLAN AHEAD.** Include periodic stops for rest, at least once every two hours.

MEDICATION

Many temporary illnesses may require medication. Whether "prescription" type - prescribed by a doctor, or "over the counter" type - purchased at a pharmacy;

ALL DRUGS MAY HAVE SIDE-EFFECTS THAT MAY AFFECT YOUR ABILITY TO DRIVE. Care should be taken to check labels, inquire from your pharmacist or ask your doctor to ensure that you will be capable of driving while taking this particular medication.

In your everyday lifestyle, there are other drugs such as nicotine or caffeine that can adversely affect your ability to drive.

Illegal drugs are just that: illegal. Driving under the influence of drugs imposes severe penalties on anyone convicted of this infraction. This usually includes the suspension of the driver's license, as well as heavy fines or imprisonment or both.

There is a chart on the next page listing various drugs and their side effects.

People who suffer from chronic illnesses (diabetes, heart disease, etc,) may be issued licenses providing their condition is under medical control. The DMV may require proof (on special forms) of their medical status.

The physically disabled can also drive provided they have special controls to compensate for their particular disability. These drivers must learn to adapt their driving habits and procedures.

DRUGS	HOW OBTAINED	POSSIBLE SIDE EFFECTS
Central-nervous system stimulants (such as diet pills, pep pills) Examples: amphetamines (Benzedrine, Dexedrine)	• Prescription only for chronic fatigue, mild depression, overweight, narcolepsy (sleep compulsion)	• Depression, headache, dizziness, decreased ability to concentrate, irritability, hallucinations, hyperactivity
Analgesics (painkillers) Examples non-narcotic - Aspirin, Exedrin, Anacin	• Over-the-counter for pain	• Bleeding in the stomach and intestines
Anti-infective agents Examples: sulfa drugs, antibiotics (Aureomycine, Penicillin, Steptromycin)	• Prescription only for infections	• Nausea
Antihistamines (in many cold pills, hay fever pills) Examples: Atarax, Benadryl, Chlortrimeton, Dramamine, Pyrilamine	• Prescription and over-the-counter for colds, motion sickness, control of allergies, nasal congestion insomnia	• Drowsiness, inattention, confusion, dizziness
Sedatives-hypnotics (sleeping pills) Examples: barbiturates Amital, Luminal, Nembutal, Noctec, Seconal, Sominex	• Prescription only for insomnia, high blood pressure, epilepsy, emotional conditions	• Mental confusion, poor muscle coordination, irritability, drowsiness
Local anesthetics	• Minor surgery, oral surgery	• Poor reflexes/judgement, fatique
Anti-anxiety agents Examples: benzodiazepines (Valium, Tanxene, Serax)	• Prescription only for mild and moderate anxiety	• Drowsiness, blurred vision, fatigue
Tranquilizers Examples: Equanil, Haldol, Librium, Mellaril, Miltown, Navane, Phenothiazine, Thorazine, Vallium	• Prescription only for severe anxiety, emotional problems, alcoholism	• Drowsiness, faintness, vomiting, tremors, dizziness
Narcotics Examples: morphine, codeine (cough syrup). Darvon, Demerol, Percodan, Vicodin (painkillers)	• Prescription and over-the counter for deadening pain, inducing sleep	• Inability to concentrate, apathy, euphoria, stupor, dimness of vision, drowsiness, nausea
Cannabinoids Examples: marijuana, hashish	• Illegal, only for medical research uses	• Less coordination, distorts distance, hallucinations, depression, panic, fear
Hallucinogens Examples: LSD, peyote, mescaline, DMT, STP	• Illegal, only for emotional illness, alcoholism (experimentally)	• Hallucinations, striking distortions in senses, hands / feet shake, floating sensation, panic, depression

Mental Health

Strong emotions can interfere with your ability to think and reason. Anger, fear, joy and depression are some examples of these. They can affect your alertness, concentration, and decision-making - all aspects central to your safety. When strong emotions take hold - postpone driving. **Wind down before you crank up!** "TAKING A DRIVE" to solve your problems may involve you in a more serious situation. The possibility of a "Road Rage" incident occurring.

While driving, realize you cannot control traffic; you can control your reactions to it! Learn to spot the warning signs of stress, fatigue as well as anger and **develop some positive coping strategies**:

- Don't drive - let someone else drive
- Drive in an organized manner - apply your concentration and skills
- Identify situations well in advance
- Adjust your expectations
- Avoid heavy traffic areas
- Stop driving and rest if emotions get out of hand.

Realize that you are also at risk from other drivers - **"Road Rage" or aggressive drivers**. Thousands are reported injured or killed in the USA every year. Do not underestimate the potential for violence. Millions are armed with weapons (firearms, knives, clubs, etc.) and **every driver is armed with a much more lethal weapon** - their vehicle. Anyone - old or young, male or female, rich or poor, from any racial background - can be an aggressive driver and attack you.

Keep your cool in traffic. **Give other driver's the benefit of the doubt.** Disassociate yourself from problems. Correct unsafe driving habits that are likely to infuriate or antagonize others. **Avoid all conflicts.** Recognize the absurdity of traffic disputes. **If you are pursued, don't go home. Proceed to a police station or location where there will be witnesses or you can get help.**

ALCOHOL

The effects of alcohol on driving have become a matter of great social concern.

Accident statistics demonstrate a drastic toll in deaths and injuries where alcohol was a major factor (in almost one-half of all fatal collisions). This is especially the case when teen drivers are involved, even though they are not of drinking age. **(The legal age for drinking alcohol is 21.)** The leading cause of death for teens aged 16 to 19 is motor vehicle crashes.

In recent years, there has been a decline in fatalities due to collisions. This is due in part to developments in vehicle safety features (air bags, ABS, etc.) and also in part because of increased police surveillance, the severity of court penalties and the actions of public groups to prevent impaired driving (MADD, SADD, etc.). There is , however, still a long way to go. One fatal collision in which alcohol or drugs are a contributing factor is one too many! There is no possible justification for a responsible driver taking the wheel unless in complete control of all of his/her faculties.

As a responsible driver, you should **NEVER DRINK AND DRIVE**.

AS A DRUG

Alcohol is a drug. It's a chemical (ethanol or ethyl alcohol) which is the result of fermentation. Fermentation is a process similar to digestion, but it occurs outside the body. When the pulp of grapes or grains has been literally digested by yeast, the result is ethyl alcohol or ethanol. Because alcohol is the result of fermentation, unlike food which must be digested, it is absorbed directly into the bloodstream. It is then absorbed by all of the fluids in the body tissues. The human brain has a larger concentration of body fluids and thus absorbs a greater percentage of the alcohol.

The liver must eliminate 90% of this absorbed alcohol, at its own steady rate. You cannot speed up the process. The liver oxidizes the alcohol present in the bloodstream - converting it into water and carbon dioxide; approximately one alcoholic serving per hour.

(1.5 OZ. HIGHBALL, 12 OZ. OF BEER, 5 OZ. OF WINE)

There is no miracle cure. Once alcohol is imbibed, TIME IS THE ONLY REMEDY!

STAGES OF ALCOHOL INFLUENCE

All of the negative consequences of alcohol **start with the first drink!** They are also aggravated by your mood and fatigue. When are you unable to drive? YOU SHOULD **NEVER DRINK AND DRIVE!**

What is the legal limit?

Drivers under 21 years of age are charged at .01 or .02 and over in most states.

Over .08 or .10, the driver will be cited and prosecuted under the Criminal Code.

BLOOD ALCOHOL LEVEL

The amount of alcohol in a person's bloodstream can be measured by a chemical analysis of the blood, urine, or breath. The amount of alcohol present is expressed as a percent and is referred to as blood alcohol concentration (BAC).

Many factors affect your BAC: your ideal weight, your sex, what you drink, if you

ESTIMATED BAC BY NUMBER OF DRINKS IN RELATION TO BODY WEIGHT

FEMALES

BODY WEIGHT LBS	NUMBER OF DRINKS									
	1	2	3	4	5	6	7	8	9	10
100	.050	.101	.152	.203	.253	.304	.355	.406	.456	.507
125	.040	.080	.120	.162	.202	.244	.282	.324	.364	.404
150	.034	.068	.101	.135	.169	.203	.237	.271	.304	.338
175	.029	.058	.087	.117	.146	.175	.204	.233	.262	.292
200	.026	.050	.076	.101	.126	.152	.177	.203	.227	.253
225	.022	.045	.068	.091	.113	.136	.159	.182	.204	.227
250	.020	.041	.061	.082	.101	.122	.142	.162	.182	.202

MALES

BODY WEIGHT LBS	NUMBER OF DRINKS									
	1	2	3	4	5	6	7	8	9	10
100	.043	.087	.130	.174	.217	.261	.304	.348	.391	.435
125	.034	.069	.103	.139	.173	.209	.242	.278	.312	.346
150	.029	.058	.087	.116	.145	.174	.203	.232	.261	.290
175	.025	.050	.075	.100	.125	.150	.175	.200	.225	.250
200	.022	.043	.065	.087	.108	.130	.152	.174	.195	.217
225	.019	.039	.058	.078	.097	.117	.136	.156	.175	.195
250	.017	.035	.052	.070	.087	.105	.122	.139	.156	.173

1 DRINK = Beer (12 oz) — Wine (5 oz) — Spirits (1.5 oz)

HOURS SINCE FIRST DRINK	1	2	3	4	5
SUBTRACT FROM BAC	.015	.030	.045	.060	.075

eat before and while drinking, how many drinks you consume, and the elapsed time while consuming them. **Consult the chart above.** Base the calculations on an ideal weight of 150 lbs. Presume you had ingested four alcoholic beverages over a two hour period. Deduct for how much time has elapsed since you started drinking. **WHAT WOULD YOUR BAC BE ?**

For a male, .086; for a female, .105.

It is commonly accepted that by a BAC of .03 to .05, a driver's abilities are impaired.

EFFECTS OF ALCOHOL ON REACTION TIME

Your ability to react to any unusual situation is reduced starting from the first drink. It deteriorates further with any increase in your BAC. Needless to say, you may be slow to understand or you may understand the wrong thing. You will be slow to decide and react (or react improperly) and then the muscles will not respond normally.

ACCIDENT POTENTIAL / STATISTICS

If your BAC exceeds .04 (yellow zone), you are five times more likely to be involved in a collision. If your BAC were above .08 (red zone), you would be twenty five times more likely to be involved in a collision. In the USA, more than twenty thousand people a year are killed in alcohol-related collisions (more than 400 a week). More than a half million are seriously injured every year and many are left permanently crippled or disfigured. The cost of alcohol-related collisions is estimated to be over ten billion dollars annually. These fatalities or injuries affect all of the parties involved, not just the impaired individuals. This is a major social problem that must be rectified.

EFFECTS OF ALCOHOL ON THE BODY

Alcohol has both immediate effects on the body as well as long term effects if the body is consistently exposed to alcohol. The immediate effects are of most interest because it is these that affect your driving ability.

ORGANS

Long term, heavy use of alcohol can lead to addiction (alcoholism). The liver, brain and other organs can become damaged. Cirrhosis of the liver usually leads to internal bleeding, liver failure and death. The brain can be damaged to the point where the individual cannot function normally in society. Problem drinkers continue to abuse alcohol and create problems for themselves, their families and their communities.

VISION

Alcohol is a depressant. It has a relaxing effect on all muscles of the body. The fine, delicate muscles of the eye that focus and move the eyes are also relaxed and the resulting image loses its sharp focus. The more relaxed the muscles, the fuzzier the picture becomes. (Double vision) Rather than scan the roadway ahead and to the sides as well as glancing at the rear-view mirror, a driver under the influence of alcohol tends to stare at a point straight ahead or any object that attracts attention.

Glare from oncoming headlights or the environment produces a greater effect on the impaired driver and the time required to recover from the glare is much longer than normal.

Possible results are:
- a tendency to stare straight ahead
- a narrowing of the field of vision
- a reduction in depth perception
- a reduction of adaptability to darkness
- increased sensitivity to glare
- a longer time to readjust after glare.

4

BRAIN

The activity of the brain is also slowed thus affecting judgement, reflexes and muscular coordination. The image from the eyes is unclear and the brain is not functioning normally due to the presence of alcohol in combination with the body fluids in the brain tissue. What a great recipe for disaster!

Other effects of alcohol are:
- reduced awareness of danger
- over-confidence (more reckless)
- difficulty recognizing potential hazards
- difficulty making decisions
- a reduction in balance (equilibrium).

HOW TO AVOID/IDENTIFY DRUNK DRIVERS

Drunk drivers identify themselves by riding the lines, weaving, driving at inconsistent speeds, intermittent braking, misjudging stops (too soon or too late), driving without headlights, etc.
When you see a driver that seems to be drunk, turn off the road into a parking lot or side street. Keep away from that vehicle; the driver could involve you in a serious crash.

Try to get the license number of the vehicle. Call the police immediately and report it along with the color, make, model, and direction of travel. In so doing, you will be instrumental in removing a drunk driver from the HTS and possibly preventing a collision involving injuries or fatalities. You are all responsible for the safety of all other road users who share the HTS.

ALTERNATIVES TO DRINKING AND DRIVING

As a responsible driver, you should **NEVER DRINK AND DRIVE**.

Many other options are open to you if you are in a situation where drinking of alcoholic beverages is occurring:

THE DESIGNATED DRIVER - The person who will drive abstains from drinking alcoholic beverages and receives complimentary non-alcoholic beverages and/or food.
Encourage your friends and favorite establishments to participate in the program. (Contact your local police department for materials/info.)

S.A.D.D. or M.A.D.D. - Organized groups that support people who have been drinking and do not wish to drive.
A contract is signed by the two parties stating they will come to get you - no matter what, no questions asked.

ABSTINENCE - Refuse to drink alcoholic beverages as you will be driving. Try to assist others who do drink.

ALTERNATE TRANSPORTATION - Take a cab! Get a ride! Call home and ask a family member to come and get you! Let someone else drive who has not been drinking. Don't ride with someone who has been drinking. Try to get the car keys. Friends don't let their friends drive drunk. Do your best to convince them not to drive; offer alternate transportation. If you can't convince them; don't ride with them.

SLEEP OVER - Stay the night at a friend's place. If you are the host, encourage impaired people to sleep over if any other alternate transportation cannot be found.

In situations where alcohol is being consumed, follow the recommendations above and encourage others to do likewise. Choose one of the options; any one you like; however, if you consume alcoholic beverages, **don't drive**.
Moreover, don't accept a ride from someone else who has been drinking.

If you host a party, plan a wide selection of non-alcoholic beverages. Serve food throughout the evening. If guests are of drinking age, don't force drinks on them; space any alcoholic beverages out. Stop serving alcoholic beverages at least one hour before the end of the evening.
Encourage any guests that have been drinking to sleep over or take alternate transportation home. Don't allow any impaired person to drive. Get their keys! If necessary, pay for the taxi.

SYNERGISTIC EFFECT

NEVER MIX DRUGS AND ALCOHOL.

Alcohol when combined with other drugs produces a result , referred to as a synergistic effect, that will be far greater than would normally have been expected. It is greater than the sum of each of the parts.

Alcohol is a primary drug. When present in your body, your system concentrates on the alcohol and ignores any other substances. Any other substance then produces a much greater effect than usual because a normal dose takes into account that some of the drug will be eliminated by your system.

Moreover, the alcohol may react with the other chemical and produce a new combination. In either case, it will have very dangerous effects and should be avoided at all costs.

4

Vision

Most of the information you need to drive is collected through the use of the eyes. The eye receives images by utilizing reflected light through the iris - like a camera - and transmits these images to the brain by the optic nerves.

Each eye captures approximately "30 to 40 images" per second.

To become a skilled driver, you must develop this eye quickness, by practice, so that you can effectively scan the roadway.

VISUAL ACUITY

Visual acuity refers to the clarity of your vision. Your ability to distinguish details up close and from afar.

Most states have certain minimum norms and require a vision test to acquire a license. Most problems can be corrected with glasses. Some defects will mean restrictions on a driver's license and in extreme cases, a license is not issued.

The responsible driver should have an eye examination at least every two years or at any time that vision becomes blurred or there is trouble focusing.

FIELD OF VISION

Your field of vision includes all the area that you can see. It includes two basic types of vision:

CENTRAL VISION: a 3 degree conic range that identifies details, color, etc.

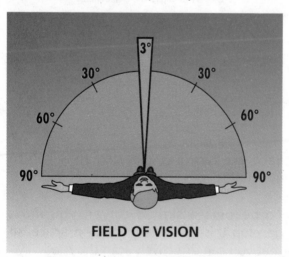

FIELD OF VISION

PERIPHERAL VISION: vision to the left and right up to a total of 180 degrees for most people. It detects movement, masses and shapes.

Your peripheral vision acts as radar to attract your attention; the central conic vision scans and identifies. The images transmitted to the brain by your two eyes are transformed into a three-dimensional image. This produces "stereoscopic vision" enabling you to judge distance, depth perception and measure relative speeds. All of these abilities are affected when driving at night. In Chapter 13, vision under many adverse conditions will be discussed in detail.

SELECTIVE VISION

The beginning driver, having developed the ability to scan the roadway, is now faced with a situation that is called **INFORMATION OVERLOAD**. The eyes are delivering images to the brain at the rate of a couple of thousand per minute. The human brain is incapable of dealing with all of these.

You must develop a technique called selective seeing. The capability of the brain to retain and concentrate on only those images it considers important to the situation at hand. The signs, hazards and signals that relate to your driving.

A pedestrian on the sidewalk is seen; a pedestrian walking towards the roadway is seen and verified again as a potential hazard.

This ability is essential to becoming a safe, smart and efficient driver.

MONOCULAR VISION

People who have suffered the loss of an eye or have an inherent eye problem have to learn to assess distance, speed and safety margins without 3-D vision. They should center their good eye on the road ahead and scan more frequently.

In cases of fatigue, monocular vision can develop. This is extremely dangerous because the affliction is temporary and the driver has not adapted to this problem.

COLOR PERCEPTION

Many people suffer color blindness. They must learn to identify signs and signals by shape and position.

TUNNEL VISION

An affliction where the normal peripheral vision is reduced to 140 degrees or less. People with this problem must scan more frequently.

AS YOU INCREASE YOUR SPEED on expressways, your normal field of vision decreases. The higher the speed, the narrower the field of vision. All drivers must learn to scan more frequently at higher speeds.

4

Carbon Monoxide

Carbon monoxide is a colorless, odorless, tasteless gas that is one of the by-products of the internal combustion engine. It is a deadly poison. The bloodstream absorbs it faster than oxygen and it sedates the person. It causes headaches, drowsiness, dizziness, and, if in a large enough quantity, death.

To protect yourself and your passengers, check your exhaust system periodically and repair any leaks. Always drive with fresh air circulating in the passenger compartment. Never run an engine in an enclosed space such as a garage or underground parking lot. In heavy traffic or tunnels be aware of the danger and limit outside air. Should anyone succumb to carbon monoxide gas by falling

asleep, move them out into fresh air immediately, lay them down, apply artificial respiration, if necessary. Call for a doctor even if they seem to revive.

Review

TERMS TO REMEMBER - WRITE A SHORT DEFINITION FOR THE FOLLOWING :

- Fatigue
- Prescription drugs
- Chronic illness
- Emotions
- M.A.D.D.

- BAC
- Visual acuity
- Field of vision
- Central vision
- Peripheral vision

- Selective seeing
- Information overload
- Monocular vision
- Tunnel vision
- Carbon monoxide

SUMMARY

Your mental and physical well-being is essential to your ability to drive properly. To ensure this, avoid drugs, alcohol, stress, fatigue and anything else that may diminish your faculties.

When either your physical or mental condition are not 100%, DO NOT DRIVE.

Practice your visual skills to develop good scanning and selective seeing habits. Since most of the data you need to drive is collected through the eyes, learn to use your eyes to their utmost.

Carbon monoxide is a toxic gas that is odorless, tasteless and colorless.

TEST A - COMPLETE THE SENTENCES BY FILLING IN THE BLANKS.

1. The most important factor in all driving situations is the _____ of the driver.

2. When a doctor prescribes medication and you know you will be driving, you should _____ the _____ or pharmacist if the medication will affect your driving ability.

3. After driving for several hours, you are feeling tired, the best solution is to stop and _____ or to _____ drivers.

4. 90% of consumed alcohol is eliminated by the _____ at its own steady _____.

5. If you drink a *mere* 2 or 3 alcoholic beverages, one hour before driving, it will _____ your judgement and your _____.

6. On the freeway, your normal field of vision _____ as you increase speed.

TEST B - MATCH THE ITEMS IN COLUMN B TO THE ITEMS IN COLUMN A BY WRITING THE CORRECT NUMBER IN THE SPACE PROVIDED.

COLUMN A	COLUMN B

COLUMN A

_____ **A)** Fatigue

_____ **B)** Prescription

_____ **C)** BAC

_____ **D)** Designated driver

_____ **E)** Synergistic effect

_____ **F)** Visual acuity

_____ **G)** Peripheral vision

_____ **H)** Information overload

_____ **I)** Tunnel vision

_____ **J)** Carbon monoxide

COLUMN B

1) The effect that a combination of drugs and alcohol will have on an individual.

2) An anagram for blood alcohol concentration.

3) Drowsiness caused by mental or physical work, emotional stress, lack of sleep, etc.

4) Vision towards the sides, up to 180°.

5) A byproduct of the internal combustion engine that is odorless, colorless and tasteless.

6) An affliction where the normal peripheral vision is reduced to 140° or less.

7) A person who abstains from consuming any alcohol in order to chauffeur partying friends.

8) The eyes deliver too many images to the brain.

9) The clarity of a person's ability to perceive objects in front of him/her.

10) Medication requiring a doctor to fill out a special form.

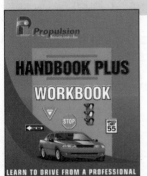

HANDBOOK PLUS WORKBOOK

*Check your comprehension and mastery of the contents of this chapter by completing the corresponding exercises that are found in the complement to the **HANDBOOK PLUS:***

HANDBOOK PLUS WORKBOOK

Complete the exercises on Pages 33 to 41 then check your responses by referring to the answer key on Pages 107 and 108.
If necessary, review the chapter for each error and refer to your instructor for further guidance.

Student notes

Knowing your Vehicle

5 - A
The Cockpit Drill

5 - B
The Instrument Panel

5 - C
The Vehicle Controls

5 - D
Comfort and Convenience Devices

5 - E
Review

Finally, the keys and the car... Your dream has come true! You climb in behind the wheel, the engine starts and purrs. Wow! Shift into gear and you're off. The sky darkens, rain starts to fall... Where is that wiper switch? Oops, not that one. Oh, There it is! And now, the headlights. What does that bright blue light mean? Why is that oncoming car flashing high beams? My gosh... the car in front is braking... You're sliding!! Your heart is pounding!

Now what?!

Good or bad habits are acquired through repetition. Familiarity with controls must be acquired before driving. Any other course of action could be fatal. Don't wait for experience to teach you, start with the right technique. Know your controls and practice.

AFTER COMPLETING THIS CHAPTER, THE STUDENT MUST BE ABLE TO LOCATE, OPERATE AND DESCRIBE:

- the information devices and symbols on the instrument panel.
- the control devices for operating the vehicle.
- the procedures when a warning device indicates abnormal operation.

The Cockpit Drill

Whether you are a novice driver or merely driving a different car for the first time, before you drive, you need to become familiar with the instruments, gauges, and controls of the vehicle.

This requires some practice. The first step: identify the location and function of all indicators/gauges in the instrument panel. Then practice glancing at them, returning your eyes to the road ahead.

The second step: identify, locate, and further, use the hand controls. Practice using them until you can do so without taking your eyes from the road ahead.

The final step: perform the same practice with the vehicle controls, the shifter lever, the ignition switch, the pedals, etc.

As a student learning to drive, this "cockpit drill" will require some time and practice. Do it on the vehicle that you will be driving once you "earn" your license. This will assist you to feel more comfortable and be more competent in your own vehicle. As well, when you take your practice lessons, the "cockpit drill" can be performed more quickly in that vehicle as you will already have this experience.

Remember, whenever you drive a new vehicle, take the time to run through your basic "cockpit drill". You'll never regret the few moments it will take. You will never be caught searching for a control device when you need to use it urgently.

The Instrument Panel

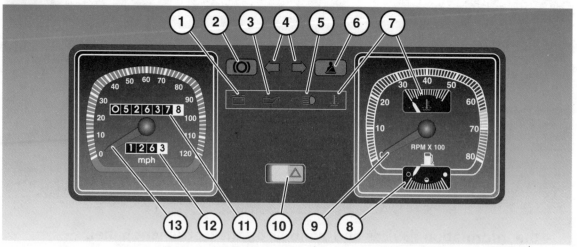

The instrument panel, part of the dashboard, is located directly in front of the driver. On it are mounted various indicators and gauges to inform the driver of the condition of the vehicle in order to drive safely. On the opposite page, there is an illustration of an instrument panel. The chart below describes the items numbered in the illustration.

INDICATOR	FUNCTION	INFORMATION
(1) ALTERNATOR (gauge or light)	Indicates intensity of electrical current	The light comes on if the current is abnormal. Turn off all unnecessary accessories, do not shut off the engine and go to the nearest service station.
(2) BRAKE LIGHT	Indicates the parking brake is activated or the brake system is faulty	Stop your vehicle and check the parking brake and brake fluid level. If these are normal, have your vehicle towed
(3) OIL PRESSURE (gauge or light)	Indicates the oil pressure in the engine	The light comes on when the oil pressure is insufficient. STOP YOUR VEHICLE AND THE ENGINE
(4) TURN SIGNALS	Flash if the turn signal or hazard lights are activated	If the light or arrow does not flash normally, this indicates a burnt bulb or faulty wiring.
(5) HIGH BEAM	When lit indicates the high beams are on	Check when activating the headlight switch
(6) SEAT BELT	Reminder to fasten the safety belts	The light comes on and a buzzer sounds for several seconds
(7) TEMPERATURE (gauge and light)	Indicates the operating temperature of the engine coolant	The light comes on when the engine overheats SHIFT TO NEUTRAL, DEPRESS THE GAS PEDAL SLIGHTLY TO REV MOTOR Set the heater at maximum heat. If no improvement, turn off engine (See Chapter 14)
(8) FUEL GAUGE (light also)	Indicates the fuel level in the gas tank	CHECK BEFORE STARTING OUT! Always keep more than 1/4 full. Keep almost full in winter (PREVENTS IMPURITIES AND GAS LINE FREEZING)
(9) TACHOMETER	Indicates the engine revolutions per minute (RPM x 100)	Check to shift at appropriate moment (standard) Avoid entering red zone - may cause engine damage
(10) HAZARD SWITCH	Activates hazard lights (disables turn signals)	Activates the turn signals in both directions simultaneously. Use to warn others of danger
(11) ODOMETER	Displays the mileage the vehicle has accumulated since it was manufactured	Check for vehicle maintenance schedule. Check when purchasing a used vehicle.
(12) TRIP ODOMETER	Displays the mileage since it was reset to zero	Useful in calculating fuel consumption and trip mileage
(13) SPEEDOMETER	Indicates the vehicle speed in miles per hour	Check frequently while driving to remain within speed limits

5

The Vehicle Controls

In additional to the instrument panel, vehicles are equipped with a number of other controls such as lights, comfort controls, and controls for safety.

HEADLIGHT CONTROL (14):
In many vehicles, the control may be located on the turn signal lever. (15)

1ST POSITION (14):
- Turns on the parking lights - amber lights in front, red in rear, use when parking if you must ensure the vehicle is visible to other road users.

- NEVER use alone when in motion.
- The instrument panel, license plate, and side marker lights will also illuminate.

2ND POSITION (14):
- Turns on the headlight as well as those mentioned in the first position.
- Always check the high beam indicator.
- High or low beams may be on.
- **DRIVE WITH LIGHTS ON AT ALL TIMES**

RHEOSTAT (14 or a separate item):
- Regulates the intensity of backlighting in the instrument panel.

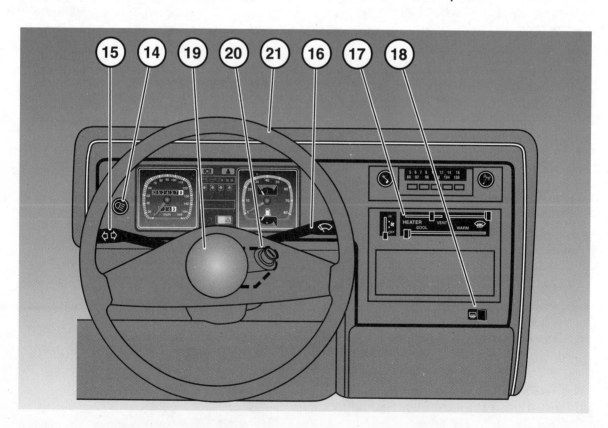

- Lower the intensity in unlit areas; raise the intensity in well lit areas.

TURN SIGNAL LEVER (15):

- Use to communicate your intentions
- Activates the turn signal lights and an indicator light in the instrument panel
- Move in the same direction as you will move the steering wheel
- HIGH BEAM DIMMER SWITCH - push or pull to change intensity of headlights
- The blue high beam indicator light informs the driver when the high beams are lit.

WIPER + WASHER CONTROL (16):

May be located on the dash or turn signal.
- Use to clear the windshield
- Several positions - OFF, INTERMITTENT (optional), SLOW, FAST. The reservoir fluid will help clear the windshield.
- Never use when the windshield is dry
- Install winter blades when necessary
- Rear-window wipers and washer are available on some models.

COMFORT CONTROL (17):

- To control the temperature in the passenger compartment
- To direct air at the windshield and windows to help keep them clear
- Air conditioner to cool air is optional
- CONTROLS PERMIT DIRECTING THE AIR - VENT, HEATER, DEFROST
- Temperature - from cold to hot
- Air recirculation or from the exterior
- Fan control - to increase air flow.

REAR-WINDOW DEFOGGER (18):

- Electric wires to clear the rear window

HORN (19):

- A warning device used to alert other road users of your presence
- May be located on the end of the turn signal lever
- Do not overuse or abuse.

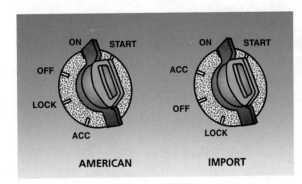

AMERICAN   IMPORT

IGNITION SWITCH (20):

The more square-looking of the two keys, the ignition key, may be inserted or removed in the lock position only.
"LOCK" POSITION:
- The steering is locked. Most electrical systems are inoperative.
"OFF" POSITION:
- Most electrical systems are inoperative. The steering is not locked.

"ACC" POSITION:
- Accessory electrical systems are operative only.
"ON" POSITION:
- All electrical systems are operative
- Indicator lights and gauges can be checked for any malfunctions.
"START" POSITION:
- Spring-loaded, a slight extra pressure must be exerted to turn the key to this position
- Activates the starter motor

- Release the key and switch when the engine is operating
- Never hold engaged for more than 10 seconds
- **IF THE ENGINE IS NOT OPERATING, WAIT SEVERAL SECONDS BEFORE RE-STARTING**
  (Some vehicles require returning to "OFF" before re-starting).

Some vehicles are equipped with a safety button that must be depressed to return to the "LOCK" position.

STEERING WHEEL (21):
- Controls the position of the front wheels
- Turning the wheel to the right will direct your vehicle to the right; to go left, turn the wheel to the left
- Avoid turning the steering when the vehicle is stationary (Dry steering).

THE ACCELERATOR PEDAL (or Gas Pedal)
- Controls the speed of the engine
- Operate using right foot, heel on the floor, exert pressure using the "ball" of the foot
- Pressure supplies more fuel to the engine causing the vehicle to increase speed when in gear
- Releasing pressure will cause the vehicle to decelerate gradually.

THE BRAKE PEDAL (or Service Brake Pedal)
- Controls the service brake system to slow or stop the vehicle
- Operate using right foot, heel on the floor (if possible)
- Exert pressure using the "ball" of the foot
- Pressure activates the service brake system slowing the wheels thus, in turn, slowing the vehicle
- Different brake systems (power brakes) may require less pressure to activate.

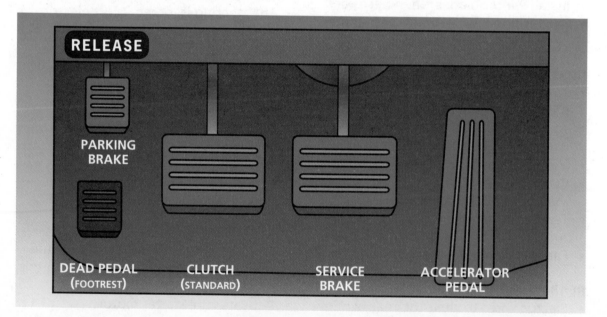

- Test the pressure required several times at slow speeds.

THE CLUTCH PEDAL:
- Found on cars with standard transmissions only
- Disengages the motor from the transmission to allow shifting (changing) gears, stopping the vehicle and during the "start" procedure
- Operate using left foot ("ball") and depress completely to disengage
- Pedal must be fully depressed to start the engine (many cars are equipped with a "clutch safety switch" that prevents starting unless the pedal is fully depressed).

THE PARKING BRAKE (or Emergency Brake)
- Controls the "mechanical" brakes

TYPE A (opposite page)
- Operate using left foot, depress firmly (foot pedal) (pump to increase pressure on some models)

TYPE B (right)
- Operate using right hand, pull firmly (hand lever) locks in the applied position.

BOTH TYPES
- Used when parking, after stopping, to restrain the

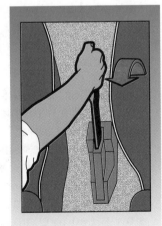

vehicle and prevent it from moving
- An instrument panel indicator light (brake) will come on when parking brake is applied.

TO RELEASE, TO SET THE VEHICLE IN MOTION, ONCE IN GEAR.

TYPE A
- Pull the release lever (located above the parking brake pedal) with the left hand

TYPE B
- Raise the lever slightly with the right hand, depress the lock mechanism, then lower the lever completely
- The indicator light should go off.

In emergency situations, if the service brakes fail, the parking brake may be used to stop the vehicle. While keeping the lock mechanism released, pump the parking brake to bring the vehicle to a stop. The stopping distance will be longer as only the back brakes are functioning; however, **the vehicle will STOP**. This maneuver should be practiced in a quiet traffic-free area.

THE AUTOMATIC TRANSMISSION:
The transmission controls the connection between the engine and the wheels. In forward motion, it will automatically change to the appropriate economical gear - hence the name. The driver may override the system by selecting a specific gear position.

SELECTOR LEVER POSITIONS:

"P"-PARK:
- After stopping, the selector is placed in park
- Locks transmission to prevent rolling
- Must be in this position for ignition switch to "lock" and remove key (most vehicles)
- Allows starting the engine
- To move out of park, must depress the lock button (red arrow). Some vehicles require depressing the service brakes. (New vehicles have a "Shifter Lock").

"R"-REVERSE:
- Used to back the vehicle
- Must be at a standstill before engaging
- Activates "REVERSE" LIGHTS (white lights) on rear of vehicle.

"N"-NEUTRAL:
- No connection to the drive wheels
- The vehicle will roll
- Allows starting the engine (if engine stalls when in motion, shift to neutral and restart while rolling).

" D " or "D4"-OVERDRIVE:
- Optional position (many newer model vehicles)

- Extra forward gear for cruising more economically at speeds exceeding 45 mph.
- in stop and go situations "D" should be selected.

"D"-DRIVE:
- Fully automatic forward gear position
- The transmission will select the appropriate gear
- May be engaged while stopped or rolling forward.

"2" or "D2" or "L2"-SECOND GEAR:
- Prevents the transmission from selecting high forward gear

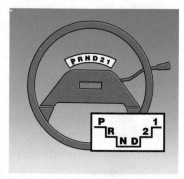

- Used to slow a vehicle at high speed or when descending a hill at higher speeds (to control speed)
- Used to obtain more power than high gear to climb a steep hill at higher speed
- Used in poor traction conditions - mud, snow, etc.

"1" or "D1" or "L1"-FIRST GEAR:
- Prevents the transmission from selecting any other forward gear
- Used to slow the vehicle at lower speeds or when descending a steep hill at slow speed
- Used to maintain maximum power at slow speed to climb a steep hill or pull a heavy load.

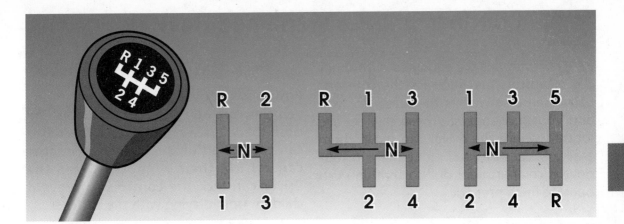

THE STANDARD TRANSMISSION:

Standard transmissions are available in three, four, or five speed models. With experience, the standard affords the driver superior control of the vehicle but requires more work by the driver.

"N"-NEUTRAL:
- The shifter lever moves easily from side to side
- Use this position to start the engine - make sure the clutch pedal is fully depressed
- The engine is not connected to the drive wheels.

"R"-REVERSE:
- Used to back the vehicle
- Make sure the vehicle is at a standstill.

"1"-FIRST GEAR:
- Lowest forward gear - most power
- Use to start from a stopped position up to speeds of 10-15 mph
- Use to climb steep hills or pull heavy loads at slow speed.

"2"-SECOND GEAR:
- Less power - more speed
- Use when shifting out of 1st up to speeds of 10-20 mph
- Use when rolling slowly to pick up speed rather than return to 1st
- Use to turn corners when in motion
- Use to climb hills or pull heavy loads at slow speeds.

"3"-THIRD GEAR:
- In a 3-speed transmission - use to cruise at speeds over 25 mph
- on a 4 or 5 speed transmission use to accelerate to 35-40 mph.

"4"-FOURTH GEAR:
- Use for steady driving in the 40 mph and over range.

"5"-FIFTH GEAR:
- Use for steady expressway cruising to save fuel and engine wear.

Comfort and Convenience Devices

Most vehicles are equipped with other controls that increase the comfort, convenience as well as the safety for you and your passengers. These devices are located where the driver can reach them easily. Make sure you include them in your driver's compartment drill so that you can operate them properly.

TILT STEERING

Many vehicles have an adjustable (tilt) steering wheel which allows you to alter the position to one that provides maximum comfort and control. Be careful not to block your view of the dash gauges and warning lights.

AIR CONDITIONING

An option on most vehicles, you can use the air conditioner to cool the interior and reduce the humidity to make driving more comfortable. Some models are computer controlled (HVAC); you set the temperature and the system adjusts.

CRUISE CONTROL

An optional feature that allows you to maintain a desired speed while removing your foot from the accelerator pedal. Tap the brake pedal or turn off the switch to deactivate the system.

Though a convenience on long trips and high speed driving, it can increase the likelihood of highway hypnosis. Compensate by searching the roadway more often.

ELECTRICAL OR LEVER REMOTE CONTROLS

Power windows, optional on many vehicles, provide switches to open and close the windows electrically. The driver can control all of them; each passenger can control their window. Often the driver can lock the controls to prevent children from playing with the switches.

Power door locks will secure all doors by means of switches. Once again the driver can lock the controls for safety purposes. Child-proof locks are available (switches located on the rear door frames) on some models preventing the rear doors from being opened except from the outside handle. Some models lock all doors when the transmission is shifted out of Park.

Power seats offer the driver, and often the front passenger, several switches that can control the position of their seat. The permutations allow for the best possible driving position. The driver should never adjust the seat position while in motion. Some vehicles provide two programmable settings which, at the touch of a button, move the seat to a prescribed position.

A trunk release button or lever, which can be locked on some vehicles, allows the driver to open the trunk.

The interior hood release lever, an additional protection against theft, opens the first latch on the hood.

Review

TERMS TO REMEMBER - WRITE A SHORT DEFINITION FOR THE FOLLOWING :

- Cockpit drill
- Instrument panel
- Headlight switch
- Windshield wiper
- Ignition switch
- Accelerator pedal
- Brake pedal
- Clutch pedal
- Parking brake

SUMMARY

THE COCKPIT DRILL:
Practice using and checking the gauges, instruments and controls of your vehicle so that it becomes "second nature". Anytime you drive an unfamiliar vehicle perform a cockpit drill before driving.

THE DASH PANEL:
Check the indicators before starting out. Make sure they are functioning. Know what they mean. Read your owner's manual if you are not sure. When purchasing a new vehicle, ask the salesperson for a copy of the owner's manual for your model while you wait for delivery; get a head start.

THE CONTROLS:
Get accustomed to the position and feel of the controls at slow speeds before venturing into heavy traffic. Don't take it for granted; your safety depends on it.

TEST A - WRITE "T" BESIDE STATEMENTS THAT ARE TRUE AND "F" BESIDE THOSE THAT ARE FALSE.

_____ **1.** The alternator warning light indicates the intensity of electrical current.

_____ **2.** The brake light only illuminates when the parking brake is applied.

_____ **3.** The oil pressure light indicates abnormal engine oil pressure.

_____ **4.** The temperature gauge indicates the temperature of engine coolant.

_____ **5.** The hazard signal switch activates the turn signals in both directions.

_____ **6.** The trip odometer (an option on some vehicles) indicates engine RPM.

_____ **7.** The tachometer indicates the vehicle speed in miles per hour.

_____ **8.** The rheostat allows the driver to change the intensity of the headlights.

_____ **9.** The horn should only be used to communicate with your friends.

_____ **10.** The START ignition switch position activates only the starter motor.

_____ **11.** The clutch safety switch prevents starting unless the clutch is depressed.

_____ **12.** The parking brake should be released prior to shifting into gear.

_____ **13.** If the service brakes fail, apply the parking brake in one motion.

_____ **14.** A shifter lock mechanism prevents shifting until the brake is depressed.

_____ **15.** A vehicle (automatic transmission) can start either in park or in neutral.

_____ **16.** The reverse position automatically activates the *back-up* lights.

_____ **17.** First gear is the most economical gear for city driving.

_____ **18.** The cockpit drill should be performed every time prior to driving.

_____ **19.** A standard transmission shifts automatically to the appropriate gear.

_____ **20.** Overdrive (automatic) or fifth gear (standard) are the most economical gears for cruising at freeway speeds.

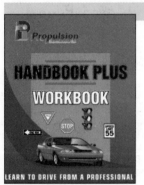

HANDBOOK PLUS WORKBOOK

*Check your comprehension and mastery of the contents of this chapter by completing the corresponding exercises that are found in the complement to the **HANDBOOK PLUS**:*

HANDBOOK PLUS WORKBOOK

Complete the exercises on Pages 42 to 47 then check your responses by referring to the answer key on Page 108.
If necessary, review the chapter for each error and refer to your instructor for further guidance.

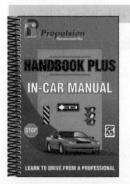

HANDBOOK PLUS IN-CAR MANUAL

*Before you start any in-car session, prepare yourself and facilitate the development of proper driving skills and habits by reading the corresponding lesson in the complement to the **HANDBOOK PLUS**:*

HANDBOOK PLUS IN-CAR MANUAL

Bring the manual to each in-car lesson so the instructor may evaluate your progress. Parents or guardians (with a valid license) should supplement the program by following the procedures in the manual and concentrating on maneuvers requiring extra practice as noted by the in-car instructor.

Preliminaries

6 - A
Approach to
the vehicle

6 - B
Pre-driving
protocol

6 - C
Blind Spots

6 - D
Pre-Drive
Inspection and
Maintenance

6 - E
Review

Before approaching your vehicle to drive, it is important to get in the habit of planning your route. Weather conditions, temporary road work areas, traffic congested areas should be taken into consideration in order to choose the safest route to your destination. Accidents, vehicle break downs etc. can create unexpected difficulties but even these tend to occur more frequently on certain roadways. Keep your radio tuned to radio stations that transmit traffic reports. Plan your route logically if several steps are required. When driving to unfamiliar areas plan the route using familiar landmarks.

Then you can approach the vehicle with a clear mind and concentrate on the task at hand. This chapter will deal with the preliminary steps involved in setting out to drive your vehicle.

AFTER COMPLETING THIS CHAPTER, THE STUDENT MUST BE ABLE TO LOCATE, DESCRIBE AND PERFORM:

- the proper approach to the vehicle, the pre-drive inspection, as well as the adjustments necessary when preparing to drive.
- the blind spots and the necessary checks thereof.

6-A Approach to the Vehicle

As you walk towards your vehicle, begin to think like a driver, make sure that nothing is in the blind zone around the vehicle.

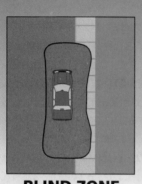   

BLIND ZONE

- Make sure that the path of travel is clear of debris, children, animals, etc.

- Check under the vehicle for any possible fluid leaks.

- Visually check the inflation of the tires and the position of the front wheels.

- Check the body of the vehicle for any damage - vandalism, hit and run, or theft.

- Check that the windows are clear and clean and the wipers are not stuck to the windshield (heat or ice).

- Verify that lights, turning signals, license plate are clean and clear.

If your vehicle is parked at the curbside, approach the driver's door from the front of the car thereby facing the traffic and

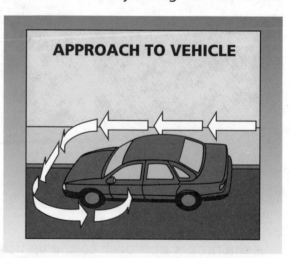

APPROACH TO VEHICLE

allowing you to check for other vehicles, bicycles, etc. before unlocking and opening your door.

Once inside, close and lock the door quickly. The key can be inserted in the ignition switch while you make the remaining pre-driving checks. (Avoid mislaying it, free your hands) make sure there are no loose objects lying about on the front or rear window ledges; the seats, the floor, hanging from the rear-view mirror, sun visors, etc. These loose objects may become "flying objects" in the event of sudden braking or a collision. Objects on the floor can roll under the pedals and prevent their proper operation. Other loose or hanging objects can create reflections and/or obscure the driver's vision.

When transporting cargo, extra care must be taken to secure the parcels in vehicles, particularly station wagons, hatchbacks,

BLOCK VISION   **"FLYING OBJECT"**

and other vehicles, where the trunk area is open to the passenger compartment. If carrying clothing on hangers, use the hook on the left rear side of the car. Never use the right one; as the clothing will obstruct your view of the right blind spot. Make sure the windows are clean inside and out.

Paying attention to these items in detail may seem like a chore at first, but if performed regularly, they will quickly become a safety habit. They will then be done automatically without thinking.

Pre-Driving Protocol

Webster defines "protocol" as "rules of etiquette" and "order of preference". With respect to pre-driving habits it is "improper" to get behind the wheel and drive without being ready to drive physically, emotionally, and having made the proper adjustments. You should develop a pattern for your vehicle that you follow every time. It may differ

slightly from that suggested here. Check your owner's manual.

A) Close and lock the doors:
To protect you against intruders
To ensure lateral integrity of the passenger compartment (Prevents the door from opening in a collision).

B) Secure loose objects:
To prevent obstruction of field of vision
To prevent reflections
To ensure free use of the controls
To prevent any "free flying objects".

C) Adjust your seat and headrest:
Your seating position determines your ability to see properly, use the controls for the vehicle, and thereby effectively command the vehicle in the driving environment. Seat yourself comfortably making sure that your back is firmly against the seat backrest and your hips are securely resting against the seat "squab". Can you see over the steering wheel comfortably? Some cars have "tilt-steering columns" or electric seats; both of these are helpful. If your car is not so equipped, you may need a firm cushion to raise your eye position.

Hold the steering wheel with one hand while using the other to release the seat locking lever (depending on the location of the "adjustment lever", you may need to use either hand). Slide the seat forward or backwards until your right foot can comfortably reach the floor under the brake pedal (as if the brake pedal were depressed to the floor) with your right leg still slightly bent, not stretching. This will permit your right foot to control the brake

and gas pedals comfortably but with good pressure when needed. On a vehicle with a standard transmission, use the left foot fully depressing the clutch pedal for this adjustment. The seat should be slightly further forward to drive a standard transmission.

Your left foot should be positioned on the far left against the foot-rest or "dead pedal". If your car does not have an actual pedal, the floor pan will have a flat plasticized area on the far left. This should be used to brace yourself in the case of any emergency maneuvers. This applies to the standard transmission as well, when the clutch pedal is released, the left foot should rest on the dead pedal.

The backrest is also adjustable on most vehicles. Place your right palm on the steering wheel at 12 o'clock (think of the steering wheel as a clock). Adjust the backrest so that your elbows are slightly bent in this position. Now lower your right hand to the 2 or 3 o'clock position and your left hand at 9 to 10 o'clock.
Adjust the headrest, if it is adjustable, so that the top of the headrest reaches just above the top of your ears. While driving, your head should not lean on the headrest.

SAFETY TIPS

Special care should be taken with the seating position, as this will determine your comfort and, more importantly, your ability to properly control your vehicle while driving.

D) Adjustment of the mirrors:

They will be used to check behind your vehicle on a regular basis (every 6-8 seconds) and also prior to braking and all other maneuvers. It is vital that they be adjusted so they can be used comfortably and easily as well as reflecting the largest view to the rear of your vehicle.

INTERIOR REAR-VIEW MIRROR: without moving your head from the driving position, grasp the mirror by the frame and adjust its position so that you can see out the rear window with the right edge of the mirror aligned with the right edge of the rear window. This reflects a clear view to the rear and to the right rear of your vehicle.

EXTERIOR LEFT REAR-VIEW MIRROR: turn your head slightly from the driving position and align this mirror with the right edge of the mirror showing a little of the side of your car. It will then reflect a view of the left rear. Use the remote control or lower the window and grasp the mirror frame.

EXTERIOR RIGHT REAR-VIEW MIRROR: turn your head and align the mirror with a little of the side of your car showing in the mirror. Remember this mirror (optional on many models) is convex and distorts distance.
RECHECK ALL MIRRORS BEFORE PROCEEDING.

E) Ensure good ventilation:

Adjust the climate controls to the preferred setting for the weather conditions. Lower the side window slightly (3/4 inch). Even with air conditioning, the danger of carbon monoxide accumulating in the passenger compartment requires that proper ventilation be maintained.

F) Fasten your seat belt:

Fasten your seat belt properly and make sure that all your passengers do likewise Chapter 11 deals with the different restraint systems in greater detail.

G) Cockpit drill

Review quickly the location and operation of gauges and controls.

6

Blind Spots

Before proceeding to the basic maneuvers of driving (Chapter 7), you must understand a vital fact. Even though you adjusted the mirrors correctly and you have a normal field of vision, there are two areas around your vehicle that you cannot see. They are called "blind spots". Located to the left and right of your vehicle just behind your normal field of forward vision, they extend to the rear on both sides until the rear-view mirrors reflect the lanes beside your car. (Trucks have three blind spots!)

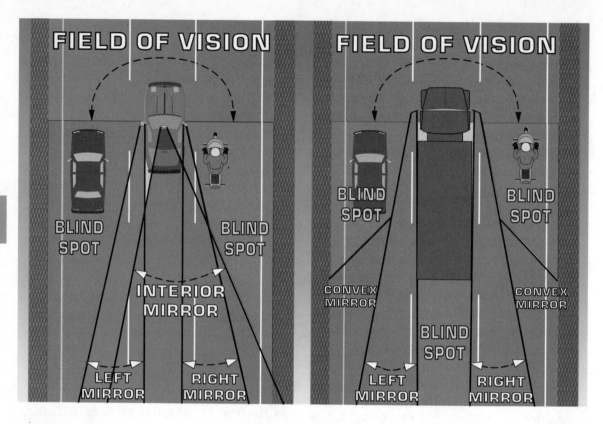

FIELD OF VISION

BLIND SPOT

BLIND SPOT

INTERIOR MIRROR

LEFT MIRROR

RIGHT MIRROR

FIELD OF VISION

BLIND SPOT

BLIND SPOT

CONVEX MIRROR

CONVEX MIRROR

BLIND SPOT

LEFT MIRROR

RIGHT MIRROR

Once you realize the size and location of the blind spots (see illustrations above), there are two things you should learn:

A) Anytime you wish to maneuver (change lanes, turn, etc.) it is essential, after checking in the mirrors, to glance at your blind spot on the side where you wish to move. To do this, you must practice turning your head till your chin reaches your shoulder and glance to the side towards the rear. Practice left and right so that it can be done quickly yet correctly. To the right, glance out the right side rear window; on the left, glance out the driver's side window. **Practice until it feels natural.**

B) Also note: if you have these two blind spots, all other drivers have them as well and large vehicles have a third just behind them. **How many drivers don't bother to check their blind spots?** Avoid driving in other people's blind spots. Reduce speed and drop back or accelerate to pass out of their blind spots. With respect to the rear blind spot on large vehicles, slow down and back off until you can see the driver in the left-side rear-view mirror.

Never place your safety in other driver's hands. They make mistakes and may involve you in a collision. **Keep your safety and the safety of your vehicle in your control.**

Pre-Drive Inspection and Maintenance

The inspection and maintenance of your vehicle is vital to the proper operation, avoidance of breakdowns and keeping your vehicle roadworthy. In the long term, this will not only reduce operating expenses and extend the span of time that the vehicle may be utilized safely; but will also help retain the value (reduce depreciation) of your vehicle when you decide to trade or sell it.

PRE-DRIVE INSPECTION

On the approach to the vehicle, as already mentioned, check for fluid leaks, tire inflation or damage and physical damage to the body or glass. If there are any abnormalities, identify (and rectify) the cause of the problem.

Should you spot a leak under the vehicle, identify whether it is coolant, brake fluid, air conditioner condensation, motor oil, transmission fluid, etc. Is it a problem that you can repair yourself? Will it cause a breakdown if not corrected immediately?

If you are not sure, do not take a chance; proceed to your service center and have a professional service technician check and repair the problem should immediate attention be recommended. Breakdowns on the roadway are much more costly than repairing a problem when your vehicle is driven to the service center: the towing charges, damaged parts, etc.

WEEKLY INSPECTION / MAINTENANCE

At least once a week, you should take the time to inspect your vehicle more completely; this could be done at the same time as you wash the vehicle. The items are:

TIRE PRESSURE: use a tire gauge to check the pressure in each tire. Note the pressure recommended on the tire sidewall (maximum) as well as in your owner's manual (smooth ride).

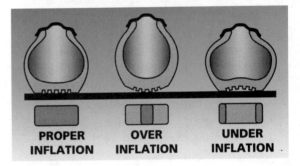

PROPER INFLATION · OVER INFLATION · UNDER INFLATION

TIRE WEAR PATTERN:
- tread wear indicator showing
- balding spots
- cuffing (uneven wear on outside or inside tread areas)
- worn tread (in middle or at side)
- stone or metal fragments.

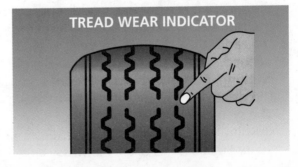

TREAD WEAR INDICATOR

6

SAFETY / COMMUNICATION ACCESSORIES:
- lights and signals
- emergency lights and markers
- emergency kit
- wipers
- HVAC

MONTHLY INSPECTION / MAINTENANCE

At least once a month, you should take the time to check:

MOTOR OIL: the engine must be off for several minutes with the vehicle on level ground; pull out the dipstick, wipe it, reinsert it fully, then pull it out and check the level of the oil slick on the gauge at the lower end. Reinsert. Add oil of the correct grade if needed. Check the color, the oil may need to be replaced. The oil and filter should be changed every 3,000 miles / 3 months (see owner's manual) and the chassis lubricated every second oil change.

WIPER FLUID: check the fluid level in the reservoir. Add fluid appropriate to the season as needed. Keep a container in the trunk so that you may add while on the road when driving conditions may require frequent use.

COOLING SYSTEM: check the level of the coolant in the expansion tank and then (only if the engine is cold) open the radiator cap and check the level in the radiator. Add anti-freeze as needed. Check the hoses (softness and swelling, brittleness and cracking) and the drive belt (condition and tension). The system requires major service - flushing and coolant replacement - every 30,000 miles or 24 months.

BRAKE SYSTEM: check the brake fluid level in the master cylinder; add when necessary. The second time you add fluid, have the brakes checked for wear and possible replacement. Lubricate and adjust the parking brake cables every second oil change. Check the operation (parking brake) every time you park by applying it and then EASING UP on the service brake while still in drive - vehicle should not move.

POWER STEERING: check the fluid in the reservoir; add if low. Check the condition and tension of the power steering drive belt.

SIX MONTH INSPECTION / MAINTENANCE

FLUID LEVELS: check the level and condition of the transmission fluid and differential fluid if so equipped (automatic- dip stick, engine running in Park; standard- access bolt on side of transmission, ask service technician)

SERVICE MANUAL PERIODIC SCHEDULE

A regular maintenance schedule is required to validate the manufacturer's warranty and to ensure that your vehicle is roadworthy. Check the owner's guide for specific requirements for your vehicle. Some items are:

TIRE and WHEEL INSPECTION / ROTATION: at 6,000 miles and then every 15,000 miles or as necessary.

IGNITION SYSTEM: spark plug replacement, EGR and plug wire inspection every 30,000 miles.

FUEL SYSTEM: inspection every 30,000 miles.

Review

6-E

TERMS TO REMEMBER - WRITE A SHORT DEFINITION FOR THE FOLLOWING :

- Blind zone
- Vandalism
- Pre-driving protocol
- Backrest
- Seat squab

- "Dead" pedal
- Headrest
- Rear-view mirror
- Left exterior mirror
- Right exterior mirror

- Convex mirror
- Ventilation
- Seat belt
- Blind spots
- Clothing hooks

SUMMARY

Proper preparation is conducive to effective driving control. Planning your route, performing the necessary checks as you approach your vehicle and once in the vehicle, following your pre-driving protocol are all essential components of this preparation. Practice doing all of these every time you drive so they will become automatic, a habit that you will eventually perform without thinking.

TEST A - STUDY THE DIAGRAM AND THEN ANSWER THE FOLLOWING QUESTIONS.

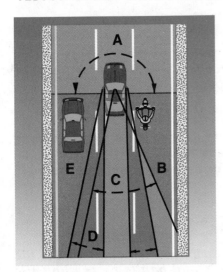

1. **Match the letters in Column A (from the diagram) with the number corresponding to the correct description in Column B**

COLUMN A

A _____

B _____

C _____

D _____

E _____

COLUMN B

1. Your forward field of vision.
2. The view in the interior rear-view mirror.
3. The view in the exterior rear-view mirrors.
4. The left blind spot.
5. The right blind spot.

2. **When should you check these blind spots?**

a)_____

b)_____

c) _____

Student notes

_____

_____

_____

_____

_____

_____

_____

_____

_____

_____

_____

_____

_____

_____

_____

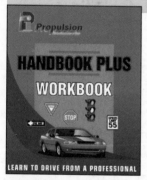

HANDBOOK PLUS WORKBOOK

Check your comprehension and mastery of the contents of this chapter by completing the corresponding exercise that is found in the complement to the HANDBOOK PLUS:

HANDBOOK PLUS WORKBOOK

Complete the exercise on Pages 48 to 52 then check your responses by referring to the answer key on Page 108.
If necessary, review the chapter for each error and refer to your instructor for further guidance.

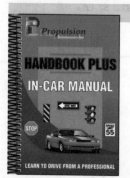

HANDBOOK PLUS IN-CAR MANUAL

Before you start any in-car session, prepare yourself and facilitate the development of proper driving skills and habits by reading the corresponding lesson in the complement to the HANDBOOK PLUS:

HANDBOOK PLUS IN-CAR MANUAL

Bring the manual to each in-car lesson so the instructor may evaluate your progress. Parents or guardians (with a valid license) should supplement the program by following the procedures in the manual and concentrating on maneuvers requiring extra practice as noted by the in-car instructor.

**7 - A
Starting
the Engine**

**7 - B
Steering and
Visual Tracking**

**7 - C
Entering Traffic**

**7 - D
Acceleration
and Braking**

**7 - E
Reversing**

**7 - F
Leaving Traffic**

**7 - G
Visual Referencing**

**7 - H
Review**

Basic Maneuvers

Once you have acquired the correct approach to the vehicle, pre-driving and "cockpit drill" habits, the real challenge begins. The driving task becomes more complicated. To build a proper house, you first must lay a solid foundation. Similarly, in driving, you have established the basics. Now it is necessary to build upon this base, one step at a time, mastering each new technique before proceeding to the next level.

Initially it's a challenge just to enter the flow of traffic, drive in a straight line, gain proficiency in the handling of the steering wheel, the accelerator pedal, the brake pedal, and then return your vehicle to a parked position.

At first, these basic maneuvers will require your total concentration. With time and practice, you'll be able to perform them easily and with confidence.

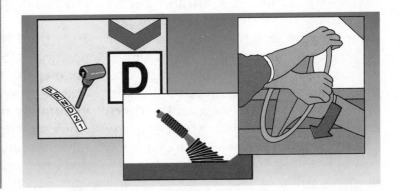

AFTER COMPLETING THIS CHAPTER, THE STUDENT MUST BE ABLE TO UNDERSTAND, DESCRIBE AND PERFORM:

- **pre-drive and starting procedures.**
- **steering input as well as brake and accelerator pedal control tasks.**
- **the basic procedures for entering, following, backing and exiting traffic.**

BASIC MANEUVERS:
To drive a vehicle in the HTS requires that you plan each maneuver, check that it can be performed safely, signal your intentions, and then proceed to actually execute the maneuver cautiously and with skill.

The sequence of actions for any maneuver will benefit by being sub-divided into three stages: ASSESS, PREPARE, and EXECUTE.

ASSESS:
At this stage, even though you should be aware of the traffic environment, examine the situation for signs and road markings, check the mirrors and blind spot, and decide whether to perform the maneuver.

PREPARE:
Having decided, signal your intentions and recheck the mirrors and blind spot to ensure that you can proceed to the final stage.

EXECUTE:
This stage involves using the controls of the vehicle to perform the actual maneuver: the steering wheel, the accelerator or the brake. As you execute the maneuver, look where you want to go, guiding your vehicle. When complete, verify the turn signal is no longer activated.

Throughout the explanation of any maneuvers in this text, this APE stage system will be applied.

Starting the Engine

Before starting any vehicle, you must have performed all the basics. The key is already in the ignition. Before proceeding, check that the parking brake is properly set and the transmission is in PARK (for an automatic). Most newer vehicles must be in the PARK position for the key to have been removed in the first place. For a standard, depress the clutch pedal, select NEUTRAL and keep the pedal fully depressed while starting.

Normally if the engine is cold, press and release the accelerator pedal to reset the electronic command module.

Turn the key in the ignition switch to the ON position. Verify the gauges and the indicator lights. (Diesel engines: wait for the GLOW PLUG light to go off before proceeding.)

Turn the ignition switch to the START position and listen to the sound of the engine; the moment the noise changes, release the switch. (Check your owner's manual as to the use of the gas pedal while starting.) Never engage the starter for longer than 10 seconds; if the engine does not start, release the switch and wait 5 to 10 seconds, then try again. (For a standard, release the clutch pedal once the engine starts.)

With the engine running, re-check the indicator lights and gauges. They should

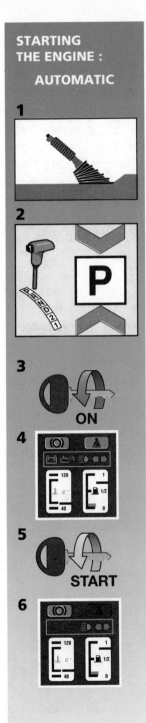

STARTING THE ENGINE :
AUTOMATIC

1

2

3
ON

4

5
START

6

indicate normal operation (lights off). The brake light remains lit because the parking brake is still applied.

IN COLD WEATHER

Activate the parking lights (5-10 seconds) before starting to "prime" the electrical production in the battery.

Keep the accelerator pedal slightly depressed while cranking the engine to facilitate starting. Allow the engine to warm up for 30 seconds to ensure oil circulation before starting off.

Drive slowly at first to improve oil circulation and the initial lubrication of bearings, gears and other moving components. To enter heavy traffic immediately, extend the warm-up time slightly to permit the engine to reach operating temperature.

A FLOODED ENGINE

The starter sounds normal, but the engine doesn't start. The odor of gasoline permeates the passenger compartment. An excess of gasoline in the engine prevents combustion.

To start the engine, depress the gas pedal fully and maintain this position even if the first attempt fails. Turn the ignition switch to "START" for 5 to 10 seconds; release if it does not start. Try again. As soon as it does start, ease up on the accelerator quickly.

This procedure will work on all gas engines (check the owner's manual).

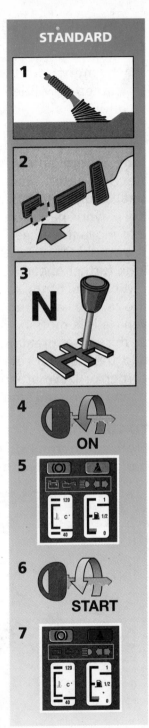

STANDARD

1

2

3

4
ON

5

6
START

7

7

Steering and Visual Tracking

As mentioned earlier, grip the steering wheel firmly at 10 and 2 (9 and 3 is also acceptable) with your thumbs resting on the wheel.

Look far ahead at the center of the lane where you wish to travel (your steering path). Even on straight roads, small course corrections will be necessary. Keep your hands on the steering wheel and move the wheel and hands together. If you are moving the steering often, look further ahead.

When turning, as much as possible, move the steering wheel while the vehicle is in motion. Avoid "dry steering" as this causes premature wear of the tires and the steering components. To turn a corner or leave a parking space, use the "hand-over-hand" method of steering.

TO TURN RIGHT

From the normal driving position, both hands turn the steering to the right.

When the right hand reaches the four o'clock position, release it and continue turning the wheel with the left. The right hand crosses over the left arm to grasp the steering at the twelve o'clock position. Continue turning with the right hand while the left returns to the normal starting position. In extremely tight maneuvers, you may have to repeat these steps to turn the wheel sufficiently.

TO RETURN STRAIGHT

At very slow speeds, such as parking maneuvers, return the steering by hand using the same technique. When driving faster, such as turning a corner, allow the steering wheel to slide through your grip on the wheel while accelerating gently. Be prepared to intervene to correct the final direction of the vehicle. The wheels will straighten with respect to your vehicle, not in relation to the direction you wish to travel.

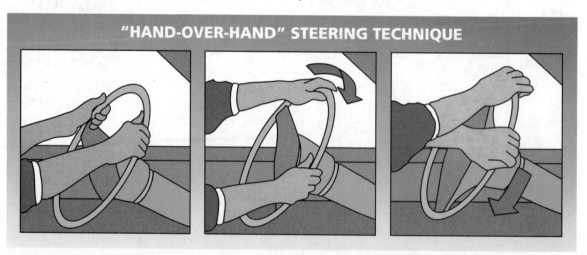

"HAND-OVER-HAND" STEERING TECHNIQUE

Entering Traffic

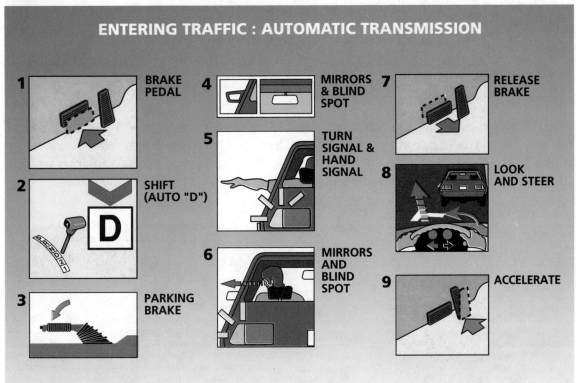

ENTERING TRAFFIC : AUTOMATIC TRANSMISSION

1 BRAKE PEDAL

2 SHIFT (AUTO "D")

D

3 PARKING BRAKE

4 MIRRORS & BLIND SPOT

5 TURN SIGNAL & HAND SIGNAL

6 MIRRORS AND BLIND SPOT

7 RELEASE BRAKE

8 LOOK AND STEER

9 ACCELERATE

AUTOMATIC TRANSMISSION

The engine is already running as described earlier, depress the brake pedal **(1)** and maintain it in this position. (make sure the pedal feels firm)

Move the selector lever to the "D" position **(2)**. (You should already know the correct procedure for your vehicle)

Release the parking brake **(3)**.

ASSESS: Make sure there is sufficient space to enter traffic
Check in the mirrors and the blind spot **(4)**.

PREPARE: Activate the turn signal, if there is any doubt as to the signal being seen, use a hand signal as well **(5)**
Re-check the mirrors and blind spot **(6)**.

EXECUTE: Release the brake pedal while looking towards your intended path **(7)**
Turn the steering as needed **(8)**
Begin to depress the gas pedal gently and increase speed as required **(9)**.

STARTING ON AN UPHILL SLOPE (AUTOMATIC)

1   **2**   **3**

When starting on a hill, the left foot may be used on the brake to prevent a rollback **(1)**. Release the brake **(2)** when the accelerator causes the vehicle to pull forward. On very steep hills, the parking brake **(3)** may be used to prevent rollback and should be released at this time instead of using the left foot.

ENTERING TRAFFIC : STANDARD TRANSMISSION

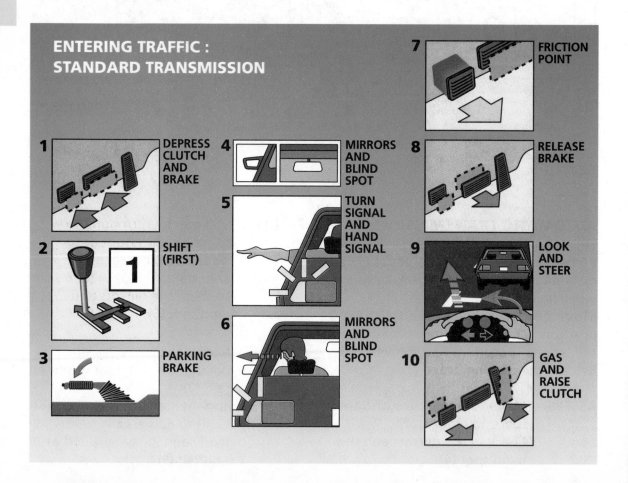

1 DEPRESS CLUTCH AND BRAKE

2 SHIFT (FIRST)

3 PARKING BRAKE

4 MIRRORS AND BLIND SPOT

5 TURN SIGNAL AND HAND SIGNAL

6 MIRRORS AND BLIND SPOT

7 FRICTION POINT

8 RELEASE BRAKE

9 LOOK AND STEER

10 GAS AND RAISE CLUTCH

STANDARD TRANSMISSION

To enter traffic, the procedure is similar. Depress the clutch pedal completely and put the gear shift lever in first; apply the brake pedal firmly and then release the parking brake.

ASSESS and **PREPARE** as for the automatic transmission. **(1 to 6)**

EXECUTE: Raise the clutch pedal to the friction point (the engine r.p.m. slows slightly) **(7)**
Release the brake **(8)**
Look towards your intended path of travel **(9)**
Lightly apply the gas while **(10)** raising the clutch pedal smoothly
Steer / accelerate as needed.

STARTING ON A STEEP UPHILL SLOPE (STANDARD)

This technique is effective in all situations except the steepest of hills. In those cases, the parking brake **(1)** may be left engaged until the vehicle begins to pull forward **(2)** then release the parking brake **(3)** thus preventing any rollback.

Acceleration and Braking

AUTOMATIC TRANSMISSION

You have put your vehicle in motion as per the steps explained earlier. Now to drive the automobile.

The speed of your vehicle is controlled by the pressure your right foot exerts on the accelerator or gas pedal. Keep your heel on the floor and depress the pedal with the "ball" of your foot. The vehicle reaction will depend on engine size, the power train, the road surface, and the weight of the vehicle. To develop a "feel" for driving, sense the change in body position (as you do when someone else is driving) and adjust your pressure on the gas pedal accordingly.

To increase your speed, depress the pedal gradually and adjust the pressure by the vehicle reaction. Always change your speed smoothly, this saves fuel and unnecessary "wear and tear" on the power train components.

Once you attain the desired speed (check your speedometer), ease up slightly and the vehicle will maintain this speed. If you ease up too much, the vehicle will begin to decrease in speed. With practice you should be able to cruise at the same speed effortlessly. Remember that any change in the inclination of the road will require an adjustment of the pressure on the accelerator pedal.

The automatic transmission will shift to the appropriate gear as you drive, whether accelerating or slowing. By looking far ahead, you may avoid having to use the brakes; releasing the gas and slowing gradually, the situation may change, and you may return to your cruising speed without stopping.

When necessary to slow the vehicle, tap the brake pedal slightly **(1)**; this lights up the brake lights on the rear of your vehicle announcing your intentions. Check the rear view mirror **(2)**. Re-apply the brake pedal firmly **(3)**, reduce your speed in relation to the space available:

- always plan to stop earlier than the intended location. You can always ease up on the brake later rather than run out of space. Just before coming to a full stop, decrease the pressure slightly **(4)** in order to stop smoothly. If it is possible in your vehicle, keep your heel on the floor while applying pressure to the brake pedal.

- To remain stopped, maintain pressure on the brake pedal.

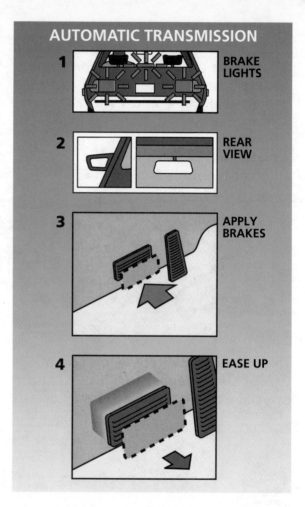

AUTOMATIC TRANSMISSION

1 — BRAKE LIGHTS

2 — REAR VIEW

3 — APPLY BRAKES

4 — EASE UP

When safe to resume, release the brake and gradually depress the accelerator.

THE STANDARD TRANSMISSION
In these vehicles, you must manually shift into the appropriate gear as the speed changes. Automobile transmissions may have 3, 4, or 5 forward speeds (gear-ratios) as well as reverse. (Trucks may have even more gears.) Most modern vehicles have the gear shift lever on the floor (some are on the steering column).

Remember the clutch pedal must be depressed completely to start the engine, to shift gears , and to come to a full stop.

1st gear 2nd gear 3rd gear 4th gear 5th gear Reverse

To begin, practice shifting into each gear with the vehicle stopped. Depress the clutch pedal completely, use the hand position illustrated for each gear and shift without looking at your hand.
Practice shifting down through the gears as well.

Once you master the shifting technique, you must accustom yourself to using the clutch pedal with the left foot and the brake pedal and the accelerator with the right foot. Choose a quiet area on level ground. Start the engine. Keep the clutch depressed **(1)**. Shift into first **(2)**. Release the parking brake **(3)**.

Rest your right foot on the gas pedal **(4)** without applying any pressure on the accelerator throughout this maneuver. Raise the clutch pedal slowly until you reach the friction point **(5)**. (The engine idle speed will decrease and the vehicle will try to move) Pause. Then slowly raise the clutch pedal **(6)** until the vehicle rolls smoothly. Release the clutch and place your left foot on the footrest **(7)**. Allow the vehicle to roll several

7

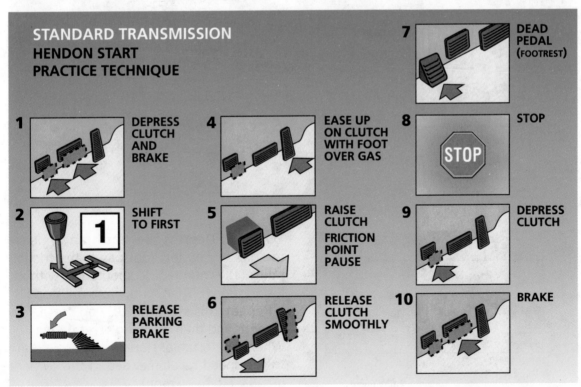

STANDARD TRANSMISSION
HENDON START
PRACTICE TECHNIQUE

7 DEAD PEDAL (FOOTREST)

1 DEPRESS CLUTCH AND BRAKE

2 SHIFT TO FIRST

3 RELEASE PARKING BRAKE

4 EASE UP ON CLUTCH WITH FOOT OVER GAS

5 RAISE CLUTCH FRICTION POINT PAUSE

6 RELEASE CLUTCH SMOOTHLY

8 STOP

9 DEPRESS CLUTCH

10 BRAKE

seconds, then depress the clutch pedal **(9)** and apply the brakes **(10)** to stop.

Practice this maneuver until you can move the vehicle smoothly and you are comfortable with the pedals. This will be useful for starting on slippery or icy surfaces and for "inching out" at intersections to check the traffic; however, this will be a little too slow for normal starting.

In normal starting, raise the clutch to the friction point, pause **(E)**, apply a slight pressure on the accelerator to raise the engine idle speed, then smoothly raise the clutch **(F)** while increasing pressure on the accelerator.

The techniques you practiced in the HENDON START practice maneuver come into play with the addition of the accelerator pedal.

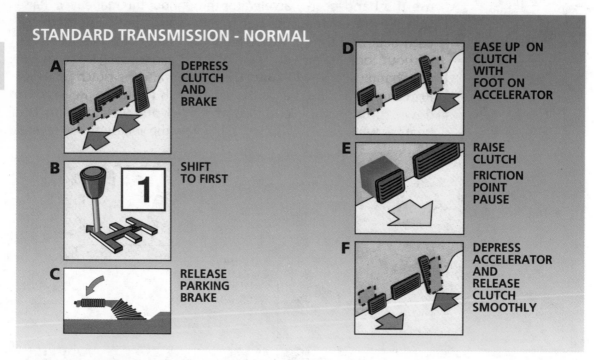

STANDARD TRANSMISSION - NORMAL

A DEPRESS CLUTCH AND BRAKE

B SHIFT TO FIRST

C RELEASE PARKING BRAKE

D EASE UP ON CLUTCH WITH FOOT ON ACCELERATOR

E RAISE CLUTCH FRICTION POINT PAUSE

F DEPRESS ACCELERATOR AND RELEASE CLUTCH SMOOTHLY

TO STOP THE VEHICLE

1 DEPRESS CLUTCH & RELEASE GAS

2 BRAKE

TO STOP: Depress the clutch and release the gas as your left foot passes the friction point **(1)**. (Your vehicle should roll without losing speed) Then, brake to a full stop **(2)**.

Repeat this starting, driving for a few seconds and then stopping several times. When comfortable, start off and accelerate to the speed recommended in the owner's manual (10 to 20 mph).

TO UPSHIFT: Depress the clutch, release the gas as practiced, then shift to second gear. Raise the clutch smoothly and apply pressure to the accelerator as you pass the friction point. (Your vehicle should roll then accelerate without any hesitation)

To shift to the higher gears follow the same procedure. Listen to the sound of the engine so that soon, you will be able to "sense" when to shift without glancing at the speedometer as often.
Notice that the standard responds more exactly to the accelerator pedal than does the automatic. For this reason you can control your speed more easily with the gas pedal. When necessary to slow your vehicle quickly, release the accelerator and tap the brake pedal **(1)** then apply it. When you reduce speed below a speed range for the present gear, downshift.

TO DOWNSHIFT: Depress the clutch **(2)** and select the correct gear with the gear shift lever **(3)**. Ease up on the clutch while pressing on the brake **(4)** if you intend to continue slowing. Otherwise, if you wish to accelerate, as you ease up on the clutch, press on the gas pedal gently **(5)**.
You must downshift before turning corners, before climbing steep hills, before descending steep hills, and at anytime that the drone of the motor signals the need for more power. Be careful when downshifting not to over-rev the engine.

TO STOP: brake as for the automatic; however, make sure to depress the clutch as you slow to a stop. Even better, depress the clutch and shift to second gear as you

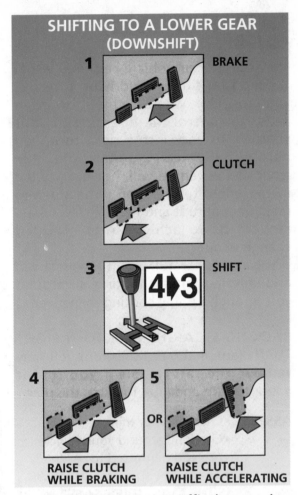

SHIFTING TO A LOWER GEAR (DOWNSHIFT)

1 BRAKE

2 CLUTCH

3 SHIFT

4 OR 5

RAISE CLUTCH WHILE BRAKING   RAISE CLUTCH WHILE ACCELERATING

approach a blockage in traffic that requires you to stop; then if the situation changes, you can accelerate from a very slow speed as long as you did not come to a full stop.

Once you stop for any extended time, shift to neutral and release the clutch. Maintain pressure on the brake pedal.

With practice and experience, you will drive a standard with ease and confidence. At first, leave extra space and aim higher than usual, in order to avoid unnecessary anxiety and shifting, or sudden maneuvers.

7-E

Reversing

Backing your vehicle requires visual tracking similar to driving forward; you must look where you wish to go in order to control the direction of your vehicle. To back into a right turn, you must turn the steering to the right. The front of the vehicle will, however, swing in the opposite direction. The steering reaction is abrupt and requires less wheel movement to achieve the intended change of direction.

You should carefully control your speed and steering while checking all around you throughout any backing maneuver.

BACKING STRAIGHT or INTO A RIGHT TURN (automatic transmission) you may remove the safety belt if you find it easier to turn and look towards the rear.

ASSESS: •Check in your mirrors
•Check all around your vehicle
•Are you permitted to reverse?
•Are there visual obstructions?
IS THE MANEUVER SAFE?

PREPARE: •Apply the brake
•Shift the selector lever to R
•Release the parking brake
(if it is engaged)
•Activate the turn signal
(if you are turning and it is
not already functioning)
•Recheck around your vehicle
•Place your left hand at
12 o'clock on the steering wheel
•Turn your torso and head to
the right until you can see
out the rear window
(when backing straight, you may
place your right arm across the
top of the passenger seat).

BACKING INTO A RIGHT TURN

BACKING STRAIGHT

EXECUTE: •Ease up on the brake pedal to
start reversing slowly
•Maintain pressure to control
your speed (walking speed)
•Glance frequently ahead and
to the sides (rear turn reference)
•When turning, check that the

left front of your vehicle clears all obstructions.
• Apply the brake to stop.

In most cases, your vehicle will roll by releasing the brake; if necessary, gently press the accelerator to start the vehicle in motion. On uphill slopes you may have to use the gas to keep it moving. The situation can change very quickly. Move slowly to allow you time to check around your vehicle easily and often.
   If you turned, begin straightening the wheel as you stop. Do not change position and look forward until after you have stopped.

BACKING INTO A LEFT TURN follow the same APE procedure except:

PREPARE: • Place your right hand at 12 o'clock on the steering
• Turn your torso and head to the left until you can see to the left rear (rear turn reference).

While backing into a left turn, the right front of your vehicle will swing out;

BACKING INTO A LEFT TURN

check that it will clear all obstructions while you turn. As well, your view to the right rear is limited in this position; include a glance to the right rear as you check ahead and to the sides.

For a standard transmission, follow the APE procedures described. To set your vehicle in motion, use the friction point. (Except on an uphill slope, when you will need to use the accelerator as well.) Ease up or depress the clutch pedal to control your speed. Cover the brake pedal, ready to stop.

Leaving Traffic

To leave the traffic lane and park your vehicle, the simplest and safest method is to steer towards the curb from the lane beside the parked vehicles. This requires a large space, at least twice the length of your vehicle. Other ways to park will be discussed in Chapter 12.

ASSESS: Locate a parking space, while still paying attention to the traffic around you **(1)**
Check for signs and pavement markings that govern parking
Check mirrors and blind spot
IS THE MANEUVER SAFE?

PREPARE: Activate your turn signal **(2)** (when parking just after an intersection, wait until you enter it to signal)

Tap your brake pedal, **(3)** then apply steady pressure to reduce your speed

Recheck your mirrors and blind spot before turning. **(4)**

EXECUTE: When the front of your vehicle reaches the space (front turn reference point), steer towards the curb **(5)**

Continue slowing while steering to a stop parallel to the side of the road (right side clearance reference point) **(6)**

Within a foot of the curb in most jurisdictions.

Make sure the turn signal is no longer activated

Make sure you are centered in the parking space. **(7)**

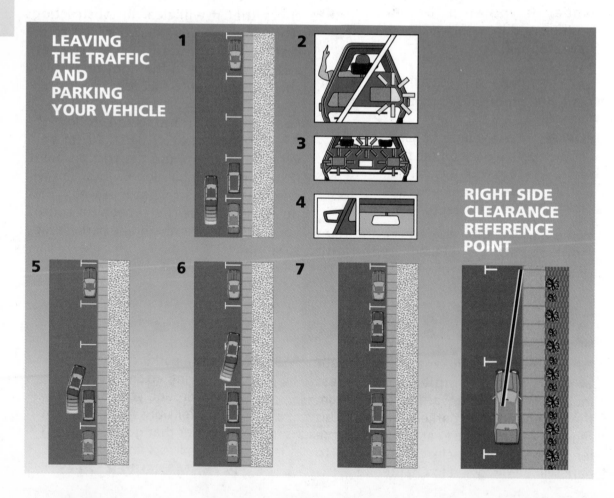

LEAVING THE TRAFFIC AND PARKING YOUR VEHICLE

1 2 3 4

RIGHT SIDE CLEARANCE REFERENCE POINT

5 6 7

EXITING THE VEHICLE

Once the vehicle is stopped **(1)** in the space, engage the parking brake **(2)**, ease up and re-apply the brake pedal to check the operation of the parking brake, then place the selector lever in PARK **(3)** (automatic) or shift into first or reverse **(3)** (standard-check owner's manual)

Release the brake pedal (4). Turn off all accessories (5), lights, comfort controls and close all windows. Turn the ignition switch to the lock position (6) and remove the key. Release the clutch pedal (7) (standard). Remove your safety belt. Check the left mirror and blind spot (8). Use your right hand to unlock and open the door (9), thus turning to check the traffic automatically. Exit carefully (10) and lock the door (11). Walk toward the rear of your vehicle facing the traffic (12).

These precautions concerning the doors and exiting should also apply to the passengers in your vehicle.

7

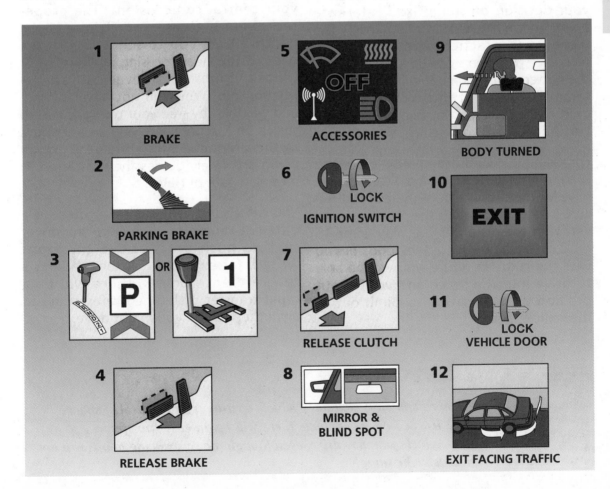

1 BRAKE	5 ACCESSORIES	9 BODY TURNED
2 PARKING BRAKE	6 IGNITION SWITCH	10 EXIT
3 P OR 1	7 RELEASE CLUTCH	11 LOCK VEHICLE DOOR
4 RELEASE BRAKE	8 MIRROR & BLIND SPOT	12 EXIT FACING TRAFFIC

Visual Referencing

Most drivers learn the operating space for their vehicle by an involved trial and error process. Sometimes they guess right and at other times they err. It is always amusing to watch an experienced driver park a new vehicle for the first time.

As a novice, some means of improving this hit or miss system is strongly advised. A method of vehicle judgment and the space required. It is critical at the outset to base your decision on some fixed reference points that are based on experience. The more you practice applying these reference points in small operating spaces, the better your judgment will become. To take advantage of this technique, you must relate some part of the roadway to a particular part of your vehicle.

For example, when driving into a parking space alongside the curb, how can you tell how far the tires are from the edge of the curb? After attempting the maneuver and verifying the distance, you may come to realize that the center of the hood lines up with the curb. In future, you will be able to drive into the space and verify your position without having to climb out of the vehicle to see.

This same concept can be applied to most driving maneuvers and will assist you in gaining confidence and skill in proper fender judgement. This will remove anxiety in tight spaces and further assist you in proper decision-making for steering input (forward visual turning point and backing alignment, as two examples).

The problem that may arise is a tendency to stare at these reference points with your central conic vision. The proper technique is to use your fringe vision which allows you to see a wider area without the clear focusing ability of your central vision. This develops a spatial relationship. You will not have to stare and will thereby free your central vision to search and target space and area changes in the driving scene while your fringe vision accurately guides the vehicle on its intended path of travel.

You will also benefit any time you drive a different vehicle (a van where the driver seating position is above the front wheels, for example). After checking a few reference points, there will be a rapid transfer of learned referencing to any other vehicle you might drive.

SAFETY TIPS

Visual referencing facilitates vehicle operation and control of space! Once learned on any vehicle there will be an easy transference to any other vehicle you may drive, even though the referencing points will not be exactly the same!

Review

TERMS TO REMEMBER - WRITE A SHORT DEFINITION FOR THE FOLLOWING :

- Assess
- Prepare
- Execute
- Glow plug

- Choke
- Flooded engine
- Dry steering
- Hand-over-hand

- Friction point
- Rollback
- Hendon start
- Downshift

SUMMARY

Apply the APE system to every maneuver. Practice starting (automatic or standard) and setting your vehicle in motion. Always drive with both hands on the wheel for maximum control. Aim high into your path of travel. Use the accelerator and brake smoothly to drive more comfortably and save fuel and brakes. Practice hand-over-hand steering. When reversing, assume the correct position and look where you wish to go. Remember to check all around your vehicle as you move slowly. Practice exiting your vehicle properly

TEST A - WRITE "T" BESIDE STATEMENTS THAT ARE TRUE AND "F" BESIDE THOSE THAT ARE FALSE.

_____ **1.** The PREPARE stage involves signalling intentions and re-checking traffic.

_____ **2.** To start an engine, turn the ignition switch directly to the START position.

_____ **3.** Once the engine is running, check the indicator lights and gauges.

_____ **4.** In cold weather, always allow the engine to reach operating temperature.

_____ **5.** To start a flooded engine, depress and hold the gas pedal while cranking.

_____ **6.** Turning the steering when a vehicle is not moving will not cause any adverse problems for the vehicle components.

_____ **7.** Release the parking brake after shifting the transmission into gear.

_____ **8.** Always accelerate smoothly to save fuel and wear of vehicle components.

_____ **9.** To reduce speed or stop, always tap the brake pedal before applying it.

_____ **10.** After applying the brake pedal firmly, always check the rear-view mirror.

_____ 11. The clutch pedal must be depressed only when you stop the vehicle.

_____ 12. When reversing, use the mirrors to guide the vehicle.

_____ 13. The speed of the vehicle when reversing should be as slow as possible.

_____ 14. Body position (reversing) should be the same for all backing maneuvers.

_____ 15. The simplest and safest parking maneuver is to drive into a large space.

_____ 16. Intending to park on the other side of an intersection, communicate your intention by activating the turn signal prior to the intersection.

_____ 17. Preparing to park, re-check the mirrors and blind spot just prior to turning into the parking space.

_____ 18. Once stopped (automatic), shift the selector lever into PARK.

_____ 19. Turn off all accessories prior to turning the ignition switch to LOCK.

_____ 20. Always exit the vehicle from the passenger side of the vehicle.

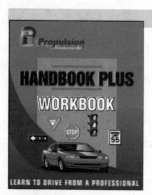

HANDBOOK PLUS WORKBOOK

Check your comprehension and mastery of the contents of this chapter by completing the corresponding exercise that is found in the complement to the HANDBOOK PLUS:

HANDBOOK PLUS WORKBOOK

Complete the exercise on Pages 53 to 57 then check your responses by referring to the answer key on Page 108.
If necessary, review the chapter for each error and refer to your instructor for further guidance.

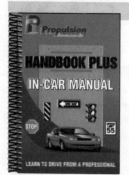

HANDBOOK PLUS IN-CAR MANUAL

Before you start any in-car session, prepare yourself and facilitate the development of proper driving skills and habits by reading the corresponding lesson in the complement to the HANDBOOK PLUS:

HANDBOOK PLUS IN-CAR MANUAL

Bring the manual to each in-car lesson so the instructor may evaluate your progress. Parents or guardians (with a valid license) should supplement the program by following the procedures in the manual and concentrating on maneuvers requiring extra practice as noted by the in-car instructor.

Defensive Driving

8 - A
The Attitude

8 - B
The SIPDE System

8 - C
Managing Time and Space

8 - D
Adapting to the H.T.S.

8 - E
Review

Driving a motorized vehicle is a most challenging activity. When you start, your prime interest may be the freedom and pleasure that a driver's license will grant you. There are, however, other aspects to driving. In addition to the complex task of proper vehicle control, you must share the road with others. You are responsible for your life, the lives of your passengers, and the lives of other road users.

Many people drive from point A to point B without a collision. This does not mean that they are capable defensive drivers, just that they were fortunate. Most are "Passive" drivers. They wait for things to happen and then they react. Hopefully in time.

This Chapter will outline a system, called defensive driving, that will allow you to develop an "Active" approach to driving. An early warning system intended to avoid potential conflicts. A method to prevent collisions in spite of unfavorable conditions and the mistakes of others.

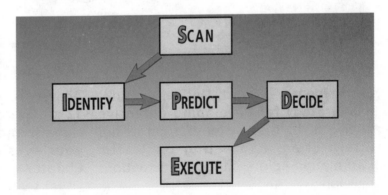

AFTER COMPLETING THIS CHAPTER, THE STUDENT MUST BE ABLE TO DEMONSTRATE A BASIC UNDERSTANDING OF:

- the SIPDE system and its strategic value.
- the management of space and time to minimize risk.
- adapting vehicle speed and position to potential hazards in the HTS.

The Attitude

It is improper to drive an unfamiliar vehicle that is mechanically defective in in the H.T.S. The attitude inherent in the defensive driver is that there is a correct manner to proceed. This applies to the vehicle, the task of driving, and the driver.

The vehicle must be in good mechanical condition, properly maintained, and adapted to the needs of environmental conditions. It can be dangerous to drive with something as "minor" as an empty windshield washer reservoir. The defensive driver ensures himself that all of the vehicle's systems are operational and ready to perform their function should the need arise.

The task of driving requires familiarity with the vehicle. Refer to "The Cockpit Drill" in Chapter 5 and the "Pre-Driving Protocol" in Chapter 6. The defensive driver will take the time necessary before starting out when driving an unfamiliar vehicle.

The driver must also know his or her own mental and physical state. You should consider it improper to drive when any factor that will negatively affect your ability to drive is present. **Even if it be over-tiredness.**

In short, the attitude of the defensive driver is **"I am ready to drive correctly".**

The SIPDE System

SIPDE

(**S**can, **I**dentify, **P**redict, **D**ecide, **E**xecute) is a strategy for developing defensive driving skills. It is a system for gathering, interpreting, and acting on traffic information before dangerous situations develop.

The "Active" driver, using this system, should not have to swerve, slam on the brakes, or take any other emergency evasive maneuver while driving.

S - SCAN

Actively scan the roadway a distance of 12 to 15 seconds ahead: looking for signs, signals, and potential problems. **Keep your eyes moving.** (Refer to Vision-Chapter 4) Develop a pattern to your visual search. Include the rear-view and side mirrors, as well as the dash. Check ahead from one side of the road to the other. You will have a complete traffic picture around you. By **aiming high** and **keeping your eyes moving**, you will center your vehicle in your lane on straight roads and in curves. At intersections, the scan should include cross traffic as far as possible before and as you enter the intersection.

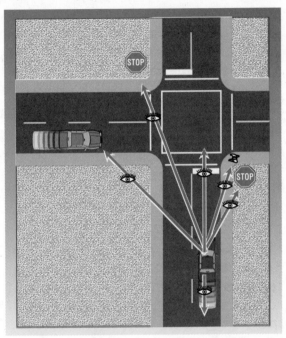

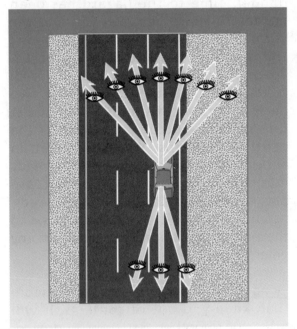

I - IDENTIFY

From all the information your eyes are scanning, you must select the critical data. The signs, signals, hazards and problems identified that require a decision on your part: your selective seeing ability.

Focus on other vehicles, pedestrians, animals, stationary and moving objects, and traffic devices that may affect your path of travel. You are in motion; you are getting closer to what you have identified. If you were scanning far enough ahead, you still have 8 to 10

seconds before you will reach the identified hazard.

P - PREDICT

Ask yourself: "What if...?" What is the "worst case scenario" for each of the identified items? You need to predict two levels - "What is the most probable?" and the "Worst case scenario". You need to know in advance what the potential paths of travel are, the timing of relative hazard movements, where and how collisions could occur, etc.

You must expect the **UNEXPECTED**. Be prepared for sudden movements of other road users. **Make sure they see you!** The use of the horn and/or flashing the high beams are effective means of getting attention. **Make "eye to eye" contact!**

Another road user looking at you, knows you are present, and is not likely to enter your path of travel. You are now 6-8 seconds from the hazard.

D - DECIDE

You must decide what you are going to do to minimize your risk. While predicting the two levels of danger from the upcoming situation, you communicated your presence and hopefully obtained "eye to eye" contact.

Now you must adapt to the potential hazard. Your path of travel and your speed are the two main aspects of control available to you. Reduction of speed will give you more time before you reach the hazard. The situation can change in this extra time. Reduced speed will lower the force of impact should a collision occur. A change of lane will create a larger "space cushion" between you and the hazard.

Decide on two levels - "What evasive maneuver will I employ?" **Leave yourself an out.** "Where will I go?" or "What will I do?" You are still 4-6 seconds away from the hazard.

E - EXECUTE

Immediately, execute stage one. Change your path of travel or your speed or both. You have minimized the probability of danger. Time to the hazard has been increased. Space between you and the hazard, in case the "worst case scenario" still develops, has also been increased. The probable danger has been reduced; however, you still have your stage two decision to execute should the "worst case scenario" occur; your "out" if the conflict develops. You have acted in anticipation and your decision is already made for your "out". You are programmed for action. In other words, you have already decided and have saved the normal decision-making time in any emergency situation.

Using the SIPDE procedure can do more than keep you out of conflicts. It will make for smoother, less stressful driving. You will make early course corrections and speed adjustments to avoid disruptions. You will avoid having to perform evasive emergency maneuvers. You will **ACTIVELY** control your vehicle in the HTS.

Managing Time and Space

The SIPDE approach is a tactical early warning and resolution system to keep you out of trouble. It enables you to control time and space. By scanning far ahead you have control of time; now let us take a further look at space.

SPACE AREAS

While in motion, there are six areas that surround your vehicle as well as the blind zone, see diagram below.

SCAN - you must constantly scan these areas for the ever-changing traffic situation. Scan for whether the areas are **open** (clear of any other road users), **closed** (occupied by others), or **changing** (about to be occupied). This will indicate if you may use an area as a path of travel and if your line of sight is clear.

IDENTIFY - What risk does the situation present? To what space area can you move to reduce the risk? Which are open?

EVALUATION OF THE SPACE AREAS

The areas of concern (space areas) can present one of the following conditions:

OPEN SPACE AREA: There is a space or area available to operate your vehicle without any restrictions to your line of sight or path of travel. No road users occupy the space and nothing impedes your line of sight through the area.

CLOSED SPACE AREA: The space area is not available for your path of travel because it is presently occupied by another road user or, of equal importance, your line of sight is restricted. You are unable to determine what the situation is.

CHANGING SPACE AREA: There is a space or area available to operate your vehicle at present, but some other road user is about to occupy the space area or your line of sight is about to be restricted. It is in the process of becoming a closed space area. It could also be a closed space area that is about to become worsened by an additional factor coming into play.

EXECUTE - without losing vehicle balance, move your vehicle to the area or lane position that reduces risk. Adjust speed to further minimize risk.

8

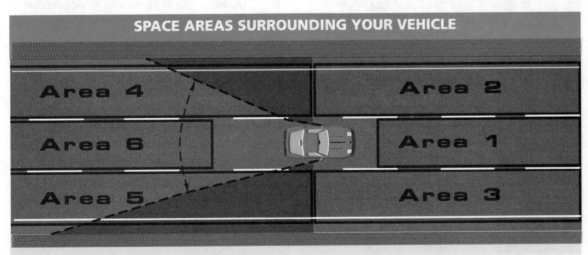

SPACE AREAS SURROUNDING YOUR VEHICLE

Area 4 · Area 2 · Area 6 · Area 1 · Area 5 · Area 3

LANE POSITION

What do we mean by change lane position? Since a lane of traffic is wider than a passenger vehicle, you must realize that it is possible to occupy more than one position in any lane without encroaching on the lanes beside you. The advantage to this concept is that it affords the proactive driver the opportunity of leaving a greater distance (more space, SIPDE system) on one side of the vehicle without changing lanes.

LANE POSITION 1

While driving, if you center your vehicle in your lane of travel, you are occupying **lane position 1** (lane center-position). In this position, you have approximately 2 to 3 feet on both sides of your vehicle (depending on the type of roadway).

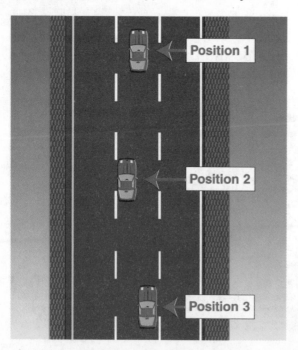

This indicates that in your judgement there is no hazard on either side of your vehicle that requires you to adapt your space to minimize a potential risk.

LANE POSITION 2

When you position your vehicle near the line on the left side of your lane, you are occupying **lane position 2** (lane left-position). In this lane position, you have approximately 4 to 6 feet of space to the right of your vehicle (contingent on road).

This position would be utilized to create more space from a potential hazard on the right or when preparing to turn left.

LANE POSITION 3

Positioning your vehicle near the right edge of your lane or near the curb will leave approximately 4 to 6 feet on the left side of your vehicle (subject to the type of roadway). This is referred to as **lane position 3** (lane right-position).

This position creates more space from a potential hazard on your left (oncoming traffic, potential danger in the left lane).

The more driving experience you acquire, the more likely you are to become a victim of seeing what you expect to see. The key to proper seeing and evaluation is to scan for what is actually present and to adjust speed, space, lane position, etc. to reduce the risk. Guided practice in the use of the SIPDE System which lasts several minutes at first, and then increased until it becomes a habit - practiced decisions that become the norm - is the only solution.

THE DANGER ZONE

A danger zone is present both in front and behind your vehicle. In front of you, a space in which it is impossible to stop; likewise behind you, the vehicle trailing yours has a certain distance in which it cannot stop. The length of these is related to many factors: speed, road conditions, the vehicle's mechanical condition, the tires, as well as the driver's condition.

THE 2 SECOND RULE
Pick a fixed reference point - the sign. As the vehicle ahead passes, count one thousand and one, one thousand and two. The front of your vehicle should reach the "sign" after you say two.

In ideal conditions (at city speeds), your danger zone dictates a **two second** *minimum* **following distance**. Don't be deceived, you cannot stop in 2 seconds at most driving speeds. This presupposes that the preceding vehicle requires the same distance to stop. **As your speed increases, 3 seconds would be advisable.**

Under adverse conditions, you should increase the space to 4-6 seconds. Your strategy is to keep this space clear in front and behind you. When anything or anyone infringes on this space, action on your part is needed. How can you keep this space clear? You need to change your speed or your lane position to regain your minimum space. It will not always be easy to maintain but it remains a key objective to safe driving.

HOW CAN YOU PREVENT SOMEONE FROM "TAILGATING"?

YOU CANNOT! But when it happens, you must react. **DON'T PANIC!** Ease off the accelerator gently. Allow your space in front to increase to at least 4 seconds. Now, you have space in front to allow you to brake gently even in a sudden stop situation. This will give your "tailgater" space to stop without hitting you. Moreover, with this large space in front, the "tailgater" will be encouraged to pass you and thus alleviate the situation behind you.

Should this occur on a multi-lane roadway, a change of lane would be an appropriate way to reduce the risk from a "tailgater". If the rear turn signals are amber colored, activating the hazard lights will also alert the tailgater, leaving no doubt as to your message.

To help manage time and space, in your decision making always consider these three basic concepts:

A-) **MINIMIZE:** reduce the risk from any one hazard by increasing time - reduce your speed; by increasing your space cushion - change lanes; and by sending a clear message or communicating your presence - tap the horn, flash the high beams or activate the hazard lights.

B-) **SEPARATE:** take each hazard one at a time, if at all possible. When multiple problems appear ahead, manage your time and space to separate them. This will make a difficult situation easier.

C-) **COMPROMISE:** when a number of hazards cannot be separated, weigh the dangers relatively. Leave more space from the most dangerous hazard without unnecessary risk from the others.

Adapting to the H.T.S.

In theory, defensive driving sounds logical. What happens when you enter rush hour traffic? Accelerate and blend with expressway traffic? **The defensive driver applies the SIPDE tactical approach in all driving situations and at all times.** Momentary lapses lead to surprises. Surprises while driving become emergency conflicts.

In the city, the visual search pattern and selective seeing will permit you to anticipate hazards. Space and time management will maintain the margin of safety needed to stay out of trouble. Remember rapid, sudden changes in speed or direction will put you in conflict with other road users, especially the **PASSIVE** type. Your early warning system gives you the edge. Your speed and direction corrections are done early and gently. Chapter 12 will discuss the urban environment and specific applications.

On rural roads and expressways, the increased speed of your vehicle and the environment changes the driving task. The tactical system adapts to these situations also. Because of the higher speeds, your eye lead time, which was calculated in seconds, focuses a greater distance ahead. The following distance, also calculated in seconds, is longer. Two seconds at 55 mph is almost double the distance at city speeds.

In adverse driving situations, whether the problem is road conditions, weather conditions, or visual conditions, you must adapt your time and space management to acquire a longer trailing distance. **At least four to six seconds is recommended.** Combinations of these conditions may necessitate even longer trailing distances. If, as a novice driver, conditions appear extreme, the decision not to drive at all

8-E

- "ACTIVE" driver
- "Worst case scenario"
- Scan
- Identify
- Predict

- Decide
- Execute
- Path of travel
- 2 second rule
- Danger zone

- "Eye to eye contact"
- Tailgater
- Minimize
- Separate
- Compromise.

SUMMARY

THE ATTITUDE:
The defensive driver makes sure the vehicle, his/her familiarity with it, and his/her physical and mental state are in the proper condition to drive.

THE STRATEGY:
The "ACTIVE" approach - aim high and scan the driving environment, "read" the traffic, identify potential hazards, predict the possible situations that may develop, decide what to do in the event of any of these situations and execute decisions early while in readiness to act further.

THE APPLICATION:
Manage your "visibility" "time" and "space" to minimize the risk. Keep space to avoid the need for rapid evasive maneuvers and at the same time provide an "out". Adapt the strategy to any and all driving scenarios.

TEST A - APPLY THE CONCEPTS OF THE SIPDE STRATEGY TO THE FOLLOWING SCENARIOS

may be wise and necessary.

1. **You are driving Vehicle A approaching a closed portion of the roadway. Vehicle B is travelling in an oncoming direction.**

    a) How can you separate these hazards?

    b) What factors will affect your decision?

    c) How should you proceed safely?

    _____

    _____

    _____

    _____

    _____

    _____

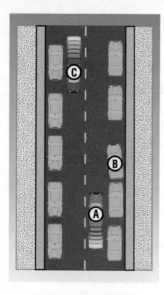

2) **You are travelling in Vehicle A on a street with parked cars. Vehicle B has a driver behind the steering wheel; Vehicle C is driving in an oncoming direction.**

   a) What are the potential hazards?

   b) What would be the "worst case scenario"?

   c) How can you minimize the risks?

   d) What should you do immediately?

   e) What would be your final solution?

_____

_____

_____

_____

_____

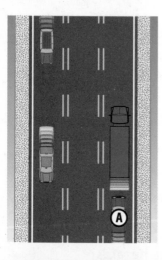

3) **You are driving Vehicle A following a slow-moving heavy vehicle in the right lane on a three lane highway. There is a long line of traffic in the oncoming lane.**

   a) What are the potential hazards?

   b) What is the "worst case scenario"?

   c) What should you do immediately?

   d) What is the final solution?

_____

_____

_____

_____

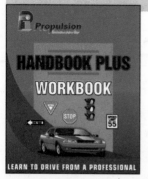

HANDBOOK PLUS WORKBOOK

*Check your comprehension and mastery of the contents of this chapter by completing the corresponding exercises that are found in the complement to the **HANDBOOK PLUS**:*

HANDBOOK PLUS WORKBOOK

Complete the exercises on Pages 58 to 61 then check your responses by referring to the answer key on Page 108.
If necessary, review the chapter for each error and refer to your instructor for further guidance.

9 - A
Friction

9 - B
Gravity

9 - C
Kinetic Energy

9 - D
Inertia

9 - E
Force of Impact

9 - F
Review

The Laws of Physics

As a passenger, you have observed the effect of natural laws on vehicle performance. Sudden acceleration or braking maneuvers have pushed you backwards or forwards in your seat. While turning a corner, you have felt the sensation of leaning towards the outside of the curve. You may have felt a minor skid on slippery pavement.

While riding a bicycle on a downgrade, you have experienced the increased acceleration that may have been exhilarating but required an extremely long braking distance. Conversely, riding uphill required extra exertion and selecting a lower gear.

All of these situations illustrate the laws of physics acting upon a vehicle in motion. As you become a driver, you must be aware of these forces and adapt your driving so that the natural forces will not adversely affect the control of your vehicle.

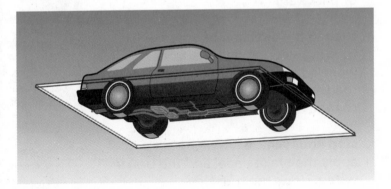

AFTER COMPLETING THIS CHAPTER, THE STUDENT MUST UNDERSTAND THE LAWS OF PHYSICS AS THEY APPLY TO THE DRIVING TASK WITH RESPECT TO:

- **friction and vehicle control.**
- **gravity and vehicle balance.**
- **kinetic energy and its impact on inertia and force of impact.**

Friction

Friction is the resistance to motion between two objects in contact with each other. This resistance to slipping between the four patches of rubber and the road surface, produces the TRACTION that is used to control your vehicle.

TIRE CONTACT WITH PAVEMENT

These four traction points are used to:
* **put your vehicle in motion**
  push the accelerator and the drive wheels turn against the pavement to move the vehicle forward
  or backward.

* **change the direction of your vehicle**
  turn the steering and the front wheels turn. They rub against the road causing the vehicle to change direction.

* **stop your vehicle**
  apply the brake pedal and the brake system slows the four tires. They react against the pavement slowing the vehicle.

The amount of traction produced is limited even when all the factors are ideal. When driving, you must avoid dividing the available traction. When you brake in a straight line, you can use all the available traction for braking. If, however, you brake and steer or accelerate and steer, you divide the available traction. If the requirements of traction exceed the amount available; then, the vehicle will skid.

THE FACTORS AFFECTING TRACTION

TIRES: Tires are designed with grooved surfaces called treads. These are designed to channel water, snow, etc. through the grooves and keep the rubber in contact with the road. Different tread patterns are intended for special uses such as snow tires.

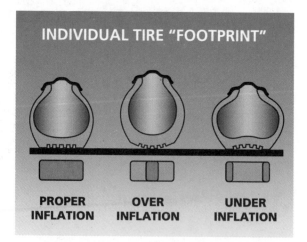

INDIVIDUAL TIRE "FOOTPRINT"

| PROPER INFLATION | OVER INFLATION | UNDER INFLATION |

As the tire wears the rubber tread thins and eventually becomes smooth (bald tire). The best traction is produced when the treads are in good condition.

Tire inflation is also very important. As shown in the diagram, properly inflated tires produce the largest "footprint" with the pavement; therefore giving the best traction. (See Chapter 16 for complete details on tires and tire maintenance.)

FRICTION FACTORS	TYPES OF SURFACE
0.9	Smooth dry asphalt
0.70	Average dry pavement
0.60	Wet asphalt-based concrete
0.50	Dry or wet gravel
0.40	Wet concrete, wet and oily gravel
0.35	Average damp pavement and melted ice
0.20	Muddy and frozen asphalt
0.05	Ice

THE ROAD SURFACE: The best traction is available on smooth dry pavement. Any variation and the friction factor diminishes accordingly. Refer to the chart, the starting point is a friction factor of 1; excellent tires stopped on a perfectly smooth surface.

SPEED: The speed at which you drive also decreases traction. As speed increases, distortions in the tire shape reduce the surface area touching the pavement. The increased air flow under the vehicle as your speed rises tends to reduce the pressure exerted by the weight of the vehicle on the tires.

Both of these factors cause a decrease in traction as the speed of your vehicle increases.

MECHANICAL CONDITION: The wheel alignment, the suspension, and the steering will reduce traction when not in proper operating condition. (See Chapter 16 for more complete details.) One example: the shock absorbers are intended to keep the tires in contact with the pavement. When in poor condition, the tires tend to skip on the pavement, causing loss of contact and premature "spotty" wear of the treads.

Gravity

9-B

The invisible force that pulls objects to the center of the earth is called **GRAVITY.** This force gives objects their weight and keeps them in contact with the ground. Without gravity a vehicle could not accelerate, brake or steer. In certain situations, uphill and downhill, you must compensate for this force acting upon the vehicle.

DRIVING UPHILL: The force of gravity will slow your vehicle; the steeper the grade, the greater the affect. Thus, as you approach a hill, you must choose the

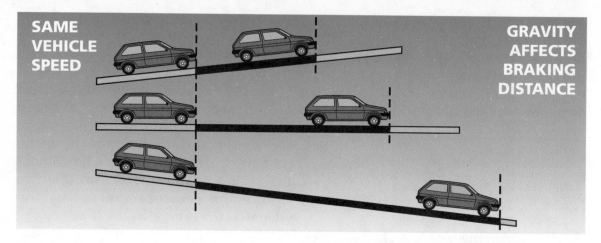

appropriate gear that will provide the necessary climbing power. In a standard, downshift; in an automatic, select a lower gear by pressing the accelerator sharply (kickdown) on a short grade or by moving the selector lever to a lower gear on a longer grade. (Second gear at 25 to 40 mph; first gear at 15 to 25 mph.) Try to avoid shifting on the hill. While going uphill, maintain your speed by increasing pressure on the gas pedal.

As you near the crest, ease up on the accelerator and keep to the right side of your lane until you can see far ahead again. When you return to a level surface select DRIVE in the automatic or shift to the appropriate gear in the standard.

Remember if you have to stop on the upgrade, your stopping distance will be much shorter. Be prepared to ease up on the brake to stop in the correct place.

DRIVING DOWNHILL: The opposite is true. The force of gravity will cause your speed to increase. The braking distance will be much longer. When you approach the downgrade, (signs will warn of the hill, length and steepness) check the brakes by applying a slight pressure. If the hill is steep, shift to a lower gear in keeping with the appropriate speed required. As you descend the slope, release the accelerator to take advantage of the engine compression for braking power. If necessary, apply the brakes as well, gently and intermittently. Increase the following distance and, if you must stop, prepare yourself by braking earlier and much more firmly than normal.

Your vehicle's **CENTER OF GRAVITY** is the point around which all of its weight is balanced. Most modern automobiles have a very low center of gravity; this gives them excellent road-handling characteristics. Pick-up trucks, jeeps, four wheel drive vehicles, and cars with rooftop carriers tend to have higher centers of gravity. This must be taken into consideration otherwise braking and steering conditions can become dangerous in these vehicles.

Kinetic Energy

Any body in motion acquires KINETIC ENERGY or momentum. (The word kinetic is derived from the Greek word meaning "to move") The formula for calculating this energy is kinetic energy equals one-half the mass (weight of the object) times the velocity (speed) squared.

$$KE = 1/2 \, M \, V^2$$

Increase in MASS (weight) proportionally increases the kinetic energy of an object.

SPEED increases kinetic energy by the square of the number of times speed is increased.

This acquired kinetic energy comes into play in all aspects of driving. To stop, you must dissipate the kinetic energy by braking (Chapter 10) or by hitting another object (force of impact).
To steer, you must overcome the momentum (inertia) of the vehicle in order to change direction.

The most important factor in kinetic energy is your speed. First of all, a small change in speed has a **tremendous effect** on kinetic energy. Secondly, this factor is **under your control**. Slow your vehicle, reduce the speed in half and the kinetic energy acting on your vehicle is only one quarter of what it was before braking.

9

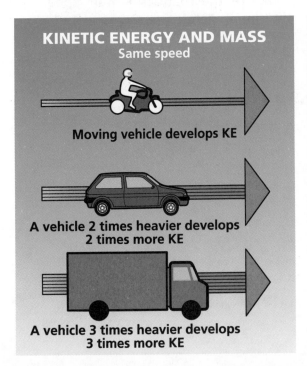

KINETIC ENERGY AND MASS
Same speed

Moving vehicle develops KE

A vehicle 2 times heavier develops
2 times more KE

A vehicle 3 times heavier develops
3 times more KE

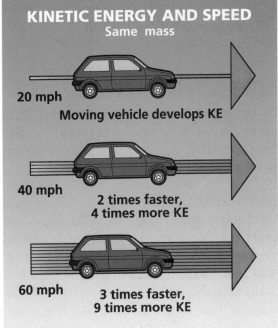

KINETIC ENERGY AND SPEED
Same mass

20 mph
Moving vehicle develops KE

40 mph
2 times faster,
4 times more KE

60 mph
3 times faster,
9 times more KE

Inertia

Sir Isaac Newton, the British scientist, stated three laws dealing with motion. The first law is called the **LAW OF INERTIA**. The law states, in part:

> A body at rest tends to remain at rest. (static inertia)

> A body in motion will continue in a straight line unless some force acts upon it. (dynamic inertia)

Vehicle control (and occupants) are affected by inertia. You have felt the effect of acceleration, of deceleration and of the vehicle turning a corner. The more kinetic energy the vehicle and the occupants accumulate the greater the effect of inertia. In a curve, the sharpness of the change of direction is also a factor. For your vehicle to turn, the traction of the tires must exceed the effect of inertia.

WEIGHT TRANSFER

Driver inputs - acceleration, braking, and steering - also cause a transfer of the concentration of weight from one point on the vehicle to another.

Acceleration transfers weight to the rear, lightening the front and reducing front traction. Conversely, braking transfers weight to the front, lightening the rear and rear traction. Steering input transfers weight to the opposite side of the vehicle; steer left - weight transfers to the right. Two inputs produce two transfers. The driver must minimize weight transfer or utilize it to increase vehicle control.

TO TAKE A CURVE PROPERLY

You have no control over the sharpness of the curve or the weight of your vehicle; **You do have control of your speed.** If you brake on a curve, you divide up the available traction that is needed to steer. As well you further upset vehicle balance (two inputs - two weight transfers) that is already reacting to the effect of inertia.

Nearing curves, **reduce speed**, respect suggested speeds, check the sharpness of the curve, and verify the slant (sideways slope) of the road. **Maintain speed on the curve. Accelerate as you exit.**

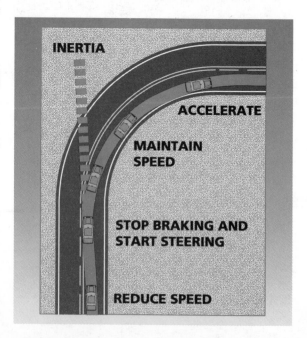

INERTIA
ACCELERATE
MAINTAIN SPEED
STOP BRAKING AND START STEERING
REDUCE SPEED

A FLAT ROAD has no slope and will not assist the vehicle to negotiate the curve.

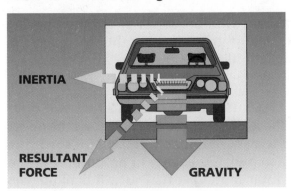

A BANKED CURVE has a higher edge on the outside of the curve and slopes down to the inside. The vehicle will lean toward the inside of the curve (similar to riding a bicycle); inertial energy partly pushes the tires into the pavement increasing traction. This allows you to negotiate the curve safely at a higher speed.

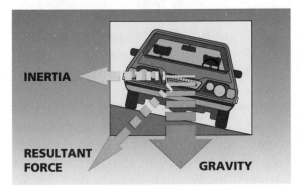

A CROWNED ROAD is higher at the center and slopes down to both sides. Approaching a right curve, this slope is similar to the banked curve; in a left turn, (see below) it is very dangerous and should be negotiated at very slow speeds.

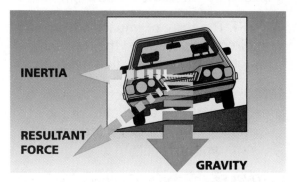

On vehicles with a higher center of gravity, special caution must be exercised on curves. Reduce speed. Remember it is better to enter more slowly, you can always accelerate gradually. If you enter too fast, a loss of control will be inevitable.

The dead pedal (footrest) should be used to brace yourself on curves or during sudden maneuvers to maintain a proper seating position, rather than relying on the seat belt or hanging on to the steering wheel "for dear life". This technique will permit you to maintain steering control in any driving situation.

SAFETY TIPS
The natural forces that act upon your vehicle do not require a police officer to ensure that they are obeyed. They are always in force. Disregard them and the result will be a loss of vehicle control and a potential collision.
The driver needs to be aware of the laws of physics and act in good time to maintain control of the vehicle.

Force of Impact

The force with which a moving vehicle collides with an object or another moving vehicle is called the **FORCE OF IMPACT**. The factors affecting this force are the kinetic energy of the vehicle or vehicles and the distance travelled after the initial impact until the vehicle stops completely.

WEIGHT: The force of impact will increase in direct proportion to the increase in weight of the vehicle . (kinetic energy)

SPEED: The force of impact increases exponentially by the square of the number of times speed is increased. (kinetic energy)

DISTANCE: The force of impact dissipates in relation to the square of the distance travelled after the initial contact.

When a collision is unavoidable, slow your speed as much as possible to reduce the force of impact dramatically and follow these basic concepts.

AVOID HEAD-ON COLLISIONS at all costs. The speed of the oncoming vehicle adds to your speed. If you are both travelling at 30 mph, the force of impact would be identical to an impact at 60 mph. (double the speed = 4 times the kinetic energy and thus 4 times the force of impact)

HEAD-ON COLLISION

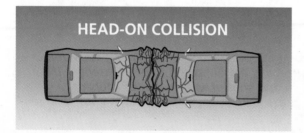

STEER TOWARDS OBJECTS that will offer the least resistance on impact. As the object yields on impact, it will absorb the accumulated energy in proportion to the distance it "gives". This will diminish the amount of energy your vehicle must absorb and increase your chance of avoiding injury.

If you must hit a solid object, try to hit so that your vehicle deflects rather than striking it directly. The construction of modern highways incorporates many features designed to reduce the force of impact. Guard rails, sand-filled canisters, cement barriers, etc. have been designed to absorb energy or deflect vehicles without throwing them back into traffic. Vehicle manufacturers have incorporated many energy absorbing features and passenger restraint systems to protect the occupants (Chapter 11). Engineers have done their utmost to make driving safer and should a collision occur, to reduce the chance of injury.

Only the *DRIVER* can avoid collisions.

Review

TERMS TO REMEMBER - WRITE A SHORT DEFINITION FOR THE FOLLOWING :

- Friction
- Traction
- Tire footprint
- Gravity

- Center of gravity
- Kinetic energy
- Momentum
- Inertia

- Banked road
- Crowned road
- Force of impact

SUMMARY

Gravity keeps the tires in contact with the road providing the traction to control your vehicle. This traction is limited by the tires, the road surface, speed and other factors. Avoid dividing the available traction by steering and braking at the same time. Foresight can control the effects of gravity on braking distance and speed on hills. Kinetic energy and inertia affect braking distance, force of impact and the stability of your vehicle in curves. Know the physical forces that affect your driving and you will maintain control of your vehicle.

TEST A - WRITE "T" BESIDE STATEMENTS THAT ARE TRUE AND "F" BESIDE THOSE THAT ARE FALSE.

_____ **1.** Different tire treads are designed for specific road conditions.

_____ **2.** All road surfaces provide the same traction.

_____ **3.** The mechanical condition of the vehicle does not affect the road holding ability (traction) of any vehicle.

_____ **4.** Gravity has no affect on a vehicle when it is travelling on a level road.

_____ **5.** The higher the center of gravity of a vehicle, the more stable the vehicle will be.

_____ **6.** Kinetic energy increases proportionally with an increase in mass.

_____ **7.** A banked curve is the safest.

_____ **8.** Braking while rounding a curve is the best method for reducing speed.

_____ **9.** Force of impact is not related to the speed of the vehicle.

_____ **10.** When a collision seems inevitable, steer towards the nearest solid object in order to reduce the force of impact.

Student notes

_____

_____

_____

_____

_____

_____

_____

_____

_____

_____

_____

_____

_____

_____

_____

_____

_____

_____

_____

_____

_____

HANDBOOK PLUS WORKBOOK

*Check your comprehension and mastery of the contents of this chapter by completing the corresponding exercises that are found in the complement to the **HANDBOOK PLUS:***

HANDBOOK PLUS WORKBOOK

Complete the exercises on Pages 62 to 68 then check your responses by referring to the answer key on Page 108.
If necessary, review the chapter for each error and refer to your instructor for further guidance.

Stopping Distances

Total stopping distance is a lot longer than most novice drivers realize. IT IS NOT POSSIBLE TO STOP "ON A DIME". From the moment a hazard appears on the roadway ahead until you bring your vehicle to a complete stop, time will pass and your vehicle is in motion. It will cover a certain distance. The length of that distance is directly related to many factors.

In the last chapter on the laws of physics, you studied some of these factors. Kinetic energy, the energy of motion, is a major factor in the actual distance needed to stop your vehicle once the brakes are applied.

In this chapter, you will examine all the factors as well as how to adapt your driving to these factors. You will learn the different braking techniques and advancements in modern brake technology.

10 - A
Time and Distance

10 - B
Danger Zone

10 - C
Braking Techniques

10 - D
ABS Brakes

10 - E
Review

10

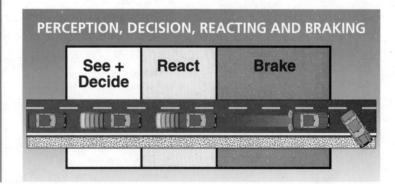

PERCEPTION, DECISION, REACTING AND BRAKING

| See + Decide | React | Brake |

AFTER COMPLETING THIS CHAPTER, THE STUDENT MUST BE ABLE TO UNDERSTAND, IDENTIFY AND BE PREPARED TO APPLY OR ADAPT TO:

- the factors in total stopping time and distance.
- the various braking techniques.
- the ABS brake system and the use thereof.

Time and Distances

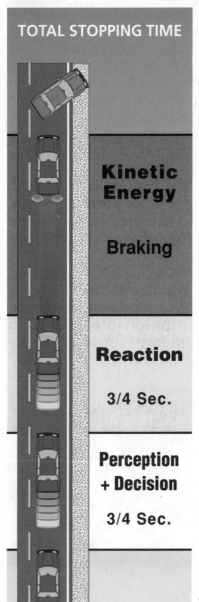

TOTAL STOPPING TIME

Kinetic
Energy

Braking

Reaction

3/4 Sec.

Perception
+ Decision

3/4 Sec.

TOTAL STOPPING TIME consists of the entire time from the moment a hazard appears ahead until you bring your vehicle to a complete stop. It can be subdivided into:

*Perception time:
   The time it takes you to spot the danger. This depends on your mental and physical state, your eye lead time (how far ahead you are scanning the road), and how quickly you identify the hazard (SCAN - IDENTIFY). In poor visual conditions, reduce your speed so that you compensate for your shorter eye lead time. (At slower speeds it will take more time to reach the hazard)

*Decision making time:
   The time it takes you to PREDICT and DECIDE what to do. Your experience, physical and mental state, as well as the attention you give to the driving task will all affect how much time will elapse. If all the factors are at their best, three quarters of a second will elapse for the perception and decision making stages.

*Reaction time:
   The time it takes you to EXECUTE your decision. Release the accelerator and apply the brakes. At best, another three quarters of a second will elapse for this stage.
   One and a half seconds in total time and only now are you starting to brake. This total can be much longer depending on the driver.

*Braking time:
   The time it takes for your vehicle to come to a complete stop once the brakes are applied. This time is related to your experience and skill in braking, the kinetic energy of your vehicle, the mechanical condition of your vehicle, and the road conditions. Let's translate this elapsed time into distances.

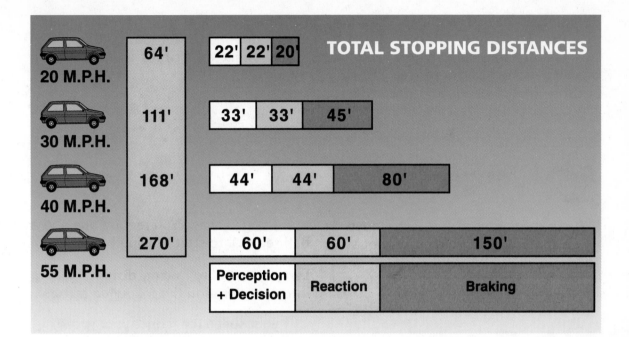

TOTAL STOPPING DISTANCES

Speed	Total	Perception + Decision	Reaction	Braking
20 M.P.H.	64'	22'	22'	20'
30 M.P.H.	111'	33'	33'	45'
40 M.P.H.	168'	44'	44'	80'
55 M.P.H.	270'	60'	60'	150'

TOTAL STOPPING DISTANCE is the distance your vehicle will travel from the moment the hazard appears ahead until your vehicle comes to a complete stop.

Look at the chart. Compare the total stopping distance at 20 mph to what it becomes as the speed increases.

Compare the braking distances (the distance your vehicle travels from the time the brakes are applied until it stops) at 20 mph and 40 mph. The speed is doubled. The braking distance ... ? This is a result of kinetic energy as it applies to braking distance. Look at the chart below for a comparison of braking distance and speed.

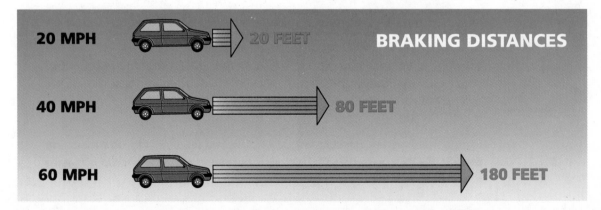

BRAKING DISTANCES

20 MPH	20 FEET
40 MPH	80 FEET
60 MPH	180 FEET

Remember these charts refer to ideal driving conditions. Change the road surface or road conditions and the braking distance increases sharply. Because of the reduced friction factor (Chapter 9), the braking distance is almost double on wet roads. It can be as much as sixteen times as long on an icy surface.

Danger Zone

Your moving vehicle is surrounded by a space within which it cannot stop. This is called its **"DANGER ZONE"**.

THE SPACE IN FRONT OF YOU IS EQUAL TO YOUR TOTAL STOPPING DISTANCE.

THE SPACE BEHIND YOU IS EQUAL TO THE TOTAL STOPPING DISTANCE OF THE VEHICLE FOLLOWING YOU.

To protect yourself, always maintain a **"SAFETY CUSHION"** around your vehicle. (Chapter 8) By utilizing the **"TWO SECOND RULE"** as a minimum, you leave a 1/2 second margin of safety from the preceding vehicle. (You require one and a half seconds to start braking.)

Lengthen this following distance taking into consideration the following factors:

- your speed (or reduce your speed)
- the road conditions (traction)
- the weather conditions (vision)
- the density of traffic

Apply these same concepts to the space behind you. When another vehicle encroaches on your safety cushion (tailgater - Chapter 8), react accordingly.

SAFETY TIPS

The key to defensive driving is to apply the SIPDE strategy and control your visibility, space and speed. Proper application of these principles will permit you to brake early and gently in complete control... in GOOD TIME.

In this manner, the need for rapid evasive maneuvers and other braking techniques can be avoided. This does not mean that you should not learn and practice all the braking techniques.

Braking Techniques

To bring your vehicle to a stop in complete safety regardless of the many factors involved, there are several techniques to master.

BRAKING IN "GOOD TIME"

The first and the best method is to constantly monitor your speed, space, and driving conditions. Then you can brake with a steady pressure on the brake as normal; braking in "GOOD TIME".

This method will keep you out of trouble though it requires a long braking distance. To succeed, this technique is based on the driver - YOU must think ahead, apply the SIPDE strategy and drive defensively.

THRESHOLD BRAKING:

This method involves applying the brake pedal more firmly, just to the point prior to "locking the wheels". Shift to neutral (depress the clutch pedal - standard transmission) to remove the unbalancing effect of the drive wheels and the differential. If the wheels lock, ease up slightly adjusting the pressure to apply as hard as you can without lock-up. As your vehicle slows to a stop, ease up gradually. To master this technique requires practice and skill. The advantages are:

- the braking distance is shorter
- you maintain your steering control
- the tires wear evenly and avoid skidding

The problem with this method is that road surfaces are rarely smooth. On wet, icy, or uneven pavement, the "lock-up point" will vary while you are braking. It requires considerable skill to maintain full braking without skidding.

"PUMPING THE BRAKE PEDAL"

This method involves applying the brake pedal completely (locking the wheels), then releasing the brake sufficiently to permit wheel rotation. Then re-applying the brake pedal again. These actions are repeated until your vehicle comes to a standstill. Shifting to neutral (depressing the clutch pedal - standard transmission) at the start of the pumping action will again remove any unbalancing effect from the power train.

This technique permits control of the steering; however, the braking distance is not as short as threshold braking.

"LOCKING THE BRAKES"

This method is not a normal stopping technique. It is intended to be used in EMERGENCY SITUATIONS ONLY; when it is a choice between a collision or stopping. The braking distance is the shortest; however, you lose steering control.

APPLY THE BRAKES SUDDENLY AND FULLY.

The immediate result is continuous braking action. The tires are skidding. Your vehicle may rotate on its axis while stopping in a straight line. **This is not a normal stopping method.**

10

ABS Brakes (Anti-lock Braking System)

The greatest recent advancement in modern automotive technology is the "ABS BRAKE SYSTEM".

This system assists the driver; allowing you to perform an emergency stop while retaining steering control. You apply the brakes fully. The onboard computer controls the brake pressure at each wheel; cycling from locked to slightly rolling in a pumping-like action many times a second.

The result is continuous braking action, under control while maintaining steering control. The vehicle will not rotate on its axis! You do not have to modulate the pressure on the brake pedal.

HAMMER THE BRAKE.

The result will be:
- The system will look after you
- Remember, you can still steer

Brake as hard as you can, look where you want to go, steer where you want to go - you will reduce speed rapidly and still change direction in full control.

REMEMBER, BRAKE AND STEER!

If you purchase a vehicle with ABS, you should practice emergency stops to learn the technique required to take full advantage of the system.

Most drivers defeat the system by easing off the pedal when the pedal begins to pulsate or by attempting to pump the brake pedal out of habit.

SAFETY TIPS

Many insurance companies offer special premium reductions for vehicles that are factory-equipped with the ABS brake system because of the tremendous advantages of this system in avoiding collisions during emergency maneuvers when used properly.

Most automotive manufacturers are including the system as standard equipment on many of their models. When you purchase a vehicle, this is an item you MUST CONSIDER. If it is not included on the model of your choice , order it as an option. If it is not available as an option, choose another make or model that has an ABS system.

Check the owner's manual for any special service requirements.

10

Review

TERMS TO REMEMBER - WRITE A SHORT DEFINITION FOR THE FOLLOWING :

- Perception time
- Decision making time
- Reaction time
- Braking time

- Total stopping distance
- Danger zone
- Safety cushion
- ABS brakes

- Braking in "good time"
- Threshold braking
- Pumping the brakes
- Locking the brakes

SUMMARY

It is impossible to stop a vehicle in motion instantly. Before you come to a complete stop, a certain distance will be required. The length of this distance depends on:

- **THE DRIVER:**
  Physical / Mental state
  Eye lead time
  Driving experience
  Reaction time
  Skill

- **THE VEHICLE:**
  Kinetic energy
  - mass (weight)
  - velocity (speed)
  Mechanical condition
  - brakes / tires / suspension

- **THE ROADWAY:**
  Traction conditions
  - friction
  - type of surface
  The slope (gravity)
  - downhill / uphill

TEST A - IDENTIFY THE FOLLOWING STATEMENTS AS TRUE OR FALSE.

_____ **1)** Perception and decision making time are the same for all drivers.

_____ **2)** Reaction time, the time to actually execute the maneuver decided upon, will require at least three quarters of a second

_____ **3)** Braking time, the time that elapses from the moment the brake is applied until the vehicle comes to a complete stop, only varies with vehicle speed.

_____ **4)** Total stopping distance includes the distance travelled while seeing, deciding and reacting as well as the distance required to stop the vehicle.

_____ **5)** If the stopping distance at 20 mph is 20 feet, the stopping distance, all other factors remaining the same, at 60 mph would be 180 feet.

_____ **6)** The "SAFETY CUSHION" equals the distance needed to stop the vehicle.

_____ **7)** The driver who tailgates, follows your vehicle too closely, is creating a hazardous situation for you as well as for himself.

_____ **8)** Applying the brake pedal suddenly and fully, "LOCKING THE BRAKES", is a normal braking technique and is used in most stopping situations.

_____ **9)** Shifting to NEUTRAL (depressing the clutch) before braking, increases control because it removes the unbalancing effect of the differential/power train.

_____ **10)** Braking in "GOOD TIME" requires the driver to constantly monitor speed, space and driving conditions in order to stop the vehicle safely.

Student notes

_____
_____
_____
_____
_____
_____
_____
_____
_____
_____
_____
_____
_____
_____
_____
_____
_____
_____
_____

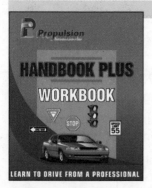

HANDBOOK PLUS WORKBOOK

Check your comprehension and mastery of the contents of this chapter by completing the corresponding exercises that are found in the complement to the HANDBOOK PLUS:

HANDBOOK PLUS WORKBOOK

Complete the exercises on Pages 69 to 72 then check your responses by referring to the answer key on Page 108.

If necessary, review the chapter for each error and refer to your instructor for further guidance.

Restraint Systems

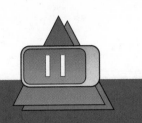

II

II - A
Safety Belts

II - B
Air Bags

II - C
Child Restraints

II - D
A Few Facts

II - E
Review

Engineers are responsible for improving vehicles, highway design, and traffic control systems. Today's automobiles are safer, more efficient, and more comfortable to drive than ever before.

In the event of a collision, the interior has been designed with a padded dash, head restraints, controls that are recessed or break away, a collapsible steering column, and shatter-proof windshields. The vehicle has energy-absorbing bumpers to minimize low speed impacts. The front and rear sections are designed to crush. Beams reinforce the side doors to reduce the possible effect on the passenger compartment in crashes.

The single most effective safety device during a collision is the seat belt!!

AFTER COMPLETING THIS CHAPTER, THE STUDENT MUST DEMONSTRATE COMPLETE COMPREHENSION OF THE IMPORTANCE AND PROPER USAGE OF:

- **safety belts.**
- **air bags.**
- **child restraints.**

Restraint Systems

When a vehicle is involved in a collision, three impacts occur in rapid succession.

- The **vehicle collides** with another vehicle or object.
- The **occupants collide** with the interior of the vehicle.
- The **interior organs collide** with the interior of the body cavity.

You have already seen how engineers design the vehicle to absorb impacts and how you as the driver can minimize the force of impact during a collision.

In a crash at 30 mph, the impact on an occupant of the vehicle is equal to falling from a three story building. The force of impact equals 35 TIMES YOUR BODY WEIGHT.

The brain and other interior organs strike the interior of the skull and body cavity with this tremendous force when the exterior of the body collides and stops instantly.

To minimize the consequences of these two impacts, the occupants should be protected by RESTRAINT DEVICES. These are designed to keep them in their seats and to cushion the stopping motion. They prevent the second impact. At the same time they slow the forward motion (effect of inertia) and bring the occupants to a stop more gradually (impact distance).

Safety Belts

A safety belt that the occupant must attach or buckle is called an ACTIVE RESTRAINT device.

The lap portion of this belt is designed to keep you in your seat. It should be adjusted to fit snugly low across your hips below the stomach.

The shoulder portion prevents your head and torso from striking the interior of the passenger compartment. It should

The result may be a more serious injury if a collision were to happen.

During a collision, the combined action of the lap and shoulder belt will maintain your seating position, cushion the impact, and distribute the force over your shoulders, hips and rib cage.

Seat belts have been proven effective in reducing the probability of serious injury by 40 percent and increasing the chance of survival by 60 percent. As a result, the majority of states have passed legislation that requires the wearing of safety belts and all states require the use of child restraints by law..

pass over the shoulder and cross your chest diagonally with a minimum of slack. Your clenched fist should barely fit between the belt and your chest, if the belt does not adjust automatically.

NEVER ATTACH THE BELT IF IT IS TWISTED!

NEVER WEAR THE BELT LOOSELY OR IMPROPERLY!

In either case, you will defeat the proper operation of the safety belt.

PASSIVE RESTRAINT DEVICES do not require the occupant to fasten or buckle these protective devices. Many vehicles are equipped with passive seat belts that are attached to the door and to the floor; they automatically fasten when the door is closed. This safety belt provides the same protection to the occupant.

SAFETY TIPS

The advantages of air bags are such that many insurance companies are already offering significant premium reductions for vehicles that are equipped with air bags.

Moreover, new vehicles are including air bag systems as standard equipment on many models. When purchasing your next vehicle, this option should be a factor in your choice of vehicle. Make sure that they are included on the model you choose whether as standard equipment or as an option.

?

Air Bags

The air bag is another passive restraint device. It can be installed in the center of the steering wheel for the driver and in the dash for other front seat passengers. Sensing devices cause the air bags to inflate instantly in any collision over 12 mph and then deflate a fraction of a second later. They further cushion the force of impact and distribute it over a wider surface of the torso. They complement the protection provided by the seat belts.

Air bags do not replace safety belts! They complement them!
- Used together, they reduce the probability of a fatality by 70 %.
- . The air bag alone - only 35 %.
- The seat belt alone - 60 %.

Caution: **Passenger side air bags can cause harm to children in all child restraints attached to the front seat!**

The safest position for passengers (even more so for children) is the back seat.

Child Restraints

It is extremely dangerous to ride in a moving vehicle while holding a child on your lap. Rather than protecting them, you are putting them at risk!
In a collision, the child will continue forward (kinetic energy - inertia) and the force required to stop this motion is beyond human capability.

IF YOU LOVE THEM, PROTECT THEM! PUT THEM IN A CHILD RESTRAINT! IT`S THE LAW IN ALL STATES!

Children should be secured in a device appropriate to their size and age. These child restraints should be properly installed in accordance with the seat manufacturer's recommendations.

THE INFANT SEAT

This restraint is intended for children weighing less than 20 lbs. The child is cushioned by the seat on all sides. At this age, the child's head is larger and heavier than the rest of his/her

No passenger-side air bag!

attached to the rear seat. Secure the toddler seat using the seat belt and in keeping with the recommendations of the manufacturer of the restraint. Your child should be facing forward and securely buckled into the toddler seat.

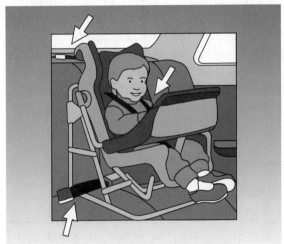

body. The seat should be positioned facing the rear with the child firmly secured to the seat which is then attached to the vehicle using the safety belt.

The safest position is on the back seat; however, attaching the infant seat to the front seat will allow the driver to check on the child without having to turn around.

Make sure that you do this by glancing and returning your eyes to the road ahead in between glances. Do not permit yourself to become distracted. If any situation arises where your infant requires attention. STOP THE VEHICLE. In a safe manner of course, then care for your child. Do not put yourself and your infant at risk.

THE TODDLER SEAT

This seat is designed for children ranging from 20 to 40 lbs. who have now become more active. This seat requires a quasi-permanent installation and is best

Accustom yourself to conversing with your child without taking your eyes off the road. Visually check him/her by using the interior rear-view mirror.

As previously mentioned, park your vehicle if you must offer physical assistance. The control of your children will become easier as they mature; the use of the seats and eventually the safety belt will have become second nature.

PRE-SCHOOLERS

Children weighing 40 to 50 lbs. are too big for the usual child restraint and yet they are not quite large enough to use the regular safety belts, especially the shoulder belt. You may often see parents allowing children to stand just behind the front seats in order to see the road. You can imagine what will happen in a collision.

There are a variety of booster seats available which raise the child while incorporating the safety belt. This raises him/her to a sufficient height that the shoulder belt may also be used.
   Engineers have also designed a shoulder harness that is adjustable, the height of the shoulder attachment can be raised or lowered to accommodate children.

 # A Few Facts

Safety belts properly used, help keep you behind the wheel in control of your vehicle in sudden maneuvers.
Seat belts help keep passengers in their seats in sudden maneuvers and therefore prevent them from hindering the driver.

MYTH! Pregnant women should not wear seat belts. **FACT:** They should wear them. Properly worn over the hips and across the chest, the belt will restrain the mother without harming the fetus. The most common cause of fetal fatalities in collisions is the death of the mother.

25 percent of traffic fatalities occur when occupants are thrown from their vehicles. The risk of death is 5 times greater in such cases.

The fear of being trapped by the safety belt in a burning or sinking vehicle is a false fear. The use of the safety belt increases the likelihood that you will be conscious and able to escape.

50 percent of all collisions occur within a 5 mile radius of your home. All the more reason to use the safety belt even on short, close to home trips.

60 percent of all collisions occur at speeds below 30 mph. What better time to be wearing a safety belt?

Fatalities have been recorded at speeds as low as 15 mph without safety belts. No fatalities have been recorded below 50 mph while using safety belts.

SAFETY BELTS WHEN WORN PROPERLY:
   • reduce the risk of injury by 40%
   • reduce the risk of death by 60%

IN CONJUNCTION WITH AIR BAGS:
   • REDUCE THE RISK OF DEATH BY 70%

Review

TERMS TO REMEMBER - WRITE A SHORT DEFINITION FOR THE FOLLOWING :

- Seat belt
- Active restraint
- Torso
- Passive restraint
- Air bags
- Infant seat
- Toddler seat
- Pre-schoolers seat

SUMMARY

Engineers are responsible for continual improvements in highway design, traffic control systems and vehicle construction. All of these improvements are useless unless you, the driver, take advantage of them. Use, and make sure that your passengers also use, the safety belts and systems in your vehicle. When purchasing your next vehicle, make new technology in safety devices one of the factors that determines which vehicle you choose to buy.

TEST A - WRITE "T" BESIDE STATEMENTS THAT ARE TRUE AND "F" BESIDE THOSE THAT ARE FALSE.

_____ 1. Collisions occur most frequently far from home.

_____ 2. In a vehicle equipped with air bags, the driver and passengers do not need to buckle up the seat belts.

_____ 3. Pregnant women should wear their seat belts as the best protection for themselves and their unborn child.

_____ 4. How you wear the seat belt does not matter, as long as you buckle up.

_____ 5. Children weighing less than 20 pounds should be restrained in a toddler's seat.

_____ 6. A booster seat is intended for children weighing 40 pounds or more.

_____ 7. The safest position for children in any vehicle is buckled in an appropriate restraint system attached to the front seat.

_____ 8. Safety belts reduce the risk of death in a collision by 60%.

_____ 9. Safety belts used in conjunction with air bags reduce the risk of death in a collision by 70%.

_____ 10. Wearing seat belts will cause the driver to be trapped in his/her vehicle in a collision.

Student notes

_____

_____

_____

_____

_____

_____

_____

_____

_____

_____

_____

_____

_____

_____

_____

_____

_____

_____

_____

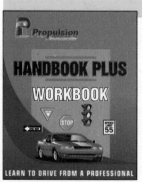

HANDBOOK PLUS WORKBOOK

*Check your comprehension and mastery of the contents of this chapter by completing the corresponding exercise that is found in the complement to the **HANDBOOK PLUS**:*

HANDBOOK PLUS WORKBOOK

Complete the exercise on Page 73 then check your responses by referring to the answer key on Page 108.
If necessary, review the chapter for each error and refer to your instructor for further guidance.

Driving Techniques

12

12 - A
Basic Rules

12 - B
Intersections

12 - C
The Urban
Environment

12 - D
The Rural
Environment

12 - E
The Expressway
Environment

12 - F
Turning About

12 - G
Parking

12 - H
Review

Drivers require good driving techniques that are second nature. Initially, concentrate and master the basic skills; develop a strategy and visual skills to adapt to the environments you will encounter when driving in the city, the country, and expressways. Each present special problems.

City driving has congested streets, intersections, road users of all kinds, as well as a multitude of signs and signals. INFORMATION OVERLOAD!

Open scenery and low volume of traffic present an idyllic picture in country driving. This can be deceiving. Higher speeds, hidden crossings, pavement variations, hills, curves, etc. are all potential hazards.

On expressways, speeds are high. There are no stop signs, no intersections, and interchanges are few and far apart. There are fewer maneuvers to perform; they are usually more dangerous.

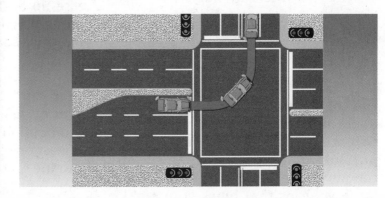

AFTER COMPLETING THIS CHAPTER, THE STUDENT MUST BE ABLE TO RECOGNIZE, EVALUATE AND RESPOND TO CHANGES IN THE DRIVING ENVIRONMENT:

- **while applying the SIPDE system and proper vehicle control.**
- **while maneuvering using appropriate risk-reduction techniques.**
- **with respect to the urban, rural and expressway environments.**

Basic Rules

COMMUNICATION

Signal your presence and what you intend to do. Sharing the road in any environment requires that others can see you and that they know your intentions. COMMUNICATE. Use the tools at your disposal early and intelligently.

Headlights: turn them on while driving, flash the high beams to communicate your presence

Turn signals: activate early to warn of turns or lane changes (avoid causing confusion)

Hazard lights: activate to warn of risk and abnormal situations

Brake lights: tap the brake pedal before applying the brakes

Horn: tap to attract other road users attention (eye-to-eye contact)

Hand signals: to warn of intentions and communicate right-of-way (Chapter 2)

Use the "TWO SECOND RULE" (Chapter 8) to maintain a minimum following distance. Increase this distance whenever possible particularly when driving conditions are not ideal, when following large vehicles that block your field of vision or when following a motorcycle.

Maintain an equal space behind your vehicle. If a following vehicle tailgates,

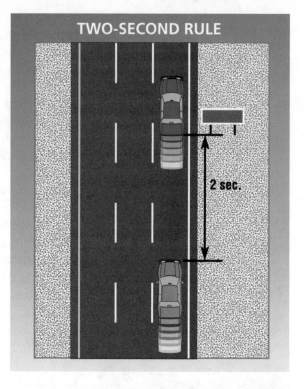

TWO-SECOND RULE

2 sec.

ease up on the accelerator and increase your following distance to at least four seconds. Look for a chance to change lanes.

Keep an "out", an open space, to the sides of your vehicle. Adjust your speed and position in traffic to keep a space on at least one side so that you could swerve into the space to avoid a hazard.

When driving in the lane beside parked vehicles, maintain the widest margin of space possible. Position your vehicle in the left portion of your lane to leave extra space (lane-left position reference).

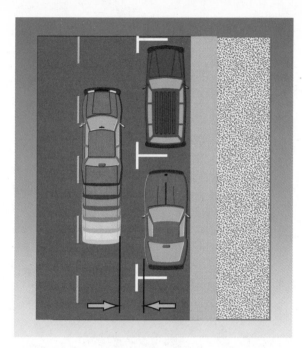

When you stop behind another vehicle, maintain a distance of at least one half a car length. You should be able to see the rear tires touching the roadway over the top of the hoodline.

This space will enable you:
- to change lanes if the lane is blocked, the vehicle stalls, or a rear-end collision is imminent

- to leave the vehicle ahead space to maneuver should the driver wish to reverse
- to avoid a roll back as the vehicle tries to advance up the slope
- to avoid carbon monoxide and hot exhaust emissions from having an adverse effect on you or your vehicle.

RIGHT-OF-WAY

It is important to understand that the right-of-way is something that must be given to you. The law specifies who must yield to whom; it never states who HAS the right-of-way. Moreover, situations are not always clear-cut. When in doubt, extend the courtesy of yielding to a vehicle with which you are in conflict. The law provides rules to go by but people create the helpful "courteous" environment. (Chapter 3)

MANEUVERS

Each maneuver should be performed applying the APE system (Chapter 7). The system sequence is ASSESS, PREPARE, and EXECUTE.

ASSESS: Scan the situation for signs and road markings, check the mirrors and blind spot, and decide whether to perform the maneuver.

PREPARE: Having decided, signal your intentions and recheck the mirrors and your blind spot to ensure that you can proceed in complete safety.

EXECUTE: Perform the maneuver, look where you want to go and guide your vehicle. When complete, make sure the turn signal is no longer activated.

CHANGING LANES

To alter your lane position, you must perform a lane change; whether to avoid an obstacle, pass another vehicle, prepare for a turn, leave the roadway, or merely to increase space from a potential hazard. Whatever the reason, plan ahead and use the APE system.

ASSESS: Check ahead in your lane and the lane you want to enter (space, speed, obstacles)
Is the maneuver permitted?
Check mirrors and blind spot (space and speed)

IS THIS MANEUVER SAFE?

PREPARE: Signal your intention by activating the turn signal
Recheck traffic ahead
Recheck mirrors and blind spot
(Standard- shift to the appropriate gear)

EXECUTE: Aim high at the center of the intended lane
Adjust speed
(gently accelerate if possible)
Steer gently (ease into lane)
Center your vehicle in the lane
Readjust speed to
the flow of traffic
Cancel the turn signal.

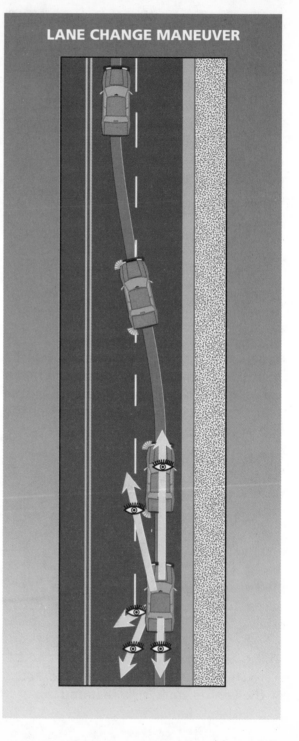

LANE CHANGE MANEUVER

Intersections

When two roadways meet, other road users may want to use the same space at the same time as you do. This may present a hazard, the risk of a collision.

Most collisions involving pedestrians, motorcycles, or bicycles with motorized vehicles occur at intersections.

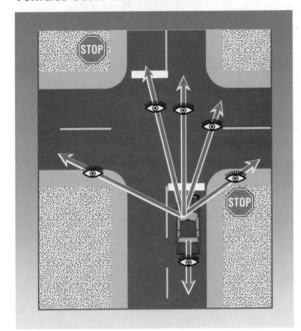

Scan the intersection to identify the situation. Controlled intersections (traffic lights or stop signs at all approaches), partially controlled (one roadway has stop signs), or uncontrolled intersections-each present different levels of danger. Check the traffic behind you.

If you are not required to stop, ease off the accelerator, cover the brake, and scan left, center, right and left again before entering the intersection. Reduce speed if your vision is blocked by large parked vehicles, trees, snow banks, etc.

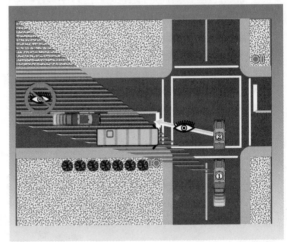

Pay special attention to the presence of pedestrians, especially children, the visually or physically impaired, or senior citizens.

Yield to any vehicle or pedestrian already engaged in the intersection.

Do not enter the intersection unless you can cross and exit in complete safety.

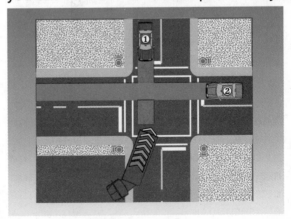

When required to stop, tap the brake, check the rear-view mirror, and then apply the brake pedal. Make a smooth stop before the stop line, the crosswalk, or the edge of the crossroad (front stop reference).

At a traffic light, wait for the green signal then check left, center, right and left again before proceeding. Be aware of road users that might enter the intersection late (Diagram below). Yield to pedestrians and vehicles that have not yet cleared the intersection.

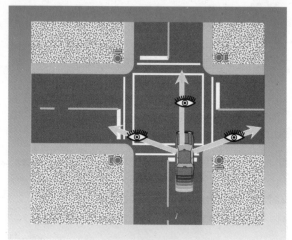

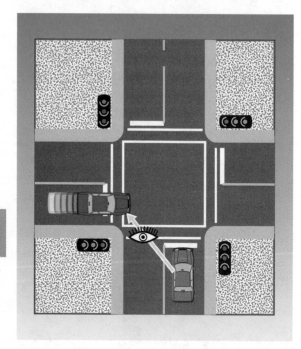

When at a stop, check left, center, and right. Apply the right-of-way rules. Ease up on the brake and advance into the intersection. Check left, center, right, and left again before deciding to cross the intersection.

RIGHT TURNS

In order to perform a right turn, you must first position your vehicle in the lane closest to the right side of the roadway. This means completing a lane change maneuver (if not in the correct lane) at least 200 feet prior to the turn.

ASSESS: Is a right turn permitted? (signs, signals)
Scan the intersection
Check the rear-view mirrors
Check your right blind spot

IS THIS MANEUVER SAFE?

PREPARE: Activate the right turn signal
Tap the brake then reduce speed
(Standard- downshift to second gear)
Scan the intersection
Recheck mirrors and blind spot
Move to the right in your lane
(3 to 5 feet from the curb)

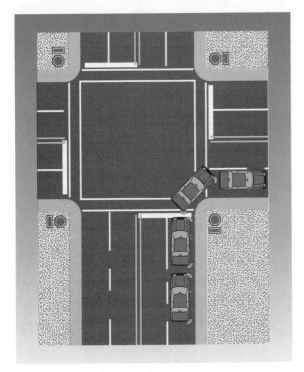

To perform a left turn, you must be in the furthest left lane that you may use.
On a two-way road, the lane nearest the yellow center line. On a one-way road, the lane closest to the left side of the road. This may necessitate one or more lane changes prior to the turn.

FROM A TWO-WAY TO ANOTHER TWO-WAY

ASSESS: Is a left turn permitted? (signs, signals)
Scan the intersection
Check the rear-view mirrors
Check your left blind spot

IS THIS MANEUVER SAFE?

PREPARE: Activate the left turn signal
Tap the brake then reduce speed smoothly
(Standard- downshift to second gear)
Advance until the front of your vehicle nears the center of the intersection
Scan the intersection and the oncoming traffic
Stop with front tires straight if pedestrians or oncoming traffic impede the turn
(Standard- shift to first gear)
Check mirrors and blind spot.

EXECUTE: As the front wheels reach the curve of the curb (turn reference)
Look through the turn (along the intended path)
Release the brake
Steer hand over hand (following the intended path)
Aim ahead into the right lane
Accelerate gently
Straighten the steering
Accelerate to normal speed
Verify the turn signal.

When performing a right turn from a stop, begin turning the steering wheel (as explained above) as you advance into the intersection to check traffic. When the way is clear, accelerate gently while steering hand over hand.

EXECUTE: Aim at the center of the intended lane (turn reference)
Release the brake pedal
Steer hand over hand

12

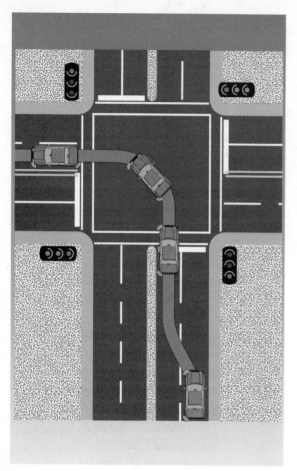

FROM A TWO-WAY TO A ONE-WAY

The intended lane is beside the curb. Stop or begin the turn when the front of your vehicle reaches the crosswalk. Otherwise follow the same procedures.

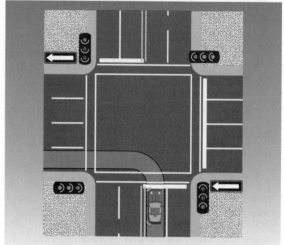

FROM A ONE-WAY TO A TWO-WAY

You must be in the lane closest to the left side of the road. Change lanes to position your vehicle in this lane at least 200 feet prior to the turn. Follow the same procedures as for a two-way to a two-way left turn.

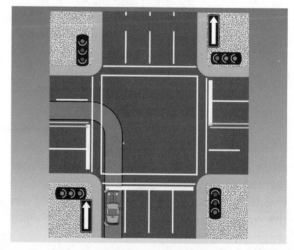

(following the intended path)
Accelerate smoothly
Aim ahead into the left lane
Straighten the steering
Accelerate to normal speed
Check the turn signal is off

As soon as possible after straightening in the left lane, perform a lane change to the right (if a lane is available to the right) to move out of the passing lane. The passing lane should be left clear whenever it is possible to do so.

12

FROM A ONE-WAY TO ANOTHER ONE-WAY

Follow the procedures for a right turn replacing the word left for the word right. When the turn is completed, you should change lanes to the right (lane of least resistance and your intended route).

WRONG LANE FOR TURN

In all turning situations, if you are close to the intersection and in the incorrect lane to turn, continue straight ahead and then change lanes into the correct lane in order to turn at the next intersection!

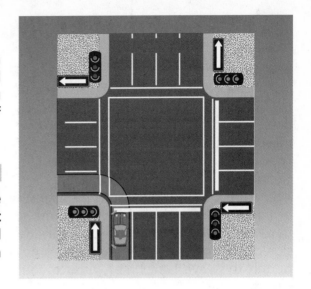

 # The Urban Environment

A city can be an exciting environment; however, crowded streets, heavy traffic, and a multitude of traffic signals can make driving a difficult challenge to the uninitiated. This is especially true for novice drivers.

The SIPDE system must be applied to manage time, space and visibility. Slow moving traffic, numerous obstacles, a wide variety of vehicles and other road users can present several hazards at the same time.

Scan the roadway, use selective vision to identify hazards, and manage your space. Try to separate hazards. Reduce your speed. Plan your route (Chapter 18) and avoid congested areas. Above all, be patient and relax.

Characteristics to be wary of:

- a multitude of intersections
- rows of parked vehicles
- off-road parking
- school buses
- school and playground zones
- changing speed limits
- traffic jams
- numerous traffic signals
- city buses, delivery vehicles and other vehicles that stop frequently

OTHER ROAD USERS MAY NOT PERFORM AS THEY SHOULD OR AS YOU MIGHT THINK; EXPECT THE UNEXPECTED.

The Rural Environment

Driving in rural areas is less hectic and more relaxing than in the urban environment. Highway driving, however, presents its own special challenges. You must adjust to higher speeds, a variety of road conditions, and traffic patterns. Accidents are fewer but more serious.

Apply the SIPDE system. Scan 20 seconds ahead and identify objects, animals, pedestrians or vehicles on or near the side of the road. When visibility does not permit this "eye lead time", reduce your speed.

Check road conditions ahead and adapt your speed to the traction available, the curves, hills, or intersections.

Particular dangers:

- slow-moving vehicles
- oncoming vehicles, especially large ones that produce air turbulence
- off-road vehicles
- crossings- animals, trucks, etc.
- railroad crossings
- wild animals
- hidden intersections
- winding roads and hills
- unpaved shoulders and no shoulders
- unpaved roads
- narrow bridges

PASSING SITUATIONS

BEING PASSED

When another vehicle is passing yours, you should cooperate:

- refrain from increasing speed
- check for an "out" to the right
- be prepared to adjust speed

If the driver of the passing vehicle suddenly decides not to do so (he starts braking) because of an oncoming vehicle, accelerate to help him re-enter the lane behind you. If he continues to complete the pass, apply the brakes to help him re-enter the lane in front of you.

PASSING

Passing is one of the most dangerous driving maneuvers. Before passing, you must decide whether it makes sense under the existing road, traffic and weather conditions. Your speed, the speed of the other vehicle, and the speed limit (which you must not exceed) must also be taken into account. If the other vehicle is driving 5 to 10 mph slower and the maneuver can be performed safely, you might decide to pass before slowing.

ASSESS: Is passing permitted
Check the situation ahead
(at right- signs, intersections
at left- off-road vehicles,
oncoming vehicles)
Check your mirrors and left
blind spot
(vehicles behind passing)

IS IT SAFE TO PASS?

PREPARE: Activate the left turn signal
Signal your presence

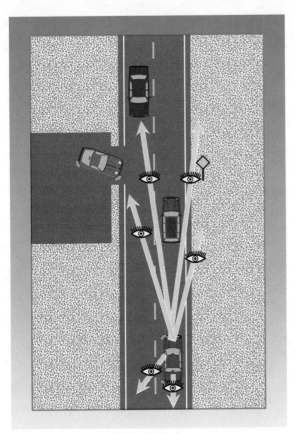

(both front tires of the vehicle you are passing should be visible)
Activate the right turn signal
Check the right blind spot
Look and steer into the right lane (lane change)
Center your vehicle in the lane
De-activate the turn signal
Ease off the accelerator
(make sure you have a safe space behind)

WHEN PASSING, NEVER PASS MORE THAN ONE VEHICLE AT A TIME!

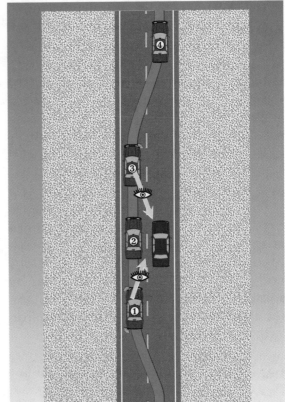

(honk or flash your high beams)
Accelerate (at least 10 mph over the preceding vehicle)
(standard- select a gear that provides power to pass)
Recheck the situation ahead
Recheck the mirrors and the left blind spot

EXECUTE: Look and steer into the passing lane (lane change)
Check the space ahead
Glance at the left front tire of the vehicle you are passing
Firmly maintain speed
Check the rear-view mirror

The Expressway Environment

Traveling on expressways, the normal traffic speed is higher than the urban or rural environment. Engineers design modern expressways with a minimum of potential conflicts to permit the high speeds in maximum safety. Drivers must adapt the SIPDE system to manage time, space and visibility in this controlled environment. Most multiple vehicle collisions occur on expressways due to vehicles following too closely.

CHARACTERISTICS
- Higher speeds
- Limited access and exits (no intersections, crossings)
- Separate roadways with two or more lanes moving in the same direction
- Gentle, banked curves
- Graded hills
- Minimum and maximum speed limits
- Uninterrupted flow of traffic

ENTERING AN EXPRESSWAY

Expressways have interchanges where cross traffic passes over or under the roadway, thus eliminating intersections and traffic lights. Access is provided by special entrance ramps with an extra lane (acceleration lane) to help drivers merge with the flow of traffic.

ASSESS: Check the access ramp (signs, speed, do not enter) Check traffic on expressway Check the flow of traffic ahead.

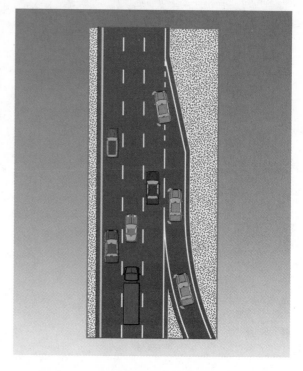

PREPARE: Adjust speed on access ramp (suggested speed, vehicles) Check for gap on expressway Activate the left turn signal.

EXECUTE: Accelerate to match traffic Check mirrors and left blind spot Look ahead and steer smoothly into the right lane Center vehicle in right lane Turn off left turn signal Adjust speed and space to the flow of traffic in your lane.

Keep extra space from preceding vehicles on the acceleration lane as many drivers brake while checking traffic as they try to enter the expressway.

If the extra lane is intended as both an acceleration and deceleration lane (entrance and exit), check for vehicles in the right lane on the expressway that may exit and reduce speed.

DRIVING ON AN EXPRESSWAY

Drive in the right lane (two lane) or the second lane (three or more lanes) as much as possible. Leave the left lane for passing. Adjust your speed to the traffic, the speed limit, and the road and weather conditions. (Minimum speed limits no longer apply in adverse driving conditions).

Scan 20 seconds ahead. Identify hazards. Keep space around your vehicle. Avoid driving in "packs". Adjust your speed and space early and gently. Avoid large vehicles that block your visibility.

Change lanes when "packs" or tailgaters approach from the rear.

If you change lanes, check the blind spot across the entire roadway as other vehicles may be changing to the same lane you intend to occupy. **Always change one lane at a time.**

POTENTIAL DANGERS

- the effect of high speed on your braking distance
- the effect of high speed on your field of vision
- the hypnotizing effect of expressway driving
- the velocitization effect of extended high speed driving
- the presence of slower moving vehicles

- entrance and exit ramps on the right and sometimes on the left
- vehicles on the shoulder re-entering the roadway
- windy sections of the roadway

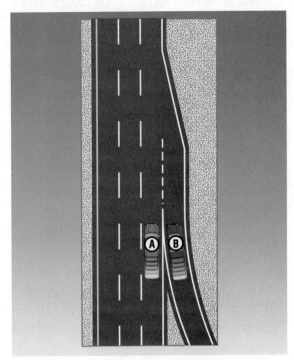

APPROACHING AN ENTRANCE RAMP

When driving in the right lane, you approach an entrance ramp and you notice a vehicle that is trying to enter the expressway. Cooperate with this driver by changing lanes to the left if the situation permits. If traffic does not permit you to change lanes safely, be prepared to adjust your speed to assist the driver to merge with the flow of traffic. When you approach an entrance ramp that is not clearly visible (curve or overpass), avoid a potential conflict by changing lanes to the left.

EXITING AN EXPRESSWAY

Plan your route ahead of time; make sure you know the highways and the exits you will be using. At least three signs will be posted to advise you of each exit. Prepare to exit by changing into the right lane (exit at right) 1500 feet prior to the exit.

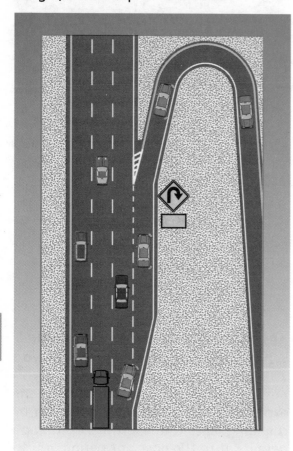

ASSESS: Verify the type of exit (entrance and exit combined) Check for traffic entering Check the exit ramp (advisory speed, curve) Check mirrors / blind spot.

PREPARE: Activate the right turn signal Maintain your speed Recheck mirrors / blind spot. (At the deceleration lane)

EXECUTE: Aim and steer smoothly onto the deceleration lane Apply the brakes firmly Verify the speedometer (velocitization) Steer along the center of the exit ramp Cancel the turn signal.

If you miss your exit, proceed to the next exit (never reverse on the freeway or the entrance and exit ramps). After exiting, check your speed frequently until you readjust to the slower speed.

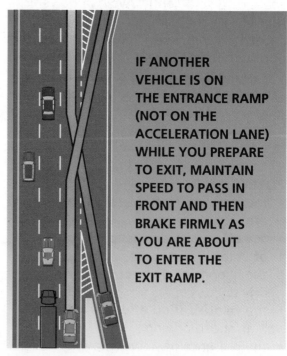

IF ANOTHER VEHICLE IS ON THE ENTRANCE RAMP (NOT ON THE ACCELERATION LANE) WHILE YOU PREPARE TO EXIT, MAINTAIN SPEED TO PASS IN FRONT AND THEN BRAKE FIRMLY AS YOU ARE ABOUT TO ENTER THE EXIT RAMP.

12

Turning About

U-TURNS

Though a relatively simple and quick way to turnabout, a U-turn requires a wide roadway and is illegal in some places. In urban areas, a turn around the block would be preferable.

ASSESS: Is a U-turn permitted?
Are you near hills, curves, or intersections?
Is the road wide enough?
Do you have a clear view 500 feet in both directions?
Will you interfere with traffic (both directions, pedestrians)?

IS A U-TURN SAFE TO PERFORM?

PREPARE: Perform a lane change to the right side of the road
Stop your vehicle
Activate the left turn signal
Recheck the oncoming traffic
Recheck mirrors and blind spot.

EXECUTE: Release the brake pedal
Steer rapidly hand over hand to the left
Accelerate gently
Aim at your intended lane
Allow the wheel to slip through your grip
to straighten
(be ready to correct)
Accelerate to normal speed
Check the traffic.

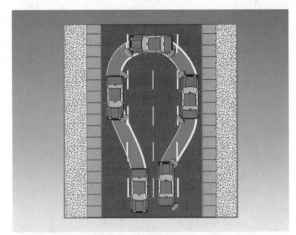

THREE-POINT TURNS

You can perform a three-point turn in a variety of ways: by heading or backing into a driveway on the right or left, or turning on the roadway. Backing across a lane of traffic or reversing into a lane of traffic can be very hazardous and should be avoided. In most circumstances, it is preferable to back into a driveway so that your forward field of vision takes in the whole roadway as you prepare to re-enter traffic.

BACKING INTO A DRIVEWAY ON THE RIGHT

ASSESS: Do you have a clear view?
Is there traffic behind you?
Is the driveway clear?
Will you interfere with traffic (both directions, pedestrians)?

IS THIS 3-POINT TURN SAFE?

12

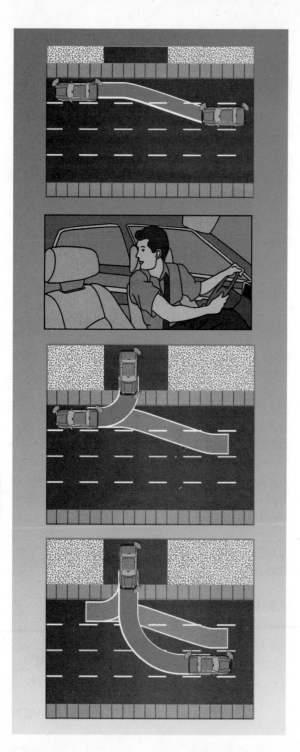

PREPARE: Tap the brake pedal
Perform a right lane change
Stop your vehicle about 3 feet from the curb with the rear just beyond the driveway
Check mirror and blind spot
Shift to reverse
Check the traffic all around your vehicle
Place your left hand at the 12 o'clock position and the right hand at the 5 o'clock position (Backing into a right turn Chapter 7)
Look over your right shoulder toward the right rear.

EXECUTE: Ease up on the brake (clutch to friction point - standard)
Reverse slowly (press gently on the accelerator to start the vehicle moving, if necessary)
Aim at the center of the driveway (rear turn reference)
Turn the steering sharply
Re-check traffic to the left
As you enter the driveway, countersteer to straighten in the center of the driveway
Stop when the front of your vehicle clears the sidewalk
Shift to drive (1st gear - standard)
Activate the left turn signal
Advance slowly to check traffic (pedestrians and other road users)
Perform a left turn.

DRIVING INTO A DRIVEWAY ON YOUR LEFT

ASSESS: Check the same items as previously
Check the driveway for hedges and other objects that may obstruct your vision when you reverse into the roadway

IS THIS 3-POINT TURN SAFE?

PREPARE: Activate the left turn signal
Check the driveway
Proceed as for a left turn.

EXECUTE: Aim at the center of the driveway (front turn reference)
Steer sharply, advance slowly
As you enter the driveway, countersteer to straighten
Stop when the rear of your vehicle passes the sidewalk
Shift to reverse
Activate the right turn signal
Check to the left, right and behind your vehicle
Use the backing into a right turn position (Chapter 7)
Reverse slowly, glancing around vehicle (ensure left front clears any obstructions) (turn reference)
Steer toward the nearest lane
Entering the lane, countersteer to straighten and then stop
Shift to DRIVE (1st - standard)
Activate the left turn signal
Check mirrors and blind spot
Aim down the roadway
Accelerate to normal speed and cancel the turn signal.

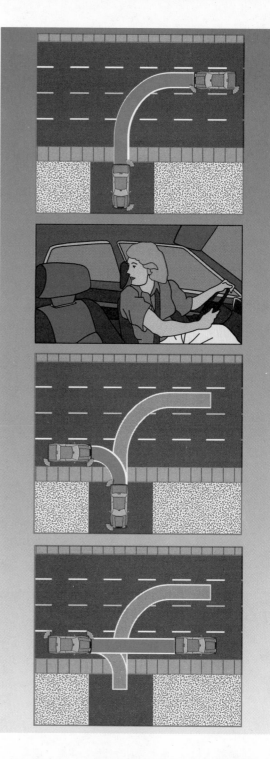

3-POINT TURN ON THE ROADWAY

ASSESS: This maneuver puts you at more of a risk and should be performed only if the street is too narrow, there are no driveways available, you cannot drive around the block, you have excellent visibility and the traffic is very light.

DO YOU HAVE ANY OTHER OPTION?
IS THE MANEUVER SAFE?

PREPARE: Perform a right lane change and stop your vehicle near the right edge of the roadway
Activate the left turn signal
Check the oncoming traffic
Check the left mirror and blind spot.

EXECUTE: Advance slowly, steer sharply
As you approach the curb, countersteer and then stop
Activate the right turn signal
Shift to reverse
Check the traffic in all directions
Assume the back into a right turn position
Reverse slowly, steering sharply
Just before stopping, countersteer to straighten
Shift to drive (1st - standard)
Activate the right turn signal
Check traffic
Aim at your path of travel
Accelerate to normal speed.

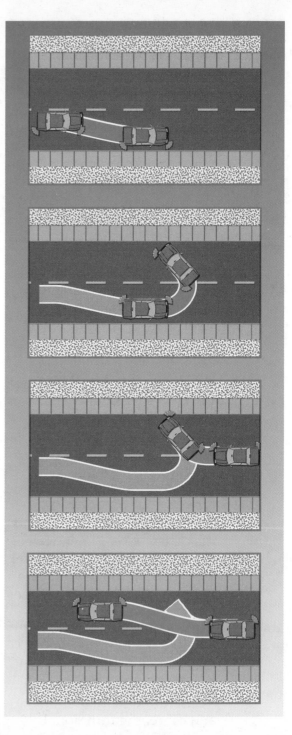

12

Parking

Though not a dangerous maneuver because of the slow speed, parking requires excellent control of your speed and steering as well as accurate judgement of space. This does not mean that there is no risk. Far too many collisions occur in parking situations. Checking the traffic constantly while maneuvering will diminish the danger. Choosing to park your vehicle, whenever possible, so that you may drive into and/or out of the parking space, rather than reversing, will also diminish the risk.

Practice the different types of this essential task so that you may perform diagonal, perpendicular and parallel parking maneuvers easily, safely and with confidence.

DIAGONAL PARKING

ASSESS: Locate a space on your right
Check for parking control signs
Check the oncoming traffic
Check the rear-view mirrors and right blind spot
Check the position of the vehicles on both sides of the chosen space
Be alert to the possible movement of any parked vehicles, pedestrians or other road users

CAN YOU PARK SAFELY?

PREPARE: Activate the right turn signal
Tap the brake pedal
Move to the left to leave about a car width from the parked vehicles
Reduce speed until you can see into the parking space
Recheck mirrors / blind spot

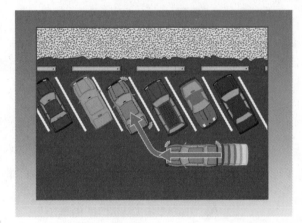

EXECUTE: Aim into the center of the space (front turn reference)
Steer sharply while rolling slowly
Glance to check your clearance on either side
Countersteer to straighten your vehicle into the center of the space
Reduce speed and stop when your vehicle is straight and in line with the other parked vehicles
Follow the procedures to exit the vehicle (Chapter 7)

12

To diagonal park on the left, keep on your side and follow the same procedures substituting left for right.

ASSESS: Check the position of the front tires as you approach
Check the flow of traffic

IS BACKING INTO TRAFFIC SAFE?

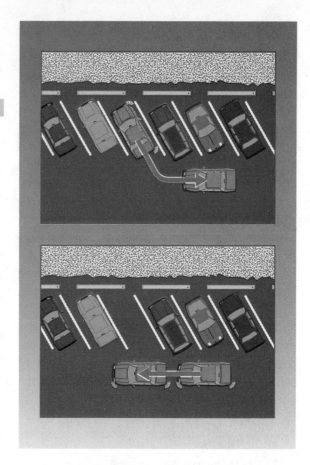

PREPARE: Follow your normal pre-driving protocol (Chapter 6)
Start the engine (Chapter 7)
Apply the service brake
Shift to reverse
Activate the right turn signal
Release the parking brake
Recheck to the left, right and to the rear
Assume the backing into a right turn position (Chapter 7)

EXECUTE: Ease off the brake pedal (Clutch to friction point - standard) a gentle pressure on the accelerator may be required to initiate movement
Reverse slowly and turn the wheel slightly
Recheck traffic to the left and right
When the front of your vehicle passes the rear of the vehicle on your left (front reference), look to the right rear and turn sharply in that direction

Recheck traffic and glance to the left rear to check your clearance
Just before stopping, countersteer to straighten the wheels
Stop, shift to drive (1st gear - standard)
Activate the left turn signal
Check the traffic in both directions
Accelerate to normal speed
Cancel the turn signal manually

DRIVING INTO A PERPENDICULAR SPACE

It is easier and safer to drive into a space on the left. Ideally, choose a space that permits you to drive forwards when you must leave so that you can avoid backing your vehicle into traffic.

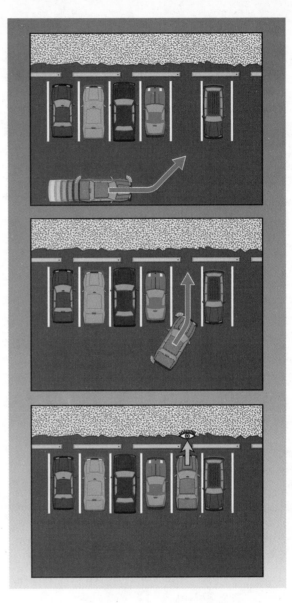

ASSESS: Choose an available space on your left
Check traffic (pedestrians as well) in both directions and your left blind spot
Check the position of the vehicles on both sides of the space
Be alert to the possible movement of any parked vehicles

IS A TURN INTO THE SPACE SAFE?

PREPARE: Activate the left turn signal
Tap the brake pedal
Move to the right slightly to leave as much space as possible from the vehicles on the left
Reduce speed until you can see into the parking space
Recheck your mirrors and blind spot.

EXECUTE: Aim at the center of the space
Steer sharply to the left
Maintain a slow speed
Glance to check the clearance from the vehicles on both sides
Countersteer to straighten into the center of the space

Stop when your vehicle is aligned with the other parked vehicles
Follow the procedures for exiting the vehicle (Chapter 7)

BACKING INTO A PERPENDICULAR SPACE

It is easier and safer to back into a space on your right. Leaving the space will be performed driving forwards into traffic which is also safer.

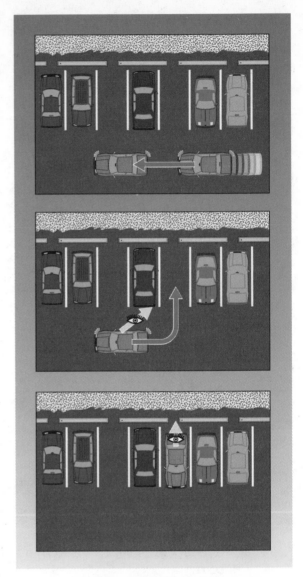

ASSESS: Locate a space on your right
Check the oncoming traffic
Check the rear-view mirrors and right blind spot
Check the position of the vehicles on both sides of the space
Be alert to the possible movement of any parked vehicles or other road users

IS BACKING INTO THE SPACE SAFE?

PREPARE: Activate the right turn signal
Tap the brake pedal
Move to the left to leave about a car width from the parked vehicles
Reduce speed and stop when the rear of your vehicle is lined up with the center of the vehicle parked after the space
Shift to reverse
Recheck your mirrors and blind spot
Assume the position for backing
into a right turn (Chapter 7)

EXECUTE: Ease off the brake
(Raise the clutch to the friction point - standard transmission)

A gentle pressure on the accelerator may be required to start rolling (rear turn reference)
Aim at the center of the space
Steer sharply to the right
Recheck traffic
Glance to check clearance on both sides of the space

12

Countersteer to straighten into the center of the space
Stop when your vehicle is aligned with the parked vehicles.
Check the space on both sides, you may have to advance straight ahead and back into the space again to center your vehicle
Follow the procedures for exiting the vehicle (Chapter 7)

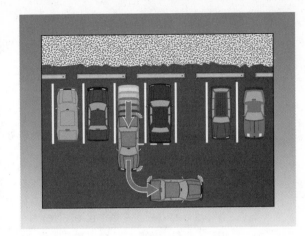

LEAVING A PERPENDICULAR SPACE

If you positioned your vehicle properly, you will drive forward out of the space. When you must back out of the space, follow the procedures for backing out of a diagonal parking space.

ASSESS: Check the position of the front tires as you approach
Check the flow of traffic (including pedestrians, bikes)

IS DRIVING INTO TRAFFIC SAFE?

PREPARE: Follow your normal pre-driving protocol (Chapter 6)
Start the engine (Chapter 7)
Apply the service brake
Shift to drive
(1st gear - standard)
Activate the left turn signal
Release the parking brake
Recheck for any other road users to the left and right.

EXECUTE: Ease off the brake pedal (Clutch to friction point - standard) a gentle pressure on the accelerator may be required to initiate movement
Advance slowly straight ahead
Recheck traffic to the left and right
When your body passes the end of the vehicle on your left, perform a left turn
Accelerate to normal speed.

PARALLEL PARKING

The ability to perform this maneuver is essential when parking in a crowded urban environment. Look for a space one and a half times the length of your vehicle on the right side of the roadway. It is possible to park in a smaller space; however, it is not recommended.

ASSESS: Locate a parking space
Make sure the space is legal (sign, driveway, fire hydrant)

Is the space large enough?
Are you in the correct lane?
Check oncoming traffic
Check mirrors and blind spot

IS THE MANEUVER SAFE?

PREPARE: Tap the brake pedal
Activate the right turn signal
Recheck mirrors and blind spot
Reduce speed
Stop beside the vehicle ahead
of the chosen parking space
(parallel to the curb, three
feet away from the other
vehicle, back bumpers in line)
Shift to reverse
Recheck oncoming traffic and
left mirror
Assume position for backing
into a right turn.

EXECUTE: Ease off the brake pedal
(Clutch to friction point -
standard) a gentle pressure on
the accelerator may be
required to initiate movement
Reverse slowly (on downgrades,
the brake or the accelerator
may be required)
Turn the steering wheel sharply
When you reach the
proper angle (30 to 45 degrees
with the curb or in line with
the front right corner of the
vehicle behind) countersteer to
straighten
Control the speed (the vehicle
has a tendency to increase
speed as you straighten)

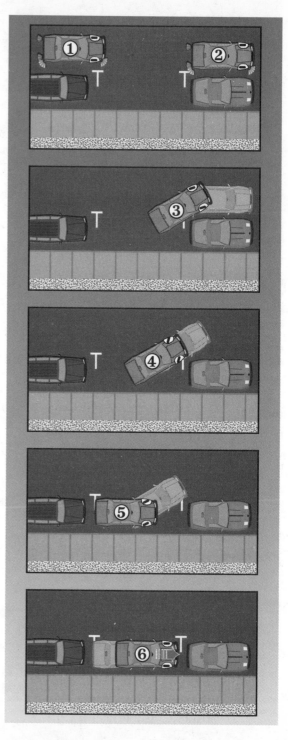

12

When your right front corner clears the vehicle ahead, look back and steer left rapidly
Just prior to stopping, countersteer to straighten
Stop without touching the vehicle behind
Shift to drive (1st gear - standard)
Advance slowly (straightening and positioning your vehicle in the center of the space)
Follow the procedures to exit.

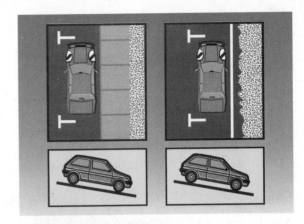

This maneuver requires practice to perform comfortably, confidently and safely. When parallel parking on the left side of a one-way street, follow the same procedures except that you assume the position for backing into a left turn at the outset and turn the wheel in the opposite direction. When you reach the proper angle and straighten the wheels, change position to assume the position for backing into a right turn.

PARKING ON A HILL

Parking your vehicle on a hill has already been explained in each of the parking maneuvers. However, the final position of your vehicle before exiting requires some explanation. The front tires must be turned in such a manner as to cause the vehicle to roll out of traffic or against the curb should the vehicle move.

When parking downhill, whether or not there is a curb, the tires should be turned toward the near side of the road.

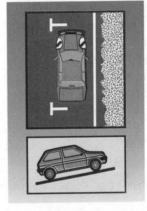

When parking uphill without a curb, the tires should be turned toward the near side of the road.

When parking uphill with a curb, the tires should be turned away from the near side of the road.

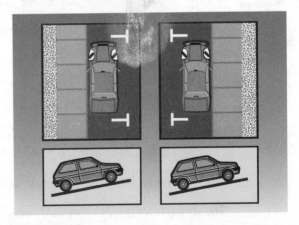

12

Review

TERMS TO REMEMBER - WRITE A SHORT DEFINITION FOR EACH OF THE FOLLOWING :

- Communicate
- Keep an "out"
- APE system
- Controlled intersection
- Uncontrolled intersection

- Urban environment
- Highway environment
- Expressway environment
- U-turn
- Acceleration lane

- 3 point turn
- Velocitization
- Diagonal park
- Perpendicular park
- Parallel park

SUMMARY

Apply the APE system to all driving maneuvers in order to perform them safely and properly: right turns, left turns and lane changes in the urban environment. Adapt the SIPDE strategy to the crowded streets while using selective seeing to identify the important data. The rural environment and its many hazards require adapting vision and SIPDE as well. Passing maneuvers benefit from the APE approach. The expressway environment presents special problems, especially entering and exiting. Parking, in all its forms, is a complex maneuver that requires practice to achieve skill and comfort.

TEST A - WRITE "T" BESIDE STATEMENTS THAT ARE TRUE AND "F" BESIDE THOSE THAT ARE FALSE.

_____ **1.** Sharing the road requires communication of your presence and intentions.

_____ **2.** The two second rule is a good following distance in all conditions.

_____ **3.** When you stop behind another vehicle, stop as close as possible.

_____ **4.** In all conflict situations, the law states who has the right-of-way.

_____ **5.** The ASSESS stage includes scanning the environment and deciding if the maneuver is safe to perform.

_____ **6.** To change lanes, the first step is to signal your intention.

_____ **7.** Most collisions involving pedestrians and cyclists occur at intersections.

_____ **8.** When a traffic signal light changes to green, check left, center, right and then left again before proceeding.

_____ **9.** To turn right, position your vehicle in the lane closest to the right.

_____ **10.** To turn left, position your vehicle in the lane beside the left sidewalk.

11. When passed on the left, ignore this vehicle as it cannot affect you.

12. When passing, return to your lane as soon as your vehicle is in front of the vehicle that you were passing.

13. Entering a freeway, you should stop on the acceleration lane.

14. On a freeway, maintain the same following distance as in the city.

15. Exiting the freeway, reduce speed once on the deceleration lane.

16. When turning about, the safest maneuver is to drive around the block.

17. Turning about using a driveway, it is preferable to drive into the space.

18. Parking maneuvers require a slow speed and accurate judgement.

19. To parallel park safely, you should select a space one and a half times the length of your vehicle.

20. When parking your vehicle on a downhill slope, the front tires should be turned towards the near side of the road.

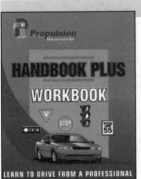

HANDBOOK PLUS WORKBOOK

*Check your comprehension and mastery of the contents of this chapter by completing the corresponding exercises that are found in the complement to the **HANDBOOK PLUS**:*

HANDBOOK PLUS WORKBOOK

Complete the exercises on Pages 74 to 86 then check your responses by referring to the answer key on Page 109.
If necessary, review the chapter for each error and refer to your instructor for further guidance.

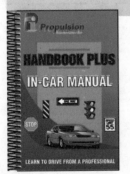

HANDBOOK PLUS IN-CAR MANUAL

*Before you start any in-car session, prepare yourself and facilitate the development of proper driving skills and habits by reading the corresponding lesson in the complement to the **HANDBOOK PLUS**:*

HANDBOOK PLUS IN-CAR MANUAL

Bring the manual to each in-car lesson so the instructor may evaluate your progress. Parents or guardians (with a valid license) should supplement the program by following the procedures in the manual and concentrating on maneuvers requiring extra practice as noted by the in-car instructor.

Student notes

13 - A
Road Conditions

13 - B
Visual Conditions

13 - C
Winter Conditions

13 - D
Review

Adverse Conditions

Foresight is a characteristic of good drivers. Each season presents specific hazards to vehicle control. Assuring your vehicle is adequately prepared to overcome these potential dangers is essential. From small details, such as windshield wiper blades and fluid to match the weather conditions, to major details, such as a tune-up and proper tires, there are many items to be considered. Anything less is unacceptable!

Foresight also relates to mental preparation. Fleet operators, who prepare their drivers for changing driving conditions with meetings, videos or memoranda, have cut vehicle "downtime" due to collisions and mechanical mishaps. You can achieve the same results. Prepare yourself mentally for the hazards of the ever-changing seasons.

Don't leave it to chance, your safety depends on proper preparation of your vehicle and yourself.

AFTER COMPLETING THIS CHAPTER, THE STUDENT MUST BE ABLE TO RECOGNIZE POTENTIAL HAZARDS AND ADAPT DRIVING STRATEGIES TO:

- road conditions.
- visual conditions.
- changes in traction due to unusual environmental conditions.

ADVERSE CONDITIONS

The good driver knows how to adapt his or her driving to the driving conditions in order to drive safely. This ability comes with experience and practice.

As a beginning driver, you must learn to recognize variables in road conditions, traction, visual conditions, etc. that require you to adapt your driving. Although techniques do not change, you must learn to be cautious. It is better to approach a maneuver too cautiously rather than too aggressively.

Road Conditions

Besides the slope and the banking of the road surface (Chapter 9), other road conditions require special adaptations.

SAND or GRAVEL on the pavement acts like tiny ball bearings between the tires and the road. Avoid turning, braking or accelerating while crossing the sand or gravel. Reduce your speed before this hazard and coast over it. Resume speed once you are safely past the danger.

FALLEN LEAVES on the pavement reduce traction (especially when wet). Maneuver gently. Increase your following distance

and, if you must brake, use a gentle pumping action to counteract the layers of leaves that slip against each other.

HEAVY VEHICLE or **TRUCK CROSSINGS**, and the immediate vicinity, may have the pavement coated with mud, earth, sand or gravel. Anticipate this possibility and reduce your speed.

POTHOLES or bumps in the pavement occur more frequently during the spring thaw season.

It is advisable to avoid them by driving around them whenever safety permits. They can prove disastrous to rims, tires, suspension and steering components. In order to maintain control of your vehicle and minimize damage, when you cannot avoid the hazard, you should:

- check your rear-view mirror
- activate the hazard lights
- slow down as much as possible
- release the brakes just prior to the hazard (allow suspension to stabilize)
- roll over the hazard (clutch depressed in standard transmission)
- return to normal speed
- deactivate the hazard lights

If you were unable to slow sufficiently to roll over the hazard at a safe speed (the impact felt severe), leave the hazard lights operating and look for a place to park. Check for damage before proceeding.

APPROACHING UNPAVED ROADWAYS,

two hazards are usually present; gravel on the paved portion of the roadway near the end of the pavement; as well as potholes on the gravel side, just after the end of the pavement.

Think ahead, reduce your speed while approaching the end of the pavement. You will avoid sliding on the gravel as you try to reduce speed and you will reach the potholes at a reduced speed.

DRIVING ON UNPAVED ROADWAYS,

traction is reduced (Chapter 9) and even more so when wet or oil sprayed. The posted speed limit is reduced. Following any vehicle creates danger from the cloud of dust obscuring vision and flying rocks damaging the windshield or headlights.

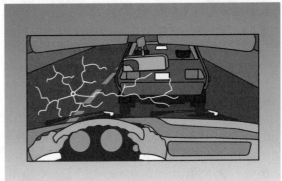

To drive safely, you should:
- drive at a much slower speed in keeping with the reduced traction
- lengthen your following distance especially when clouds of dust or large vehicles block your vision
- avoid the ruts in the road especially when raining

13

- drive well over to the right
- allow a larger safety margin if you must pass (the space needed to pass and advance further than normal before returning in front of the vehicle you passed)
- cooperate with other road users move over or stop to assist others in passing you

When you return to normal pavement, you should take a few moments to stop and check your vehicle as well as clean the headlights and windshield.

HILLS

On hills, gravity affects the movement of your vehicle - uphill reduces speed and shortens the braking distance, downhill increases speed and lengthens the braking distance. When the hill is quite steep, a warning sign may be posted.

SHIFTING GEARS

Uphill, shift to a lower gear (even with an automatic transmission) to make the engine turn faster and develop more power to climb more easily. Downhill, shift to a lower gear as well (without pressing the accelerator) and the engine compression will help control the speed so that you will not have to press the brake pedal firmly and continuously.

VISIBILITY AND SPEED

As you approach the crest of the hill, your visibility will be reduced. Keep your vehicle positioned to the right in your lane and ease off the accelerator until your line of sight allows you to see the other side (your lane and oncoming traffic). Expect the unexpected! Reduce speed in relation to your line of sight.

BRAKE FAILURE OR OVERHEATING

Check the brakes by tapping on the pedal prior to downgrades. If they were to malfunction, you will have time to perform an emergency stop before gravity will increase your speed and thus the danger.

Moreover, continuous braking on steep slopes (if you don't downshift) causes the brakes to heat up and brake "fade" may occur. As a result of brake "fade", a normal pressure on the brake pedal will not result in normal speed reduction.

Uphill, the transmission and the engine are both working harder than normal, especially if you don't downshift. (On shorter hills in an automatic, the transmission "kickdown" may suffice to climb without over-straining.) If you don't downshift, the excessive straining that results will cause both the engine and the transmission to overheat and can lead to a breakdown.

MOUNTAIN DRIVING

Driving in the mountains affects both the driver and the vehicle. High altitude can cause drowsiness, shortness of breath and headache. Plan rest stops or change drivers regularly.

VEHICLE CONDITION

The carburetor (if you still have one of these) and the cooling system may require adjustment. Otherwise you might get poor response from them. Computer controlled systems adjust automatically to the change in altitude. In either case, have your vehicle checked.

SPEED

Use the techniques (downshifting) just mentioned in the "Hills" driving section to control your vehicle's speed.

ALLOWING OTHER VEHICLES TO PASS

Whenever you notice vehicles behind that want to pass, look for pull-out areas or use a wide shoulder rather than impede their progress. If you meet an oncoming vehicle and the road is too narrow for both to get by, the vehicle on the downgrade should back up the hill to a wider area. Co-operate!

PASSING SLOWER VEHICLES

Be patient and careful. Make sure you can see far enough to ensure the maneuver is safe or wait for the vehicle to reach a pull-out area. The thin air and lower atmospheric pressure reduce vehicle acceleration. It will take longer to pass than you would normally expect.

SPECIAL PROBLEMS IN HIGH ALTITUDES

Driving in the mountains often presents very sharp curves called switchbacks (see illustration for warning signs). These curves are similar to U-turns and require a very slow speed to negotiate them safely. Be prepared to reduce speed to the (suggested) posted limit and look out for any oncoming vehicles that may inadvertently cross the center line.

OVERHEATING

The engine might overheat; check the temperature gauge frequently. Stop to allow it to cool. (Activate the heater in the HOT position with the fan on HIGH and some of the engine heat will enter the passenger compartment.)

VAPOR LOCK

This raised operating temperature can also lead to a condition called "vapor lock". The fuel can vaporize in the gas lines near the engine (especially when you turn the engine off) and the system cannot pump this vaporized fuel into the engine. The vehicle will not restart. Let the engine cool and then try again.

13

DESERTS

Desert areas are also stressful for drivers and vehicles; they are larger and hotter than most people realize. Prepare your vehicle. Put heavier oil in the engine: at least S.A.E. 50 grade. Have the engine cooling system double checked.

Drive at night, when it is cooler, if at all possible. If not, plan rest stops every few hours or change drivers frequently. Check all fluid levels every time you stop. Never open the radiator cap when the engine is hot. Carry a water supply for the occupants as well as for the vehicle, just in case. Check the tire pressure every morning when the tires are cool.

Wear a good quality pair of sunglasses to protect your eyes from the glare. If they forecast strong winds, delay your departure, since dust or sand storms could cause a lot of problems in addition to damaging the paint of your vehicle.

Storms, though rare, cause flash floods. If a storm occurs, drive to higher ground and avoid stopping in natural drainage areas. Wait for the water level to return to normal before continuing on your way

RAIN

Rainfall reduces traction (Chapter 9) as well as visibility (visual conditions later in this chapter). Roads become especially slippery during the beginning of a rainfall (even more so after a hot dry spell). The water causes the oil and dust on the pavement to float creating an oily film that will wash away as the rain continues. The lighter the rain the longer the washing-away process takes. As the rain continues, water may accumulate on the road. Puddles, sheets of water and, in extreme cases, flooded pavement become possible hazards. (Wet snow and slush also reduce traction, hide potholes, and clog the tire treads.)

DRIVING IN THE RAIN

To counteract these hazards:
- reduce speed
- lengthen your following distance
- drive in the tracks of other vehicles
- brake sooner and more gently (if tires skid, ease up, re-apply gently)
- accelerate more gradually
- steer with smooth gentle motions
- use windshield wipers (blades in good condition; full fluid reservoir)
- activate the defroster and rear window defogger to prevent fogging or condensation (keep a window slightly open as usual)
- make sure the tires have good tread and are properly inflated

When approaching puddles and sheets of water, they may be deeper than they seem or they may hide potholes. Avoid them if possible. Be aware of and try to minimize the splashing that will ensue for your vehicle and also for pedestrians.

When you cannot avoid the situation:
- check traffic behind you
- reduce speed as much as possible
- activate the hazard lights
- hold the steering wheel firmly (water resistance varies with depth and may pull the wheels off course)
- release the brakes and coast through the water slowly (in deep water, accelerate gently to maintain the slow speed)

CROSSING DEEP PUDDLES

After crossing, apply the brakes gently (check the rear-view mirror first). If the brakes respond normally, turn off the hazard lights and proceed on your way.

If the brakes are wet, the vehicle will not reduce speed. If this is the case, continue (right foot on the accelerator) and apply the brakes simultaneously (using your left foot). The friction produced by braking steadily will dry the brakes. As soon as they respond normally, release the brakes and turn off the hazard lights.

When you approach a stop (stop, light, blockage in traffic), begin braking earlier than normal and check the rear view mirror. The driver behind you may not have checked his/her brakes and is only now discovering that the brakes are wet. By anticipating this problem, you can avoid a rear-end collision (Chapter 14) before you come to a complete stop.

HYDROPLANING can occur when a combination of speed, tire wear, tire inflation, or the depth of the water on the pavement causes the tires to lose traction. In wet weather (water, wet snow, slush), the tires cut through and maintain contact with the pavement at speeds of less than 30 mph.

NORMAL WET TRACTION
(tire in contact with the road)

Unless the tires are excessively worn (bald tires) or underinflated, or the water is very deep; in any of these cases, you may still hydroplane at slow speeds.

13

At higher speeds (40 mph and higher), the wedge of water in front of the tires may pass under the tires and the tires will ride on the cushion of water. Traction will be lost completely.

HYDROPLANING
(cushion of water - loss of contact)

To prevent hydroplaning:
- check your tires and tire inflation regularly
- reduce your speed even more when facing standing water and puddles
- drive in the tracks of preceding vehicles

Should your vehicle hydroplane:
- shift to neutral (depress the clutch for a standard)
- activate the hazard lights
- grip the steering wheel firmly
- avoid braking or accelerating
- check your rear view mirror

The water resistance will slow your vehicle. As soon as the tires regain contact, brake gently to reduce your speed, re-engage the transmission, resume driving at a slower speed and turn off the hazard lights.

WIND by itself does not affect the road conditions; however, in combination with rain or wet snow and cold temperatures, the wind can create icy patches. Handle this hazard in the same fashion as sand or gravel on the roadway. Slow before the danger, coast over the icy area and proceed. Scan the pavement ahead for other patches especially when nearing or driving on raised expressways, bridges, tunnels, wide open areas, or between tall buildings.

AIR TURBULENCE
ONCOMING LARGE VEHICLES

Gusty or high winds can push at your vehicle making it difficult to remain in your lane. This effect is even greater on large boxy vehicles, vehicles towing trailers, and vehicles with luggage on the roof.

To maintain control, you should:
- reduce your speed
- grip the steering wheel firmly
- compensate gently for the wind

gusts as soon as the vehicle moves off course even slightly
- avoid passing
- increase your following distance
- keep away from other vehicles on either side (multi-lane road)
- position your vehicle close to the right in your lane (on roads with one lane in each direction)

Besides the wind, large heavy vehicles generate air turbulence as they drive at high speeds. Passing or meeting an oncoming vehicle of this type can affect your vehicle control. Compensate by reducing speed and changing your position within the lane to leave as much space as possible from these vehicles.

 # Visual Conditions

Anything that reduces your ability to see; reduces your ability to control your vehicle. Automotive engineers have done their utmost to design vehicles and accessories to assist your vision. You must learn to use them to your advantage and to minimize any other obstructions.

The headlights should be turned on whenever you drive (Chapter 8). Daytime automatic headlight laws (like Canada) are being considered. If they become law, check your owner's manual. The parking, side marker and taillights may not come on automatically. The intensity of the headlights may be reduced. Drive with your normal headlights on at all times to make your vehicle more visible.

PASSENGERS or **CARGO** in your vehicle can become visual obstructions if not seated or stored properly. Try to minimize the blockage. When driving, if your view is not clear, double check and maneuver more gradually.

13

A FILM OF DIRT on the windows reduces vision, reflects light and causes glare. Keep windows clean (inside and out) to eliminate this danger and realize that the lights and taillights also require cleaning so that you can see and be seen to full advantage.

NIGHT VISION

Reduced lighting at night makes driving more difficult and dangerous. The effects on your vision are:

- reduced visual acuity
- distance and depth perception decrease
- colors and contrasts are less distinct
- eyes must constantly adjust to changes in light intensity (oncoming lights, trailing vehicles, area lighting)
- fatigue and its affects on vision

Your field of vision is more or less restricted to the narrow beam of light provided by the headlights.

HEADLIGHTS AT NIGHT

The most dangerous time to drive is at dusk. The eyes are subjected to a bright horizon (and sky) and a dark road and sky. The partial light condition reduces the effectiveness of headlights as an aid to your vision.

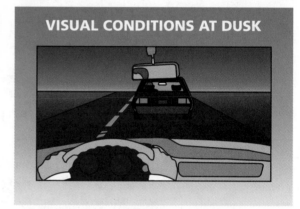

VISUAL CONDITIONS AT DUSK

To drive safely at night:

- reduce your speed in accordance with the range of your headlights (about 200 feet for low beams)
- increase your following distance
- allow a larger safety margin as all maneuvers take longer and your ability to judge distance is diminished
- use your high beams on unlit roads (dim to low beams when meeting or following another vehicle)
- scan beyond the range of the headlights to identify hazards as early as possible
- adjust the dash lights to the exterior lighting conditions
- clean windows and lights
- avoid interior glare (lighter, matches, dome light)
- communicate to make sure you are

13

seen (flash your high beams, flash your brake lights then brake, use the hazard lights, turn signals)
- activate defroster and defogger as needed

Eyes that are exposed to glare over an extended period of time develop a diminished capacity to adjust to the dark and to recover from exposure to glare. You must protect your eyes by wearing sunglasses during the day in order to retain the ability to adapt to night driving.

When driving at night, if your speed requires a total stopping distance that exceeds the range of your headlights, **you are over-driving your headlights**. You will not be able to stop your vehicle before reaching the hazard; you will have to perform an emergency evasive maneuver to avoid the danger. Instead of creating this situation, reduce your speed so that you can stop comfortably within the range of your headlights.

In curves and turns, the headlights are aimed straight ahead. You must scan into the curve or turn beyond the path that is illuminated by the lights and reduce speed more than usual.

Cooperate with other road users on right curves, dim the high beams to minimize the glare from the headlights.

HEADLIGHTS ON A CURVE

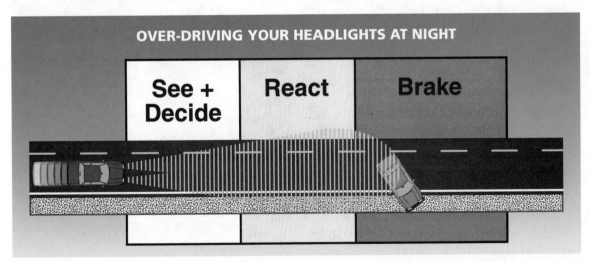

OVER-DRIVING YOUR HEADLIGHTS AT NIGHT

See + Decide	React	Brake

13

IN URBAN AREAS

On most major arteries, the eyes are bombarded by stimuli (neon signs, street lighting, advertisements). Utilize your selective vision to identify the data needed to drive safely. Increase the intensity of the dash lighting in order to easily see the information displayed.

On quiet dark residential streets, lower the intensity of the dash lighting to reduce glare and allow the eyes to better adapt to the exterior darkness. Scan ahead and to the sides of the road beyond the narrow beam of your lights. Use your high beams to verify hazards and communicate your presence.

IN RURAL AREAS

Poor lighting and higher speeds are a dangerous combination. Dim the dash lighting and use the high beams while maintaining a safe speed. Scan beyond the lighted zone and to the sides ahead. Take advantage of all possible data, the line of utility poles, the tree tops, the reflection of oncoming lights, etc.

GLARE

Glare is a problem caused by too much light, the reflection of bright light, or the sudden change from darkness to light. At night, glare causes temporary blindness while the eyes re-adjust to the dark.

As already mentioned, avoid glare from the dash lighting, matches, the dome light, and all other interior sources.

When the lights of a vehicle following you are blinding in the rear view mirror set the mirror to the night position. Return to the daylight position as soon as the offending headlights are gone.

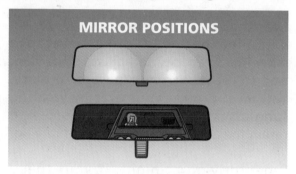

MIRROR POSITIONS

Cooperate with other road users:
- use your low beams on well-lit roads
- dim to your low beams when you approach another vehicle from the rear as soon as the range of the lights nears the rear of the other vehicle.

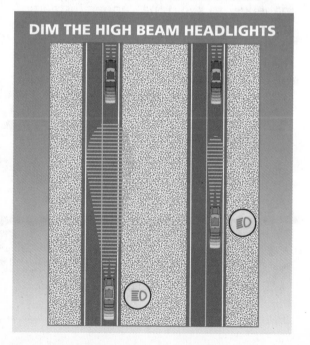

DIM THE HIGH BEAM HEADLIGHTS

13

- dim to your low beams when you meet an oncoming vehicle (500 feet). Don't dim your lights too soon and leave a large unlit area between the vehicles. Dim the lights before the oncoming lights become bothersome to you. Return to the high beams once you pass the oncoming vehicle.

- when passing at night, dim the high beams as you approach (200 feet). In addition, flash the high beams to warn the preceding driver and then keep using the low beams as you begin to pass. Return to the high beams when your vehicle is abreast of the vehicle you are passing.

MEETING AN ONCOMING VEHICLE

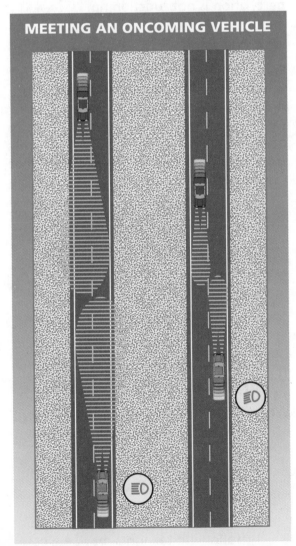

PASSING ANOTHER VEHICLE

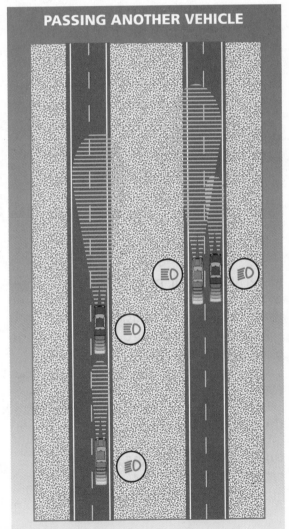

- when another vehicle is passing you, maintain the high beams to light the way for both of you until the other vehicle is abreast of yours.
Return to your high beams when the other vehicle is far enough ahead that the range of your high beams will not reach this vehicle.

- when approaching curves and climbing hills, flash to your low beams and back to the high beams. Look for a return signal from an oncoming vehicle.
Be prepared to dim your lights.

WHEN FACED WITH ONCOMING BLINDING LIGHTS:
- flash your high beams
- check your rear view mirror
- look ahead towards the right edge of the pavement
- reduce your speed

Never leave your high beams on to "get even", this merely increases the glare and the possibility of a collision.

Reduce your speed if there is no danger from the rear.

Maintain your reduced speed until your eyes recover from the glare.

Looking to the right ahead minimizes the effect of the glare.

WHEN FACED BY GLARE FROM BOTH SIDES:
- flash your high beams
- check your rear view mirror
- reduce your speed considerably

- close one eye and look ahead to the center of your lane

Reopen the eye once you have passed the multiple sources of glare. This eye has not been blinded and can be used to guide your vehicle at the reduced speed until the other eye recovers. Leave a longer following distance as your depth perception is not functioning.

FOG AND SMOG

Fog results from rapid condensation of humidity in the air as the temperature drops quickly. Smog includes dust or smoke particles with the fog. The density of these air masses can vary considerably from small patches to dense clouds that reduce visibility to zero.

When faced with patches of fog or smog:
- slow your speed in relation to density
- drive at a steady speed
- use your low beam (high beams reflect back at you)
- increase your following distance
- use the lane markings as a guide (following taillights may be a case

of "the blind leading the blind")
- use the defroster, defogger, and windshield wipers as needed
- avoid passing
- be alert to faster vehicles approaching from the rear
- use hazard lights or flash brake lights to warn of imminent danger

Special fog lights which penetrate the fog should be installed if you drive in foggy areas consistently. They should be mounted as low as possible so they will be most effective and should be used only in the fog.

In very dense fog (zero visibility):
- safely move as far off the road as possible and stop your vehicle.
- activate the hazard lights and the dome light. Turn off the headlights.
- do not return to the roadway until there is a marked improvement in the visibility conditions.

Rain and snow can create similar visual problems and require similar adaptation of your driving as does fog conditions.

When the sun is low on the horizon, the glare from the sun and the reflection off the roadway reduces visibility. The cleanliness of the windshield can further deteriorate the visual situation.

If you are driving into the sun, wear polarized sunglasses and adjust the sun visor to block the glare without restricting your view ahead. Oncoming vehicles will be difficult to identify especially if driving without using their headlights. Reduce your speed.
The brake.lights and turn signals of preceding vehicles will be less visible. Increase your following distance.

If you are driving with the sun behind you, oncoming vehicles have the glare problem and will have difficulty seeing you. Your headlights should be turned on whenever you are driving and, in this situation, it is essential in order to be seen properly. Communicate your intentions early and monitor traffic ahead and behind to ensure that you have been understood.

13

 # Winter Conditions

Winter can be very harsh in most parts of the country. This exacts a heavy toll on a vehicle. It is intelligent to make sure that your vehicle is well prepared and ready to cope with all of its rigors. Protocol requires the following precautions and they may save you a great deal of trouble and inconvenience.

•**ENGINE TUNE-UP** to ensure that the fuel and ignition systems will perform in all conditions. The engine oil should be replaced with an engine oil of the correct viscosity for cold-weather. A block heater is a good investment to ensure starting in extreme cold.

•**THE FUEL SYSTEM** should be protected from gas line freezing by keeping the fuel level as full as possible. Allow at least fifteen minutes of driving time to elapse after a fill-up before turning off the engine. This ensures moisture will pass through the system rather than collect at the bottom of the tank and in the fuel lines and freeze. In extreme cold, add gas line antifreeze at each fill-up.

•**THE ELECTRICAL SYSTEM** should be checked to make sure that the battery is charged and operates at maximum strength.The terminals should be cleaned. The alternator should be tested and the V-belt adjusted to ensure maximum efficiency.

•**THE TIRES** should be of the correct type for the winter conditions in your area. All season or snow tires are recommended and should be installed before the onset of winter. The inflation pressure must conform to manufacturer's specifications and should be checked regularly.

•**THE COOLING/HEATING SYSTEM** should be tested and the coolant anti-freeze level and concentration added to as needed. The system should be flushed every third year. The air ducts and fan should perform properly. Keep outlets clear.

•**THE BRAKE SYSTEM** should be verified, adjusted and repaired as needed. It must respond effectively and precisely to pedal pressure to ensure control in critical winter driving conditions. The parking brake is part of the system and must also function properly.

•**THE WINDSHIELD WIPER/WASHER SYSTEM** should have special winter wiper blades installed. The wiper arms should be checked to make sure they will last the season. Make sure that the washer fluid in the reservoir and in your trunk is appropriate for winter temperatures.

•**THE EXHAUST SYSTEM** should be checked for leaks and looseness all the way to the tailpipe. Winter conditions test the system severely.

•**THE LOCKS AND SEALS** should be prepared for the rigors of winter. The locks should be lubricated with a product recommended by the manufacturer. The rubber seals around the doors and the trunk (hatchback) should also be treated with an appropriate product to prevent sticking and freezing.

INDISPENSABLE ACCESSORIES

- Brush and scraper
- Snow shovel
- Traction aids (anti-skid grids or mats)
- Sand or salt
- Lock de-icer fluid (carry it with you)

INDISPENSABLE ACCESSORIES

IN CASE OF A MECHANICAL FAILURE

Booster cables; flares or reflectors; a flashlight; a small tool kit; and spare fuses and bulbs. It is a good idea to have these on hand at all times; however, winter requires a few extra items.

SURVIVAL KIT

In case of an out of town trip, a long stop will necessitate the following items to combat the cold:

- Candles, matches and/or lighter, and a metal candle holder. A lit candle will provide light and heat thus reducing the need of operating the engine.
- Non-perishable food with a high caloric content.
- A thermos of hot, sweet, non-alcoholic beverage.
- Space saver blankets, warm clothes gloves and plastic bags.
- A first aid kit.

APPROACH TO THE VEHICLE

Besides the normal procedures, start the engine and activate the defroster and defogger. Then clear the snow from your vehicle - windows, roof, hood and trunk lid, all lights, and license plate. scrape all the windows to remove ice accumulation, If necessary. Unstick and clean the wiper blades. Remove any packed snow or ice in the wheel wells that may inhibit the normal movement of the wheels. This will also permit the engine to warm up before putting your vehicle in motion.

REMOVING SNOW AND ICE

When re-entering, kick the snow from your footwear to ensure that your soles will make firm contact with the pedals.

After performing the preliminaries, tap the accelerator pedal to disengage the automatic choke before moving the selector lever (automatic) or gearshift lever (standard). Remember to drive slowly for the first few minutes to allow the entire power train to become lubricated and warm up.

WINTER DRIVING

To get your vehicle moving follow the normal steps; however:
- Straighten the front wheels
- AUTOMATIC - release the brake pedal and apply a gentle pressure (if needed) on the accelerator pedal. STANDARD - raise the clutch to the friction point and gently engage, add a slight pressure on the accelerator, if necessary.
- Once in motion, press more firmly on the accelerator as needed to gradually increase your speed and steer in the desired direction. Should your vehicle get stuck, reverse in the path already created and try again. Avoid spinning your tires - they sink in the snow and melt the snow forming a layer of ice under the wheels.

While driving test the traction from time to time by lightly applying the brake pedal. On slippery surfaces, drive more slowly. Look further ahead and to the rear more often and keep a longer safety margin both in front and to the rear. Be gentle with the accelerator, the brakes and the steering. Sudden or quick maneuvers are the most common cause of loss of control on slippery surfaces.

Plan your maneuvers sooner so that you may reduce your speed more than usual in "good time". When turning, start at a much slower speed and accelerate later than usual and more gently. While driving, activate the windshield wipers (if not already operating) before you meet oncoming vehicles, a vehicle passes you or you pass another vehicle. Avoid passing unless it is absolutely necessary; make sure that the driver ahead is in no danger of steering off course and the space available for passing is much longer than normal.

In snow or blowing snow, travel in the lane with the least snow or ice. In fact, follow the path of the preceding vehicles even though it may not coincide with the center of a lane. Avoid driving in ruts; do not attempt to get out of them at high speeds.

Wet roadways are especially slippery as the temperature nears the freezing point (32 degrees Fahrenheit). Extra caution should be exercised on bridges, elevated expressways and shaded areas as these surfaces freeze more quickly.

SLOWING OR STOPPING

- Allow a longer braking distance.
- Ease off the accelerator gradually. A sudden release of the gas may cause an un-balancing effect - drive wheels and differential. Should the vehicle deviate from its course, shift to neutral (automatic) or depress the clutch pedal (standard) and steer where you wish to go. Normally, the engine compression, while still in gear, will assist you to slow your vehicle.
- Apply the brake pedal gently. If one or more of the wheels skid, release the brakes and re-apply more gently. If they still skid, shift to neutral and pump the brakes.

13

PARKING

In heavy snow, create a path for your tires by driving past the parking space and then reversing. Leave your vehicle in the middle of the tire tracks thus facilitating your departure.

It is always preferable and safer to park your vehicle (parking lots, driveways, etc.) so that you can leave the parking space by driving forward. In winter, this is even more important.

The parking brake can stick in freezing temperatures. To disengage when this occurs, reverse slowly while releasing the lock mechanism.

WHEN STUCK ON ICE OR SNOW

- Make sure the front tires are straight
- Drive slowly. Spinning tires dig deeper and create ice.
- Limit your movement forward and backward to the range attainable without spinning the tires.
- Accelerate gently when the tires grip, then shift to neutral and coast. Brake when you reach the limit of travel even if it is only a few inches. Repeat in the opposite direction. You will slowly rock your way out without damaging the power train.

WHEN ONE TIRE SPINS

Rear wheel drive vehicles, if the tires are straight and one of the rear tires is spinning, apply the parking brake (keeping it unlocked) while accelerating gently. Release the parking brake slowly and you will move forward.

THE PRINCIPLE
The differential reacts to the resistance of the drive wheels. It transfers power to the wheel with the least resistance.

SPINNING TIRE (REAR WHEEL DRIVE)

EXAMPLE
If one wheel rests on a dry surface and the other on ice, the one on ice will spin while the other doesn't turn. The parking brake intervenes by mechanically giving both wheels the same resistance.

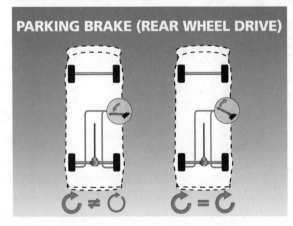

PARKING BRAKE (REAR WHEEL DRIVE)

RESULT

The differential transfers the same amount of power to both wheels. The resulting traction will get your vehicle moving forward.

USING TRACTION AIDS

- Place the mats or grids against the traction wheels with the spikes towards the ground. To move forward place them in front of the wheels and vice versa.
- Advance or reverse cautiously onto the grids. Once in motion, maintain your momentum without spinning the wheels.
- Make sure no one is standing near the vehicle as the traction aid may be thrown out from under the wheels.

TRACTION GRID (REAR WHEEL DRIVE)
Note use of red ribbon
to locate grid in snow after use.

WHEN STALLED OR SNOWBOUND

- If possible, drive onto the shoulder
- Use your hazard lights.
- Keep a window slightly open for air circulation.
- Get your survival kit from the trunk.
- Turn off the engine to conserve fuel. Do not use any electrical accessories while the engine is not operating.
- Run the engine for ten minutes every hour to charge the battery and warm the interior; check that the exhaust pipe is clear. (Carbon monoxide gas)
- Use the plastic bags to encase your feet and legs to retain body heat.
- Use the blankets and clothing to further insulate against the cold.
- Keep awake. If accompanied, take turns sleeping for short periods.
- Unless you are CERTAIN that you can reach help nearby; do not leave your vehicle. It provides shelter and is more visible.
- Use the candles, food and beverage sparingly.

Following these procedures, you and your passengers can wait out any situation until help arrives.

13

Review

TERMS TO REMEMBER - WRITE A SHORT DEFINITION FOR THE FOLLOWING :

- Foresight
- Adverse conditions
- Potholes
- Hydroplaning
- Air turbulence

- Over-driving your headlights
- Dash lighting
- Night mirror
- Glare

- Smog
- Fog lights
- Booster cables
- Survival kit
- Traction aids

SUMMARY

Proper preparation of your vehicle and attention to small details will permit you to drive safely in adverse conditions. Adapting to road, weather and visual conditions will diminish the risks. Learning to handle poor driving situations is part of the learning to drive process. Until you gain experience, choosing not to drive may be the correct choice in some situations.

TEST A - WRITE "T" BESIDE STATEMENTS THAT ARE TRUE AND "F" BESIDE THOSE THAT ARE FALSE.

_____ 1. When driving on a slippery roadway, your minimum following distance should be increased.

_____ 2. If your vehicle hydroplanes, you should shift to neutral.

_____ 3. To start off in deep snow, the tires should be turned as much as possible.

_____ 4. Ice on the pavement is most slippery when the temperature is near the freezing point.

_____ 5. In foggy weather, you should drive with the high beam headlights.

_____ 6. On a windy day, you should reduce speed, keep extra space and be prepared to correct the steering.

_____ 7. On a gravel road, you should decrease your following distance so that you can see the preceding vehicle better.

_____ 8. When a vehicle passes you at night (from the rear), you should dim your high beams when the other vehicle is abreast of your vehicle.

_____ 9. Near the crest of a hill at night, you should flash your high beams, then proceed more slowly with low beams until you can see over the hill.

_____ 10. Approaching a curve at night, you should activate the high beam headlights to see further into the curve.

Student notes

_____
_____
_____
_____
_____
_____
_____
_____
_____
_____
_____
_____
_____
_____
_____
_____
_____
_____

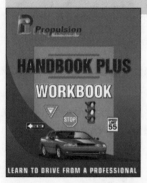

HANDBOOK PLUS WORKBOOK

Check your comprehension and mastery of the contents of this chapter by completing the corresponding exercises that are found in the complement to the **HANDBOOK PLUS**:

HANDBOOK PLUS WORKBOOK

Complete the exercises on Pages 87 to 93 then check your responses by referring to the answer key on Page 109.
If necessary, review the chapter for each error and refer to your instructor for further guidance.

14

14 - A
Vehicle Failures

14 - B
Driver Error

14 - C
Road Sharing
Errors

14 - D
Emergency
Vehicles

14 - E
Unusual
Occurrences

14 - F
Review

Emergency Situations

Driving in normal weather and road conditions is a challenge of itself.

There are times when driving becomes even more difficult. The hood may FLY OPEN! A tire may suddenly BLOW OUT! Another vehicle may approach HEAD-ON in your lane.

Foresight in the proper maintenance of your vehicle can prevent many possible emergency situations. Applying the SIPDE system and active visual habits while driving can evade many others.

Despite the best of intentions and precautions, you are most likely to face at least one critical situation at one time or another during your driving career.

Avoid panic! Easier said than done!

14

AFTER COMPLETING THIS CHAPTER, THE STUDENT MUST BE ABLE TO RECOGNIZE PROBLEMS AND PERFORM LOSS CONTROL TECHNIQUES IN RELATION TO:

- **vehicle failures and the value of preventive maintenance.**
- **driver and road sharing errors.**
- **emergency vehicles and unusual occurrences.**

What is panic? When the brain receives input from the senses either too quickly to assimilate or concerning a totally unknown situation; it is incapable of reaching a decision. A weighty, telling pause ensues... !

A decision will then be rendered which has no factual basis. It is highly likely to be an incorrect response.

This chapter is intended to mentally prepare you for the possible emergency situations which might arise. Then the brain will have the necessary information. You will not panic. The correct response will be readily available and the situation can be resolved safely.

Vehicle Failures

BLOW OUT

A blow out is a rapid loss of tire inflation (explosion or reaction to driving over an object on the roadway). A flat while driving produces a similar effect.

The result: the vehicle pulls to the side where the front tire has deflated. If a rear tire deflates, the rear of the vehicle swerves back and forth.

WHAT TO DO
- Maintain speed - DO NOT BRAKE!
- Grip the steering firmly and steer to keep the vehicle in a straight line.
- Activate the hazard lights
- When under control, ease off the accelerator
- Check traffic and select a safe path
- Change lanes to move off the roadway as far as possible to change the tire.

PREVENTION
Check tire inflation regularly. Check the tire tread and sidewall each time you approach the vehicle (have a more thorough examination performed when the vehicle is being serviced - oil change). Replace tires when worn, bulging, or cracked. Avoid driving over objects on the roadway

14

ACCELERATOR PEDAL STICKS

If the gas pedal is released and the vehicle maintains speed or continues accelerating, the accelerator control is stuck. A broken spring or engine mount, a sticking linkage, a crumpled floor mat or ice around the pedal could cause this problem.

WHAT TO DO
If you must stop quickly:
- Apply and maintain pressure on the brakes (until you are stopped)
- Shift to Neutral (depress the clutch)
- Turn off the ignition switch
- Activate the hazard lights.

If you do not have to stop:
- Without looking, try to free the pedal with your right foot - if no success
- Activate the hazard lights
- Shift to neutral
- Turn off the ignition switch
- Check traffic, choose a safe path, and steer off the roadway
- Apply the brakes in a continuous manner until the vehicle is stopped.

Have the problem corrected before restarting the engine.

PREVENTION
Check the floor mat and foot pedals. Have the accelerator cable lubricated. Check the accelerator control at the first sign of any abnormality.

HEADLIGHT FAILURE

Usually one light will burn out; however, both headlights can fail due to dimmer switch failure, a blown fusible link, a relay failure or a short circuit. Your ability to see and be seen is compromised.

WHAT TO DO
- Activate the hazard lights
- Reduce speed
- Maintain your lane position using the image you have imprinted in your brain
- Turn the headlight and dimmer switches on and off several times
- If the lights function, proceed to the nearest service center. Be careful to dim the high beams (even to no lights) for oncoming traffic.
- If the lights do not function, check traffic and select a safe path
- Change lanes to move off the roadway as far as possible
- Install flares, flashing lantern, or reflectors if you cannot stop in a lit area

14

HOOD FLIES UP

While driving, the hood pops open. Stop the vehicle in a safe place, open the hood and re-close it making sure that it is securely latched. If it flies up blocking your forward vision, depending on your speed, it may fold back against the roof and/or crack the windshield. An improperly closed hood or faulty hood locks are the usual causes. Engineers design most modern vehicles with a double lock to prevent this possibility.

WHAT TO DO
- Maintain your forward vision - look through the space between the hood and the dash or lean to your left to look past the side of the hood.
- Activate your hazard lights
- Reduce your speed while maintaining your lane position
- Check traffic, choose a safe path, and steer off the roadway

- Park in a safe location
- Close or tie down the hood firmly
- Drive slowly, checking the temporary fastener frequently, to the nearest service center.

PREVENTION
Lubricate the hood lock and hood release mechanism when washing the vehicle.

Check that the hood is securely latched whenever you close it.

DEFECTIVE WINDSHIELD WIPERS

While driving, the wipers stop working or don't start working when the switch is activated. The cause could be a defective switch, burnt fuse or the wiper linkage.

WHAT TO DO
- Activate the hazard lights
- Reduce your speed
- Turn the switch on and off several times
- Check traffic, choose a safe path, and steer off the roadway
- Park in a safe location
- If the problem cannot be corrected on the spot, and if the rain or snow continues, have your vehicle towed.

PREVENTION
Never use the wipers to clear the windshield after a snowfall, after freezing rain or when the windshield is dry.

Have the wipers checked and repaired as soon as they operate abnormally.

14

THE ENGINE STALLS

The engine of your vehicle stops suddenly while driving. Mechanical failure, empty fuel tank, water or cold are the normal causes of this situation.

WHAT TO DO
- Shift to neutral (depress the clutch)
- Activate the hazard lights
- Activate the starter using the ignition switch several times
- If the engine restarts, shift to the appropriate gear, accelerate and turn off the hazard lights.
- If the engine does not restart, check traffic, choose a safe path, and steer off the roadway or near the curb
- Apply the brakes with continuous pressure until you stop
- Park in a safe location

Power steering becomes more difficult to turn when the engine stalls. Grip the steering firmly and you can control your vehicle. (Low power steering fluid level, a broken V-belt or a defective pump may also cause power steering failure)

Power brakes work normally for one more application when the engine stalls. Apply the brakes in one continuous application, modulating the pressure, without releasing. If you brake then release the brakes completely, the brakes will require a much greater pressure to work.

PREVENTION
Follow the recommended service intervals in your owner's manual.

Check the fuel gauge every time you start your engine.

Check the fluid levels every time you refuel.

Allow the engine extra time to warm-up in extreme cold conditions before driving in heavy traffic.

Avoid, when possible, puddles and splashing.

BREAKDOWN ON RAILROAD TRACKS

Should the engine stall, try to coast over the tracks or perform an emergency stop before the tracks.

WHAT TO DO
- Check if a train is or is not approaching
- If a train is approaching, get all occupants out of the vehicle
- Move at least 100 feet away from the vehicle in the direction from which the train is approaching
- If a train is not approaching, try to restart the engine
- Shift to neutral and then push the vehicle off the tracks.

14

ENGINE OVERHEATS

The gauge or indicator light shows the engine temperature is rising above the normal level. This may occur in slow-moving traffic during hot weather or due to a mechanical defect in the cooling system. Lengthen your stopped distance from the preceding vehicle, activate the heater in the hot position with the fan on high, shift to neutral while stopped and rev the engine slightly. The temperature should return to the normal range, if not...

WHAT TO DO
- Check traffic, select a safe path and steer onto the shoulder or near the curb
- Park in a safe place; turn off the engine
- Activate the hazard lights
- Open the hood to allow heat to escape (cover your hand with a glove or cloth)
- Visually check hoses, belt, etc. while the engine cools
- If the coolant level (overflow tank) is low or empty, get a container of water
- Unlock the radiator cap (1/4 turn) and step back from the front of the vehicle

- After the pressure has been released, push and turn the radiator cap to remove completely
- Add some water slowly
- Restart the engine and fill the radiator as needed
- Close the cap and proceed to the nearest service center to have the cooling system verified.

PREVENTION
Proper maintenance of the cooling system as outlined in Chapter 15.

TOTAL STEERING FAILURE

Though a very rare occurrence, if you lose steering control completely, a breakdown in the front suspension or steering is the reason.

WHAT TO DO
- Activate the hazard lights
- Shift to neutral (depress the clutch)
- Hold the parking brake release mechanism and pump the parking brake firmly to reduce speed quickly
- Be prepared for a collision as you cannot control the direction in which the vehicle will move

PREVENTION
The steering and suspension will not breakdown without warning. Any abnormal looseness, shimmy, wandering or noises should be verified immediately.

Following the recommended service intervals in your owner's manual will permit early diagnosis and repair.

BRAKE FAILURE

Complete service brake failure is rare in modern vehicles as they have a dual braking system (Chapter 16). Should one fail, the other will stop your vehicle and a warning light will advise you of the problem. Partial or temporary brake failure can occur due to lack of brake fluid, overheating, wet brakes, V-belt failure (on some models only), etc.

WHAT TO DO

- Downshift to use the engine compression
  (taking advantage of engine braking)
- Pump the brake pedal several times
  (to restore braking power)
- Activate the hazard lights
  (to warn of your situation)
- Pump the parking brake while releasing the lock mechanism
  (to use the rear brakes to stop)

- Select a safe path while slowing (steer around obstacles).

If none of these permit you to stop, look for an uphill slope, guard rail or curb to further reduce your speed. As a last resort, select objects that will give on impact (Chapter 9) to bring you to a complete stop.

PREVENTION

Check the brake fluid level monthly.
In wet weather (Chapter 13) and on steep hills (Chapter 2 and 9), follow the aforementioned procedures.

Have the brakes verified at recommended intervals - owner's manual.

Verify the proper operation of the parking brake by using it every time you park.

Practice emergency stops using the parking brake.

POWER BRAKE FAILURE

When the engine stalls, the power brake unit will be affected. However, the power brake will function normally for one more application of the pedal. Apply the brake in one continuous motion, modulating the pressure without releasing, and your vehicle will stop normally. Release the pedal and you will have to press harder on the brake to obtain the desired result, but it will still function.

14

FIRE

Vehicle fires rarely occur, but when they do, you must act quickly to minimize danger to people and property. While driving, if you see or smell smoke in the passenger compartment, the ashtray, under the dash or under the hood, your vehicle has a fire.

WHAT TO DO
- Activate the hazard lights
- Select a safe path and move your vehicle out of the traffic flow
- Park away from crowds, vehicles and buildings (especially service stations)
- Turn off the ignition
- All occupants should move at least 100 feet away from the vehicle.

A CIGARETTE OR MATCH
Don't over-react, the materials used in the passenger compartment are non-flammable. When stopped, locate the cigarette or match and put it out. Make sure that any smoldering embers are out as well. Proceed on your way.

AN ASHTRAY FIRE
Close the ashtray while driving, this will cut off the oxygen supply somewhat. When parked, remove the ashtray and extinguish the fire outside the vehicle.

UNDER THE HOOD
Once the vehicle is safely stopped, have someone call the fire department. Decide how serious the fire is: high heat and flames - wait for the fire department.

If you have a fire extinguisher (ABC type) and the fire appears to be minor, cover your hands with cloth or gloves. Release the hood latch. Approach the front with your head below the hood line, pull the hood release and raise the hood slightly. Aim at the base of the fire through the narrow opening and smother the flames. Open the hood and smother the area completely.

A fire extinguisher should be mounted in the passenger compartment within reach of the driver. It should never be stored in the trunk because of the proximity of the trunk to the fuel tank.

UNDER THE DASH
This is an electrical fire and can be very difficult to extinguish. Wait for the fire department.

Driver Error

TIRES DROP OFF THE PAVEMENT

Due to fatigue, lack of concentration or to avoid an oncoming vehicle, the right tires of your vehicle have dropped off the pavement onto the shoulder.

HEY... DON'T BRAKE!!

WHAT TO DO
- Grip the steering firmly
- Stabilize your vehicle parallel to the pavement
- Ease off the accelerator and allow the vehicle to reduce speed
  (do not brake - traction is unequal)
- Check traffic, mirrors and blind spot
- Activate the left turn signal
- Turn the steering a quarter turn towards the roadway
- When the right front wheel climbs the edge, countersteer towards the center of the lane
- Accelerate and turn off the signal.

Should you leave the pavement completely to avoid an oncoming vehicle, follow the same procedures.

AVOIDING AN OBSTACLE

When driving at such a speed that an obstacle which appears in the road cannot be avoided by stopping, the only alternative is to swerve around the object.

WHAT TO DO
- Apply the brake to perform an emergency stop
- Activate the hazard lights
- Select a safe path around the obstacle (avoid crossing the center line as you may encounter oncoming traffic)
- Look and steer in the desired direction
- Ease up on the brake to allow the steering to direct your vehicle in the chosen direction
  (vehicles equipped with ABS brakes will steer during hard braking)
- Stabilize your vehicle
- Check traffic and return to your lane.

14

SKIDS

When a wheel or wheels slide against the roadway due to insufficient traction, the vehicle is skidding. Poor traction conditions (Chapter 9), a sudden change of acceleration, hard braking, a sudden change of direction or a combination of these factors cause skids. The usual result is a loss of directional control.

FRONT WHEEL SKIDS
The front wheels slide and your vehicle continues straight ahead.

1) Excessive brake pressure locks the front wheels (not with ABS brakes), your vehicle will not respond to the steering. It continues straight.

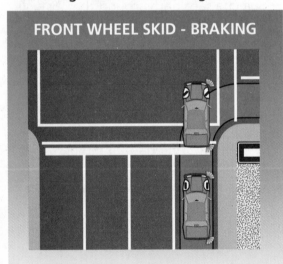

FRONT WHEEL SKID - BRAKING

WHAT TO DO
- Look and steer in the desired direction
- Release the brake pedal
- Reapply the brake more gently to continue reducing speed

2) A sharp turn of the steering and your vehicle continues straight (understeer).

FRONT WHEEL SKID - STEERING

WHAT TO DO
- Unwind the steering slightly to regain steering control
- Look and steer in the desired direction

3) With a front wheel drive vehicle, while accelerating, you turn the steering and your vehicle continues straight (understeer).

WHAT TO DO
- Shift to neutral (depress the clutch)
- Look and steer in the desired direction
- Reduce your speed after the turn
- Engage the transmission and proceed at a slower speed.

14

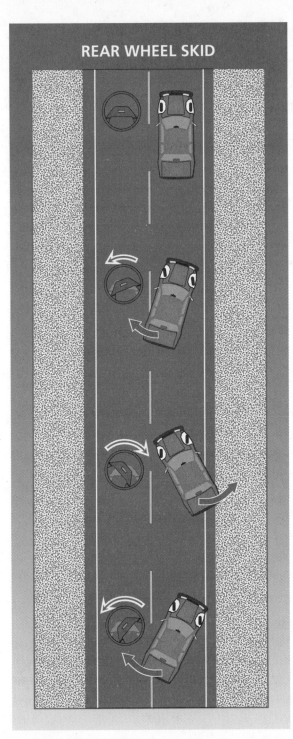

REAR WHEEL SKID

REAR WHEEL SKIDS

The rear wheels slide and the rear of your vehicle moves to the right or left.

1) While turning, the rear of your vehicle slides towards the outside of the curve (oversteer).

2) While driving in reduced traction conditions, you downshift, release the accelerator quickly or accelerate sharply and the rear of your vehicle begins to skid to the side.

WHAT TO DO

- Shift to neutral (depress the clutch)
- Look and steer in the desired direction

As you straighten from the skid, the rear of your vehicle may begin to slide in the opposite direction (fishtail).

- Keep looking ahead in the desired direction
- Steer, quickly and smoothly, to direct your vehicle where you are looking
- When under control, reduce your speed
- Engage the transmission and proceed at a slower speed

ABORT - RETRY

As is the case in all driving maneuvers, if at first you don't succeed, don't give up. Keep trying to correct the situation and you will succeed. Some experience or practice in skid control, such as taking a course, would be well advised before driving in areas of slippery or icy conditions.

14

Road Sharing Errors

HEAD-ON COLLISION

This is the worst type of collision as the force of impact is the highest (the combined energy of both vehicles). Avoid a head-on collision at all costs.

WHAT TO DO
- Begin an emergency stop (reducing your speed reduces the force of impact, gives you more time and may give the other driver time to recover)
- Signal with your horn and headlights
- Select the safest path (the shoulder, off the road completely)
- Ease off the brake pedal
- Look and steer in the desired direction

If a collision is inevitable, choose objects that will "give" on impact or sideswipe rather than hit directly (Chapter 9).

REAR-END COLLISION

While stopped at an intersection, you notice a vehicle approaching from the rear. It does not seem to be able to stop in time.

WHAT TO DO
- Check traffic and select an "out" (turn right, cross the intersection, climb the curb)

If there is no safe "out"
- Ease up on the brakes to move forward slightly
- Brace your head and body against the headrest and seat using the dead pedal
- On impact, re-apply the brakes fully

SIDE-IMPACT COLLISION

While crossing an intersection, another vehicle approaches in the transverse lane (on the cross street) at high speed.

WHAT TO DO
- Accelerate quickly to free the intersection

Side-impact collisions require a rapid decision to brake or accelerate quickly. Whichever seems more likely to avoid the collision. If a collision cannot be avoided, try to receive the impact towards the rear of your vehicle thus protecting the passenger compartment.

Emergency Vehicles

Any emergency vehicle (police, fire, ambulance) that has its siren operating and its lights flashing, must be given the right of way.

APPROACHED FROM THE REAR

While driving on a two-way roadway or a multilane highway, an emergency vehicle requesting passage approaches from the rear.

WHAT TO DO
- Check traffic and select a safe path
- Change lanes to the right side of the road
- Stop your vehicle safely
- Wait for the emergency vehicle to pass
- Safely proceed on your way

Be especially careful to drive at least 500 feet behind any emergency vehicle.

MEETING AN ONCOMING VEHICLE

While driving, an emergency vehicle requesting passage approaches in an oncoming direction.

WHAT TO DO
- Check traffic
- Change lanes to the right
- Slow your vehicle
- Wait for the emergency vehicle to pass
- Proceed safely

STOPPED AT AN INTERSECTION

While stopped at an intersection, an emergency vehicle approaches from the rear with its siren and lights operating

WHAT TO DO
- Check the position of the emergency vehicle in your rear-view mirror
- Remain stationary until it passes

If the emergency vehicle nears your vehicle in your lane, check traffic and proceed in a safe manner to clear its path.

14

Unusual Occurrences

ELECTRICAL WIRES CONTACT YOUR VEHICLE

Due to an accident or a storm, live electrical wires are in contact with your vehicle.

WHAT TO DO
- Remain in your vehicle
  (the tires insulate you from danger)
- Activate the hazard lights
- Turn off the ignition
- Advise people not to touch the vehicle
- Request that someone call for help
- Wait for qualified assistance

If you must leave the vehicle (a fire breaks out), be sure to jump out, as far as possible with both feet simultaneously. Make sure you are not in contact with the vehicle and the ground at the same time. Do not touch any of the wires lying on the ground.

IMMERSION IN WATER

If you drive or plunge into water, the vehicle will float for several minutes before sinking. Act quickly.

I CAN FLOAT FOR A FEW MINUTES!!

WHAT TO DO
- Occupants should unfasten seat belts
- Open the window farthest out of water
- Leave the vehicle while it is floating
- Swim away from the vehicle to avoid being pulled down by the wake of the sinking vehicle

If the vehicle sinks, air will be trapped in the highest part of the vehicle. Float in the vehicle, get a couple of deep breaths, open the door nearest the air pocket and leave the vehicle.

WASPS, BEES OR OTHER INSECTS

If a bug threatens to sting you or is buzzing around in your vehicle, remain calm.

WHAT TO DO
- Roll down your window
  (All windows, if power windows)
- Select a safe path and park
  (if the bug does not fly out)
- Shoo the bug out of the vehicle.

Review

TERMS TO REMEMBER - WRITE A SHORT DEFINITION FOR THE FOLLOWING :

- Panic
- Blow out
- Fusible link
- Short circuit
- Hood latch

- Engine stalls
- Breakdown
- Engine overheats
- Power steering failure
- Power brake failure

- ABC fire extinguisher
- Emergency stop
- Skid
- Head-on collision
- Side-impact

SUMMARY

A wide variety of emergency situations could arise while you are driving. The first concept is prevention. Maintain your vehicle properly to prevent most of these occurrences. Should a situation arise despite the best of precautions, do not panic. Study the outlined procedures carefully now and, when the situation occurs, you will be capable of responding quickly and easily. Thus, avoiding the potentially dangerous results.

TEST A - WRITE A "T" FOR TRUE OR AN "F" FOR FALSE IN THE SPACES PROVIDED

_____ 1. When a blowout occurs, you should immediately pump the brake.

_____ 2. When the right front wheels of your vehicle drop off the pavement onto the shoulder, you should brake firmly then re-enter the roadway.

_____ 3. If the hood of your vehicle flies open while driving, swerve towards the shoulder immediately.

_____ 4. If the brake system fails, fully apply the parking brake immediately.

_____ 5. If the engine stalls while driving, shift to neutral and try to restart while your vehicle continues to roll forward.

_____ 6. If your vehicle is equipped with power steering and the engine stalls while driving, the steering will not turn.

_____ 7. When the engine stalls, the power brakes will function normally for one more application of the brake pedal.

_____ 8. Approaching a railroad crossing and the engine stalls, coast over the tracks or make an emergency stop before reaching the tracks.

_____ 9. The rear wheels slide and the rear of the vehicle moves to the left, you should release the accelerator pedal and steer towards the right.

_____ 10. You notice an approaching vehicle in your lane (head-on); brake sharply to reduce speed, then release the brake and steer onto the shoulder.

Student notes

_____

_____

_____

_____

_____

_____

_____

_____

_____

_____

_____

_____

_____

_____

_____

_____

_____

_____

_____

HANDBOOK PLUS WORKBOOK

Check your comprehension and mastery of the contents of this chapter by completing the corresponding exercises that are found in the complement to the **HANDBOOK PLUS:**

HANDBOOK PLUS WORKBOOK

Complete the exercises on Pages 94 to 100 then check your responses by referring to the answer key on Page 109.
If necessary, review the chapter for each error and refer to your instructor for further guidance.

15

15 - A
Engine

15 - B
Cooling System

15 - C
Lubrication System

15 - D
Electrical System

15 - E
Fuel System

15 - F
Exhaust System

15 - G
Power Train

15 - H
Boosting a Vehicle

15 - I
Review

The Engine and Power Train

As a vehicle owner, you are responsible for keeping it in proper operating condition and ensuring that it is equipped to handle the different seasons and driving conditions.

An engine that is properly maintained will operate at maximum efficiency. It is less likely to break down and cause inconveniences. In this chapter, we will review the components and support systems of the automobile engine as well as the maintenance that each may require.

Far from intending that you become a mechanic the intention is to remove the mystery that surrounds the automobile. The owner's manual should also be consulted for specific information related to your make and model and its maintenance schedule.

A well maintained vehicle is safer and cheaper to drive as well as producing less pollution!

AFTER COMPLETING THIS CHAPTER, THE STUDENT MUST BE ABLE TO LOCATE THE COMPONENTS, DESCRIBE THE GENERAL FUNCTION OF AND TAKE RESPONSIBILITY FOR:

- **the internal combustion engine and proper maintenance thereof.**
- **the engine support and power train systems.**
- **basic maintenance procedures as well as owner manual requirements.**

Internal Combustion Engine

The engine in your automobile is an internal combustion engine; that means it burns fuel in a combustion chamber inside the engine. The energy produced is converted into mechanical energy. Let's begin by examining the major components.

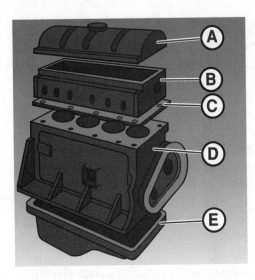

THE MAIN (NON-MOVING) COMPONENTS:

A) VALVE COVER: prevents oil leakage and permits adding oil through the filler cap.

B) HEAD: forms the combustion chambers, conducts the fuel mixture to and exhaust gases from the engine and supports the valve train.

C) HEAD GASKET: seals the head to the block to prevent any leakage.

D) CYLINDER BLOCK: contains the four cylinders and the major moving parts.

E) OIL PAN: acts as a collector and reservoir for the engine oil.

THE MAIN MOVING ENGINE COMPONENTS:

1) PISTON: moves in the cylinder using piston rings to seal against the cylinder wall.

2) CONNECTING ROD: converts the reciprocal piston motion to crankshaft rotary motion.

3) CRANKSHAFT: transmits the power to the support systems and power train.

4) CAMSHAFT: opens the valves at the correct time. An overhead camshaft (OHC) is mounted on the head above the valves.

5) VALVES: open and close to control the flow of gases into and out of the engine.

6) FLYWHEEL: balances engine operation; engaged by starter to crank engine and transmits power to the transmission.

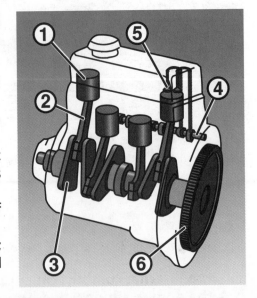

15

THE FOUR STROKE CYCLE

Most motorized vehicles are equipped with engines that operate on a four stroke cycle. Some motorcycles and a few diesel engines are the exception; they use a two stroke cycle.

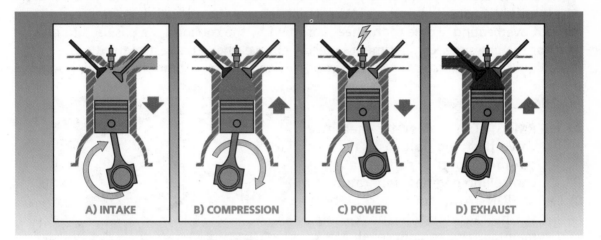

A) INTAKE STROKE: The intake valve opens. The piston is descending in the cylinder and the air fuel mixture enters the cylinder.

B) COMPRESSION STROKE: Both valves are closed and the piston ascends in the cylinder. The fuel-air mixture is forced into the space at the top of the cylinder and compressed (combustion chamber).

C) POWER STROKE: A spark from the spark plug ignites the highly explosive air-fuel mixture initiating combustion, thereby pushing the piston down in the cylinder.

D) EXHAUST STROKE: The exhaust valve opens and the fumes begin to escape. The piston rises forcing the burned air-fuel mixture out of the cylinder.

This sequence repeats thousands of times per minute in each cylinder. Each cylinder operates on a different stroke of the cycle in order to smooth out the engine operation. The more cylinders an engine has; the more power it produces (it also uses more fuel). Engines may have 3, 4, 5, 6, 7, 8, 10, or 12 cylinders.

MAINTENANCE TIPS

Keep the exterior of the engine clean in order to spot any leaks as soon as they appear.

Check your owner's manual for the recommended service intervals for the engine components - valves, tune ups, timing chain, etc.

Whenever engine performance or noise are abnormal, have your vehicle verified. This will prevent costly breakdowns.

The Cooling System

The engine cooling system brings the engine to its most efficient operating temperature as quickly as possible and maintains that temperature in all operating conditions without overheating. Some of the heat absorbed by the cooling system is used to provide heat for the passenger compartment in inclement weather. The vast majority of vehicles use a liquid cooling system. Most motorcycles and some automobiles are air-cooled.

THE BASIC COMPONENTS

A) THERMOSTAT: a temperature-sensitive valve that regulates the flow of coolant to the radiator, thus controlling engine temperature.

B) EXPANSION TANK: connected by hose to the radiator filler neck, helps maintain the coolant level. Marks on the tank permit verifying the coolant level without opening the radiator cap.

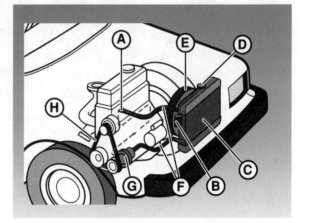

C) RADIATOR: reservoir of coolant, transfers heat to the air passing through the core. The coolant can then return to the engine when needed to absorb more heat.

D) RADIATOR CAP: seals the radiator, pressurizing the cooling system, to increase the coolant boiling point and thereby improve the ability of the system to perform efficiently.

Remove the radiator cap only when the engine temperature is cold!

E) COOLING FAN: provides a powerful draft of air through the radiator fins. It may be driven by a belt (rear wheel drive) or an electric motor with a control switch (front wheel drive).

F) RADIATOR HOSES: reinforced rubber hoses that conduct the coolant to the radiator and, after cooling, back to the engine. Two smaller hoses connect the system to the heater radiator.

G) WATER PUMP: circulates the coolant (a mixture of water and anti-freeze) through the engine (block and head) and sends the coolant to the radiator when the thermostat opens as the temperature rises.

H) DRIVE BELT: drives the water pump and the fan (rear wheel drive).

GAUGE / INDICATOR LIGHT: mounted in the instrument panel (not shown), informs the driver of the operating temperature of the engine.

15

MAINTENANCE TIPS

Check coolant level regularly, adding some to the expansion tank if necessary. Should this occur frequently have the system checked for leakage.

Check the condition and tension of the drive belt at the same time. The operation of the entire system relies heavily on the proper action of the belt.

Check the hoses as well. Softness and swelling or brittleness and cracking are all signs that replacement is required.

When washing your vehicle, take the time to wash the radiator by spraying water with the hose from the fan side towards the exterior. This will clean the radiator core removing dust, insects, etc.

Test the anti-freeze every year prior to the winter season. Every third season, have the system flushed (cleaned) and new anti-freeze installed. The anti-corrosive additives and the anti-freeze lose their effectiveness after a couple of years.

The Lubrication System

The engine lubrication system circulates oil, a liquid lubricant, under pressure to all the moving engine components. The oil must perform a number of important functions:

1. Reduce friction to minimize wear and loss of power.
2. Cool the moving components (especially those not in contact with the cooling system).
3. Clean the moving components to remove dirt and metal that will cause increased wear and tear.
3. Cushion the shock between moving parts.
4. Create a seal between the rings and the cylinder wall.
5. Coat the components with residual oil to prevent rusting and provide initial lubrication during starting.

THE BASIC COMPONENTS

A) GAUGE OR INDICATOR LIGHT: in the instrument panel (not shown), informs the driver of the pressure in the system.

B) OIL FILLER CAP: removable cap on the valve cover permitting access to the crankcase to add engine oil.

C) DIPSTICK: an oil level indicator to check the level in the oil pan.

D) OIL PAN: encloses the bottom of the engine block to collect the oil dripping from the components and acts as a reservoir when the engine is not operating.

E) OIL PUMP: draws oil from the pan and circulates the oil (under pressure) to the filter, then to all moving components through the galleries (lines or passageways in the block, head and engine components).

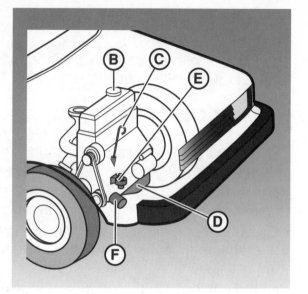

F) OIL FILTER: removes impurities from the oil, while passing through the filter under pressure, before it enters the oil galleries to circulate to all the moving components.

ENVIRONMENTAL TIPS

Engine oil contaminates soil and water, affects water in the water table and may affect water treatment facilities. Used oil may also contain particles of metal. Recycle used oil at hazardous waste collection sites.

MAINTENANCE TIPS

Check the oil level each time you gas up. The engine should be off for a few minutes and the vehicle should be on level ground to obtain an accurate reading.

Pull out the dipstick, wipe it, reinsert it fully, then pull it out again and check the level of the oil slick on the gauge at the lower end of the dipstick. Reinsert the dipstick. Add oil only if the gauge indicates the need for one liter.

As all oil refiners meet the American Petroleum Institute standards, you may use any brand of oil. Check your owner's manual for the grade and viscosity ratings. Verify the recommended service intervals (max. 3,000 miles [5,000 kilometers]).

15

The Electrical System

The electrical system includes the ignition, charging, starting systems, and the accessory circuits.

THE IGNITION SYSTEM converts the 12 volt battery current to high voltage surges directed to the spark plug at the proper time to initiate combustion.

The system consists of the ignition switch, the distributor assembly, the ignition coil, spark plugs, wiring and the battery.

THE CHARGING SYSTEM produces electrical power while the engine is running to operate all the electrical components and recharge the battery.

The system consists of a drive belt, the alternator, the voltage regulator, wiring and the battery.

THE STARTING SYSTEM permits the driver to turn the ignition switch to activate an electric motor to crank and usually start the engine.

The system consists of the ignition switch, the starter motor, a solenoid switch, wiring and the battery.

THE ACCESSORY CIRCUITS power the lights, safety systems, and accessories. This system includes the fuse box, wiring and any electrically powered equipment.

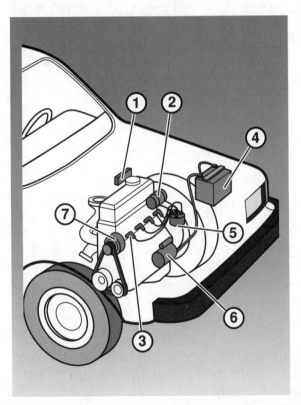

BASIC COMPONENTS

1) THE FUSE BOX: protects the electrical equipment. Spare fuses should be stored in your vehicle.
2) THE IGNITION COIL: transforms the 12 volt current to a surge of current of many thousands of volts.
3) THE SPARK PLUGS: produce a spark to ignite the air-fuel mixture.
4) THE BATTERY: stores energy in chemical form so that it can supply the electricity to start the engine.
5) THE DISTRIBUTOR: controls the production and distribution of the surges to the spark plugs.
6) THE STARTER: an electric motor that cranks the engine (turns the flywheel) during starting.
7) THE ALTERNATOR, driven by the belt, charges the battery and operates electrical components.

15

MAINTENANCE TIPS

Spare fuses should be stored in your vehicle. It is a fairly simple matter to replace a fuse. Should a particular fuse need replacement more than once, consult a mechanic.

Check the battery regularly. Make sure the terminals, clamps, or connectors are clean and properly tightened. Most new batteries are sealed and maintenance free. (Older types require checking the fluid level and the addition of distilled water when necessary.)

Check the condition and tension of the belt that drives the alternator.

Check your owner's manual for the recommended tune up and electrical service intervals.

DIESEL ENGINES DO NOT HAVE AN IGNITION SYSTEM AS THE FUEL IS IGNITED BY THE HEAT OF THE COMPRESSED AIR. They are, however, equipped with components called GLOW plugs. These are intended to heat the combustion chamber or the air entering the combustion chamber for cold starting. When the ignition switch is turned to the "ON" position, a light is illuminated on the dash to signify that the GLOW plugs are warming up. When the light is extinguished, you may start the engine.

 # The Fuel System

The automotive fuel system is designed to provide the correct amount of fuel and air to the engine under all operating conditions and power demands. It must be linked to a driver operated control - the accelerator pedal. It must also provide fuel enrichment for starting cold engines (the choke) and compensate for hot engine and high altitude operating factors. All of this must be achieved without diminishing performance in both power and economy while complying with exhaust emission standards.

Many vehicles use a fuel injection system (replacing the carburetor) to deliver the fuel under pressure into the combustion chambers or into the airflow just as it enters each individual cylinder. This maximizes power and economy.

THE BASIC COMPONENTS

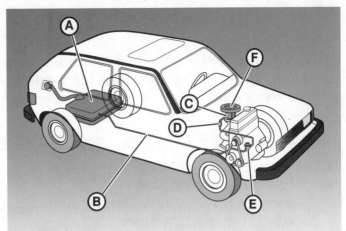

A) **FUEL TANK:** a reservoir for fuel. A tank device controls the fuel gauge to inform the driver of the fuel available.

B) **FUEL LINE:** tubes connect the tank to the carburetor or injection system.

C) **CARBURETOR:** mixes the fuel and air and supplies it to the cylinders. Gas pedal controls the carburetor.

D) **FUEL FILTER:** removes dirt and other contaminants from the fuel.

E) **FUEL PUMP:** electrical or mechanical device that forces fuel from the tank to the carburetor.

F) **AIR FILTER:** removes dirt and dust particles from air entering engine.

CHOKE: (not shown) restricts air flow and increases idle speed (when cold).

TURBO: (not shown) turbine to increase the air entering the cylinders.

ENVIRONMENTAL TIPS

Gasoline contaminates soil and ground water and poses a risk of explosion and/or fire. Care in storage (never for an extended period of time) and try to use it up entirely. If not, bring to a hazardous waste disposal. Conservation of fuel - a non-renewable resource - by proper driving habits and eliminating unnecessary trips (ride sharing) as well as maintenance of your vehicle will all reduce fuel consumption and pollution.

MAINTENANCE TIPS

Check the fuel gauge every time you start your vehicle. Keep the fuel level above the one-quarter mark to avoid: • Condensation in cold weather • Fouling or clogging the system with contaminants • Running out of gas

IN WINTER, keep the fuel level above the one-half mark. Never fill-up just prior to parking your vehicle (this can lead to a frozen gas line). IN SUMMER, avoid filling the tank completely in order to leave space for gasoline expansion.

When you refuel (fill-up with gas): • Turn off the engine. • Make sure no one smokes near the vehicle. • Do not overfill as drips can damage the paint.

Check your owner's manual for recommended service intervals.

15

The Exhaust System

The exhaust system collects the burned gases from each cylinder, directs the harmful gases and heat through the exhaust pipes and releases them behind the vehicle. At the same time, the exhaust system reduces noise and exhaust pollution.

THE BASIC COMPONENTS

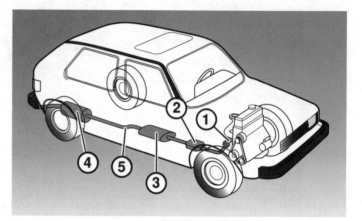

1) **THE EXHAUST MANIFOLD:** a collector pipe with several passageways through which the exhaust gases leave the engine and enter the exhaust system.

2) **THE CATALYTIC CONVERTER:** converts harmful exhaust gases by promoting a chemical reaction thus catalyzing the pollutants.

3) **THE MUFFLER:** reduces noise and produces an engine back pressure.

4) **THE RESONATOR:** auxiliary muffler on many vehicles to reduce the noise.

5) **EXHAUST PIPES:** are tubes that interconnect all of the exhaust system components and extends past the rear of the vehicle.

 ENVIRONMENTAL TIPS
The exhaust system helps minimize air pollution when it meets manufacturer's specifications. Government requirements are becoming more and more demanding in this area. Do not modify the system.

MAINTENANCE TIPS

Check the exhaust system periodically to make sure that it is intact and leak-free all the way to the tailpipe. Should exhaust noise start to become louder, have the system verified. Carbon monoxide gas, one of the by-products of combustion, may seep into the passenger compartment if there are any leaks in the exhaust system.

Do not alter the exhaust system of your vehicle in any way. State laws prohibit the operation of a vehicle that does not conform to specified standards.

Power Train

The power train carries the engine power (mechanical energy) to the vehicle drive wheels. Vehicles may be rear, front or four wheel drive. Each of these types of power trains may be equipped with an automatic or a standard transmission.

BASIC COMPONENTS

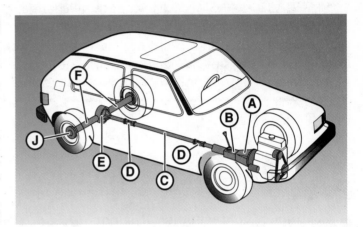

A) POWER COUPLING: connects engine to transmission. Automatic uses a fluid coupling (torque converter). Standard uses a clutch.

B) TRANSMISSION: an assembly of gears that permit different ratios as well as neutral and reverse.
An automatic selects the appropriate forward gear. Standard must be shifted manually.

C) DRIVE SHAFT: transmits rotation to the differential and permits a change in angle and length when the rear wheels move up and down.

D) UNIVERSAL JOINTS: change drive shaft angle while transmitting power.

E) DIFFERENTIAL: permits each drive wheel to turn at different speeds.

F) AXLE SHAFTS: connect the differential to the wheels within a housing (rear wheel drive).

G) TRANS AXLE: the combination of the transmission and the differential on front drive vehicles.

H) AXLE SHAFTS: connect the trans-axle externally to the front wheels.

I) C.V. JOINTS: connect to the front wheels while sharply changing in angle so the front wheels can steer and move up and down.

J) DRIVE WHEELS: receive the power to push (rear wheel drive) or pull (front wheel drive) the vehicle.

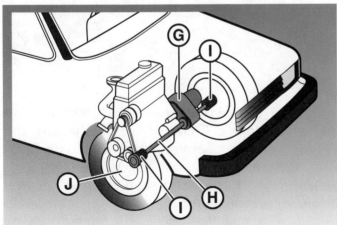

15

MAINTENANCE TIPS

The transmission fluid level should be checked regularly.

AUTOMATIC TRANSMISSION: The selector lever in park, parking brake engaged and the engine idling. Use the transmission dipstick (as for the engine oil). If necessary, add the appropriate oil.

STANDARD TRANSMISSION: At each oil change, ask the mechanic to verify the level and condition of the oil. (At the same time, have the clutch checked)

The differential fluid level should also be checked at every oil change.

At the first signs of slippage, clunking, abnormal noises or uneven shifting have a service technician check the power train completely.

Boosting a Vehicle

In extremely cold weather, it is not uncommon for a battery to go "dead". In order to start the vehicle, you will have to "JUMP START" or boost it using another vehicle. Make sure:
- the two vehicles are not touching
- the batteries have the same voltage
- the dead battery is not frozen
- the fluid level is not low

WHAT TO DO:

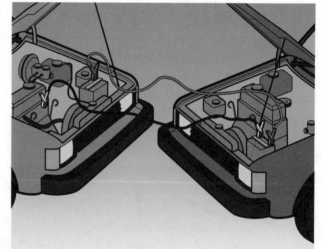

- Turn off accessories, engine and apply parking brakes
- Remove battery caps, if so equipped (Cover with a heavy cloth)
- Connect both ends of the red cable to the positive terminals (+ or marked P) of both batteries
- Connect the black cable to the negative terminal (– or marked N) of the battery being used to boost
- Attach the other end to the engine block or frame of the vehicle with the "dead" battery (avoid moving parts)
- Start the booster vehicle and fast idle
- Start the other vehicle and run for several minutes
- Reverse the order to disconnect.

15

Review

TERMS TO REMEMBER - WRITE A SHORT DEFINITION FOR EACH OF THE FOLLOWING :

- Internal combustion
- Cylinder block
- Piston
- Flywheel
- Intake stroke

- Compression stroke
- Power stroke
- Exhaust stroke
- Radiator cap
- Starter

- Choke
- Catalytic converter
- Oil pump
- Dipstick
- Differential

SUMMARY

The operation and components of the engine and power train should be understood in at least a very basic manner to encourage the correct use and maintenance of your vehicle.

You will save money, in the long run, by maintaining and servicing your vehicle properly. A well maintained vehicle is also safer to operate.

TEST A - WRITE "T" BESIDE STATEMENTS THAT ARE TRUE AND "F" BESIDE THOSE THAT ARE FALSE.

_____ 1. Your engine may overheat if you do not check and adjust the fan belt.

_____ 2. The radiator cap should be removed only when the engine is cold.

_____ 3. The coolant, water and antifreeze, should be replaced every year.

_____ 4. Check the oil level using the dipstick while the engine is operating.

_____ 5. The oil filter should be changed as well as the oil every 3,000 to 5,000 miles.

_____ 6. If the oil light comes on and stays on while driving, you should stop and turn off the engine.

_____ 7. When filling the fuel tank the engine should be turned off.

_____ 8. The fuel system does not require service as long as it operates properly.

_____ 9. The exhaust system should be checked only if it becomes noisier than usual.

_____ 10. The differential permits the drive wheels to turn at different speeds.

Student notes

_____
_____
_____
_____
_____
_____
_____
_____
_____
_____
_____
_____
_____
_____
_____
_____
_____

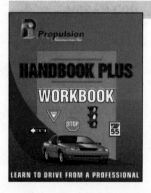

HANDBOOK PLUS WORKBOOK

*Check your comprehension and mastery of the contents of this chapter by completing the corresponding exercise that is found in the complement to the **HANDBOOK PLUS:***

HANDBOOK PLUS WORKBOOK

Complete the exercise on Pages 101 and 102 then check your responses by referring to the answer key on Page 109.
If necessary, review the chapter for each error and refer to your instructor for further guidance.

16 - A
Tires

16 - B
The Suspension
System

16 - C
The Steering
System

16 - D
The Brake
System

16 - E
The Body

16 - F
Review

The Chassis

When you own a vehicle, you are responsible for keeping it in proper operating condition.

In this chapter, we will examine the different units that are part of the chassis: the tires, the suspension system, the steering system, the brake system, and the body.

These systems are essential to the operation of your vehicle. The stability and road-worthiness of a vehicle depend on basic maintenance performed at regular intervals. Once again, if these systems are properly maintained, the cost of operation will be reduced. Check your owner's manual for specific requirements.

You also have a social responsibility to be a "GREEN" driver; one who avoids polluting the environment as much as possible. Proper maintenance procedures will reduce pollution.

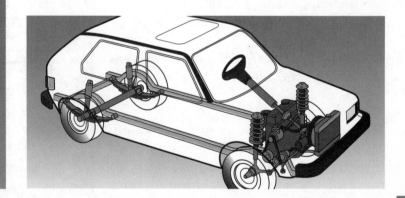

AFTER COMPLETING THIS CHAPTER, THE STUDENT MUST BE ABLE TO LOCATE THE COMPONENTS, DESCRIBE THE GENERAL FUNCTION OF AND TAKE RESPONSIBILITY FOR:

- the tires and suspension systems.
- the steering and brake systems.
- basic maintenance procedures and owner manual requirements.

Tires

Improved tire design has reduced the incidence of tire troubles on modern vehicles; yet, the tires are still one of the most neglected parts of the vehicle.

Tires have two functions. First, they are air-filled cushions that absorb most of the shocks caused by road hazards. The tires flex, or give, as they meet these irregularities. Thus they reduce the effect of the shocks on the vehicle and the passengers. Second, the tires grip the road to provide traction. This enables the driver to accelerate, brake, and steer the vehicle.

TIRE CONSTRUCTION

The tire casing is composed of plies (layers of cord impregnated with rubber) shaped on a form. The rubber treads and sidewalls are then applied to give the desired form, wear characteristics and flexibility.

There are two basic tire types: the bias ply (also belted bias ply) and the radial ply design.

THE BIAS PLY has the plies criss-crossed. This makes the casing strong in all directions; however, the plies tend to move against each other. This generates heat and tire "squirm". The tires wear more rapidly and provide less traction.

THE RADIAL PLY has the plies parallel and perpendicular to the tread. Belts (usually steel) are then attached in the same position as the tread which is then applied with the sidewall. This results in more flexibility. The tread stays in contact with the road producing greater traction. Radial tires also wear more slowly.

NEVER MIX BIAS AND RADIAL TIRES ON YOUR VEHICLE. EVEN MIXING RADIAL TIRES OF DIFFERENT MAKES AND TREAD DESIGNS IS NOT RECOMMENDED.

TIRE SPECIFICATIONS

By law, details about each tire must be molded into both sidewalls - tire size, maximum inflation pressure, load rating, construction, number of plies and manufacturer. The two most common formats are the metric and alphanumeric types (see illustrations).

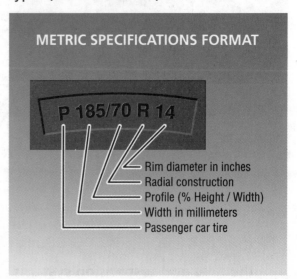

METRIC SPECIFICATIONS FORMAT

P 185/70 R 14

- Rim diameter in inches
- Radial construction
- Profile (% Height / Width)
- Width in millimeters
- Passenger car tire

16

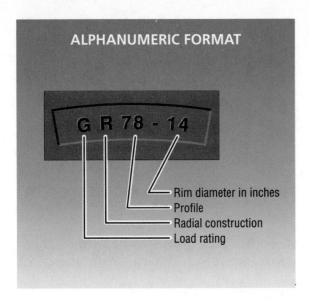

ALPHANUMERIC FORMAT

G R 78 - 14

— Rim diameter in inches
— Profile
— Radial construction
— Load rating

Most tires have wear bars or tread wear indicators, which are filled-in sections of the tread grooves. When the tread has worn down enough to reveal the wear bars as a line of rubber across the tread, the tire should be replaced.

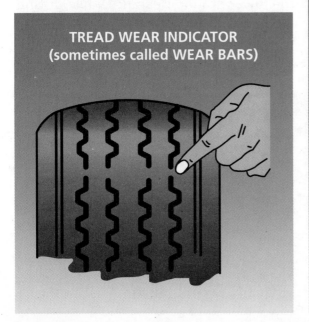

TREAD WEAR INDICATOR
(sometimes called WEAR BARS)

TIRE ROTATION

The amount of wear a tire gets depends on its location on the vehicle and the type of vehicle. Turning, accelerating, braking, the slant of the road surface, etc. cause each tire to wear differently. One tire can wear out as much as twice as fast as another. To equalize wear and extend the usage of all the tires, the tires should be rotated every 12,000 miles. Check your owner's manual for the recommended interval for your vehicle.

Passenger vehicle tires can be rotated using different methods. Two patterns (no full size spare) are shown below (check your owners manual); also, check the tire inflation when rotating as the front and rear may require different tire pressures.

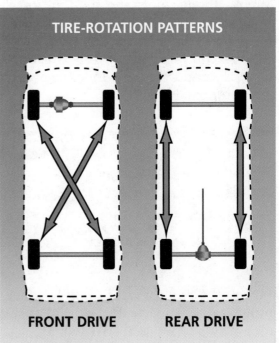

TIRE-ROTATION PATTERNS

FRONT DRIVE   **REAR DRIVE**

16

CHANGING A TIRE:

Too many injuries and deaths occur while changing tires every year. To proceed safely, activate the hazard lights, position the vehicle on a hard flat surface as far off the roadway as possible.and apply the parking brake. Set out reflective warning devices 100 feet in both directions.

Take the jack, jack handle, lug wrench and spare out of the trunk. Block both the front and the rear of the wheel diagonally opposite the flat using stones or blocks. Position the jack (trunk lid diagram or owner's manual) and jack up the vehicle slightly. Remove the wheel cover, use the lug wrench to loosen the bolts a couple of turns, then raise the vehicle until the flat clears the ground.

Remove the lug nuts and the flat. Install the spare and the bolts by hand. Tighten the bolts slightly. Lower the vehicle and remove the jack. Retighten the bolts (every second bolt until they have each been tightened twice).

CHANGING A TIRE

Note the position of the jack and the blocks preventing the wheel from rolling.

Store the jack, jack handle, lug wrench, wheel cover, flat tire and reflective warning devices in the trunk.

DRIVING WITH A COMPACT SPARE:

To save space, most vehicles have an under-sized, limited mileage spare. Do not exceed 50 mph, avoid sudden change in speed or direction, and be aware of the lower ground clearance while driving with this type of spare. Stop at the nearest service station to repair and reinstall the regular tire.

MAINTENANCE TIPS

Check the tire pressure regularly preferably while the tires are cold.

UNDER-INFLATED TIRES PROVIDE POOR TRACTION. (CHAPTER 9 - LAWS OF PHYSICS) DRIVING ON AN UNDER-INFLATED TIRE WILL MAKE THE TIRE TEMPERATURE RISE AND MAY CAUSE A BLOW-OUT!

Check the tires for wear, bulges and/or splits in the tread or sidewall whenever the vehicle is serviced (oil change).

Uneven wear may signal problems:
- Center tread wear- over-inflation
- Shoulder tread wear- under-inflation
- One side wear- alignment problems
- Patchy uneven wear- shocks, brakes, etc.
- Abrasive wear- high speed cornering

If you notice abnormal wear, have a service technician correct the problem. Always have the tires balanced before installation on the vehicle.

The Suspension System

The suspension system supports the weight of the vehicle, absorbs the shocks caused by road irregularities, and provides flexibility while ensuring vehicle stability and drivability.

BASIC COMPONENTS

A) SPRINGS: whether leaf (rear), coil (front and rear), or torsion bars, support the weight of the vehicle and flex to absorb road shocks.

B) SHOCK ABSORBERS: one installed at each wheel to control the oscillating action of the springs to minimize movement and stabilize the wheel contact with the road.

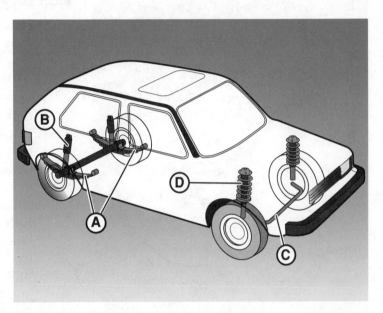

C) STABILIZER BARS: (sway bar) added to the front and sometimes the rear suspension to minimize body roll (lean or sway) on turns and bumps.

D) MACPHERSON STRUT: a suspension unit that combines the shock and the spring into one component (front and rear on many small vehicles).

MAINTENANCE TIPS

Have the shocks checked for leakage whenever your vehicle is in for service.

If your vehicle tends to bounce while driving, check your shocks by pushing down on the corners of your vehicle. The vehicle should stabilize after rebounding once. If it continues to oscillate, change the shocks.

Whenever your vehicle does not appear to be level (unloaded), have the springs checked for sag, wear and/or breakage.

The Steering System

The steering system controls the position of the front wheels in order to permit the driver to change the direction of the vehicle.

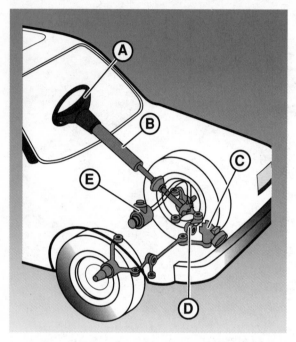

BASIC COMPONENTS

A) **STEERING WHEEL:** driver control that may be adjustable. (tilt and/or telescoping steering)

B) **STEERING COLUMN:** connects the wheel to the gearbox. Collapsible on impact to protect the driver.

C) **STEERING GEARBOX:** converts the rotary motion of the wheel into linear motion of the steering linkage: various types.

D) **STEERING LINKAGE:** a series of arms, rods and tie-rods that transmit the linear motion to the front wheels to change their position.

E) **POWER STEERING:** hydraulic pump impelled by a belt connected to the engine that facilitates steering.

ENVIRONMENTAL TIPS

Power steering fluid is toxic, contaminates soil and water, can cause eye and skin irritation and combustion produces carbon monoxide. Unused fluid can be shared with others or brought to a hazardous waste site.

MAINTENANCE TIPS

Check the power steering fluid level and the condition and adjustment of the belt regularly.

Avoid turning the steering if the vehicle is not in motion (dry steering); premature wear of steering components and tires will result.

Never force the steering at the limit of travel; back off slightly and the wheels will still be fully turned. Forcing causes early failure of power steering / steering components.

Avoid deep potholes, curbs and any other sudden or hard impacts that may damage the steering components.

Have the steering aligned at least once a year and after any serious impacts.

The Brake System

The brake system permits the driver to slow or stop the rotation of the tires. The friction of the tires against the road surface will then slow and/or stop the vehicle. Modern vehicles are equipped with two braking systems: a dual hydraulic brake system (service brakes) and a mechanical brake system (parking or emergency brake).

BASIC COMPONENTS

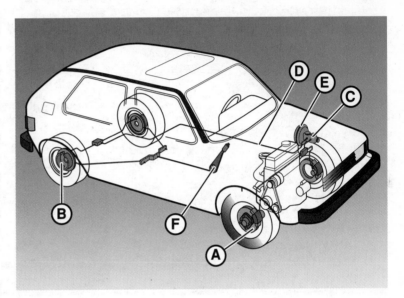

A) DISC BRAKES: superior (cool faster) brakes that utilize a pinching action on a metal disc to slow or stop rotation of the tire. Usually at the front wheels (the front does 70% of braking) but is available as an option at all four wheels.

B) DRUM BRAKES: brake shoes (hemispherical type) push outward on a rotating drum. (Because they are enclosed, they retain heat.)

C) DUAL MASTER CYLINDER: brake pedal applies pressure on two pistons that pressurize the brake fluid. The fluid transmits this pressure to each wheel where it activates the disc or drum brake mechanisms. A reservoir (sometimes two) supply extra fluid when needed. The dual systems operate independently in case one should fail.

D) BRAKE LINES: double walled steel tubes full of brake fluid that conduct the hydraulic pressure.

E) POWER BRAKE: an engine-activated booster unit that reduces the effort required to apply the hydraulic brakes. Will operate one more time if the engine should stop functioning.

F) PARKING BRAKE: a lever or foot pedal that mechanically (cables and levers) activates the rear brakes only (most vehicles). Can be used for parking and if the hydraulic brakes fail.

INDICATOR LIGHT: (not shown) comes on if one of the dual hydraulic brake systems should fail or in some vehicles, if the brake fluid is low.

MAINTENANCE TIPS

Check the brake fluid level at least once a month. The second time you add (correct) fluid, have the brakes verified.

Lubricate and adjust the parking brake cables every oil change.

Check the operation of the parking brake every time you park by applying them and then EASING UP on the service brake while still in drive. Your vehicle should not move.

A brake system warning light (some vehicles have more than one) on the dash informs you:
- the parking brake is engaged
- there is a brake system malfunction
- the brake fluid level is low

Most drum brakes are self-adjusting - while reversing and braking or, in some recent models, as the parking brake is applied.

If the brake pedal feels low or "spongy" (is soft but firms up when pumped), the vehicle pulls to one side during braking, or makes any unusual noises (grinding or squealing) have the brake system checked by a service technician.

Have the brake system cleaned, verified and adjusted every spring even if it does not demonstrate any unusual symptoms.

With ABS brakes, check the owner's manual for service (brake fluid must be replaced at specified intervals).

16-E

The Body

The exterior body components, windows and interior of your vehicle also require service and maintenance on a regular basis.

- Wash your vehicle once a week. Check your owner's manual for soaps and recommended solvents.
- Wax the exterior of your vehicle once a year to protect the paint finish.
- Lubricate all hinges, locks, etc. to ensure smooth operation.
- Enquire about special rust-proofing to protect the vehicle against rust.
- Purchase touch-up paint to repair small chips and nicks before rust has a chance to start.
- Proper maintenance will maintain the value of your vehicle as well as improving its looks while you are driving it around town.

16

Review

TERMS TO REMEMBER - WRITE A SHORT DEFINITION FOR EACH OF THE FOLLOWING :

- Tire tread
- Radial ply
- Tire specifications
- Tread wear indicator

- Tire rotation
- Springs
- Shock absorber
- Stabilizer bar

- Power steering
- Disc brakes
- Master cylinder
- Parking brake

SUMMARY

The operation and components of the chassis should be understood in a very basic manner to encourage the proper use and maintenance of your vehicle.

You will save money, in the long run, by maintaining and servicing your vehicle properly. A well maintained vehicle is also safer to operate.

TEST A - WRITE "T" BESIDE STATEMENTS THAT ARE TRUE AND "F" BESIDE THOSE THAT ARE FALSE.

_____ 1. Tires should be rotated to extend the life span of the tires.

_____ 2. When the tread wear indicator appears in the tread, you should have the tires replaced by new ones.

_____ 3. It does not matter what kind of tires you install on your vehicle as long as the tread is in good condition.

_____ 4. When the shock absorbers show signs of leakage, they must be replaced.

_____ 5. If you must add brake fluid to the master cylinder, this indicates there is a problem.

_____ 6. The parking brake applies on the front wheels only.

_____ 7. A "spongy" brake pedal is an indication of air in the brake lines.

_____ 8. The brake indicator light is illuminated when the parking brake is in the applied position.

_____ 9. It is normal for the suspension system of an older vehicle to bounce and rebound many times after passing over a bump.

_____ 10. You should align the steering system of your vehicle at least once a year.

Student notes

_____

_____

_____

_____

_____

_____

_____

_____

_____

_____

_____

_____

_____

_____

_____

_____

_____

_____

_____

_____

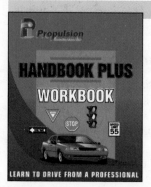

HANDBOOK PLUS WORKBOOK

*Check your comprehension and mastery of the contents of this chapter by completing the corresponding exercises that are found in the complement to the **HANDBOOK PLUS**:*

HANDBOOK PLUS WORKBOOK

Complete the exercises on Pages 103 and 104 then check your responses by referring to the answer key on Page 109.
If necessary, review the chapter for each error and refer to your instructor for further guidance.

17 - A
Deciding to Buy

17 - B
**Choosing
a Vehicle**

17 - C
**Financing
your Purchase**

17 - D
**Insuring
your Vehicle**

17 - E
Review

Owning a Vehicle

Driving a vehicle is a great responsibility. As you have already seen, you are accountable for your own safety, the safety of your passengers, as well as the safety of the other road users who share the HTS. Becoming the owner of a vehicle means even greater responsibilities.

Today, the purchase of a vehicle, whether new or used, is a major spending decision. It consumes a major portion of the household budget. And, for many people, the transaction is paid for with borrowed money- loan, lease, or financing.

On top of the purchase price, you must be financially capable of paying the sales taxes, the registration fees, and the insurance coverage required in most states. This coverage should be considered when deciding to purchase as it varies considerably with the type of vehicle. In addition, everyday operating expenses include the cost of fuel, tolls, parking, and maintenance.

AFTER COMPLETING THIS CHAPTER, THE STUDENT MUST UNDERSTAND ALL THE FACTORS INVOLVED IN AND BE ABLE TO ACCEPT PERSONAL RESPONSIBILITY FOR:

- **deciding to buy and choosing a vehicle.**
- **arranging financing for the purchase.**
- **vehicle insurance (types and purposes for).**

Deciding to Buy

When you're young, "wheels" represent liberty. The freedom to go where you want, when you want. Later on, vehicles may become status symbols or extensions of your personality with glitter and gadgets added to the basic product to create your personal "dream machine". For the more practical minded, vehicles represent transportation, nothing more. The first step is to determine whether or not you are able to afford a vehicle.

Evaluate honestly how much of your budget is available to spend on the purchase, insurance and upkeep of a vehicle. Will you have to work extra hours to pay for it? If you are a student and you intend to pay for the vehicle yourself, these extra hours will be lost from your studies and other activities. Can you afford the time?

TRANSPORTATION NEEDS

Do you need transportation for work, school, weekday and weekend activities? Is public transportation readily available at a reasonable cost? If you live in a city core, you may find a vehicle to be more of a bother than a convenience since parking can be hard to find and expensive. Public transit, taxis or biking may provide adequate alternatives. The occasional rental of a vehicle can cover special requirements.

Will you transport other people and equipment regularly? A good way to establish your needs is to keep track of your transportation usage over a three to four week period. Keep a record. Is a family vehicle at your disposal? Include these trips on your list. Will the time saved balance the cost of owning your own vehicle? Remember, a personal vehicle that is not in use, still costs you money in terms of depreciation and insurance.

A mature evaluation of these needs will determine if purchasing a vehicle is really necessary and economically feasible.

Choosing a Vehicle

People are increasingly conscious of the need for quality in the vehicles they choose to drive. Quality of construction, corrosion protection, warranty protection, emission standards, and good mileage are important items to consider. You must also take into account the maintenance schedule, repairs, and the availability and cost of replacement parts. At today's prices, there is good reason for hoping you can keep your vehicle a long time.

17

From your transportation study, you can determine what kind of vehicle you will need to purchase. How many passengers did you usually have? What were their ages? How much baggage and equipment did you transport regularly? Will you need a two-door or a four-door vehicle?

TYPES OF VEHICLES

There are several categories of vehicles to choose from:

SUBCOMPACTS - small, easy to maneuver, economical to operate. Seating for two adults and limited trunk area. Good for short distances and light loads.

COMPACTS - good mileage, easy to handle. Seating for four adults for short periods of time. Limited trunk space.

INTERMEDIATES - more expensive to operate with seating for five or six adults comfortably. Perform well in city and highway environments. Larger trunk space.

FULL-SIZED - the largest models. Power and comfort for trips, loads and large families. More compact and fuel efficient than in previous years.

SPORTY MODELS - personality vehicles with performance and luxury features. Most expensive to purchase, operate, maintain and insure. Generally, seating for two adults.

TRUCKS, VANS, JEEPS, RV VEHICLES - Specialty vehicles that are expensive to operate, maintain, insure, and repair.

VEHICLE PERFORMANCE RECORD

You should consult consumer information magazines or services in your area before making your choice. The "track record" for repairs, service, costs of operation, fuel mileage and safety as well as the suggested retail price can all be verified from these sources.

SAFETY EQUIPMENT

Safety is a prime consideration in deciding what to buy. Larger vehicles are safer though more expensive to operate. Is the vehicle equipped with air bags? How did this vehicle perform in crash test and accident studies? Does the vehicle have an ABS brake system? What is the advertised braking distance?

SAFETY FEATURES
Seat belts and air bags

You may spend a lot of time in your vehicle, so try it out. Perform the "cockpit drill". Make sure the seats, controls, and instrumentation are suitable or adjustable to suit you. Take it for a test drive. Can you check the blind spots easily? Are all the controls within easy reach? Do the seats support you comfortably? Check the road-handling and maneuverability; try parallel parking.

As you can see, there are many factors to consider when deciding to buy a vehicle. Do not rush into this purchase. Think carefully. Do your research. You will own this vehicle for some time, make sure your choice is a mature one.

NEW OR USED VEHICLES

Once you have given careful thought to the kind of vehicle you will purchase, the next step is to consider whether to buy a new or used one. A new vehicle costs more than a comparable used model; however, warranties and guaranties usually mean the new model will cost less

in maintenance. If properly maintained, it will last longer. The used model has a lower purchase price, lower depreciation per year and lower insurance cost.

BUYING A NEW VEHICLE

With the make, model and options already chosen, you must find a reputable, reliable and, if possible, conveniently located dealer. This will permit you to receive competent and courteous service at the time of purchase, during the warranty period and when routine maintenance is required. Check local consumer groups and/or ask people that you know for suggestions.

Visit a local showroom. Check out and test drive the vehicle as mentioned earlier. Get quotes on the model and the desired options. Don't be pressured into buying a vehicle in stock with extras if a base model is sufficient.

DEALER SHOWROOM

VEHICLE INFORMATION STICKER

If a low financing rate is offered, ask if you can have a rebate on the price if you pay cash. Ask to see an owner's manual and check required maintenance schedules and warranties thoroughly.

Leave the showroom and prepare to visit several others. Be prepared to negotiate the final price. The final price should be somewhere between dealer cost and the suggested (sticker) retail price. Keep in mind that you can often get a good deal at the end of the month or the end of the model year. After several quotes, negotiate the best possible price.

BUYING A USED VEHICLE

Shopping for a used vehicle can provide good service for less money, but it is a little more complicated. You can buy a used model from a dealership, a used-car dealer or a private owner. The dealers offer a warranty for a limited amount of

time which is not the case with a private owner, where the price is usually lower. The price of used vehicles will vary depending on the model year, wear and tear, mileage and general condition.

USED VEHICLE
SUGGESTED RETAIL PRICE

Check the "Blue or Red Book" (dealers, banks and insurance agents) as well as the local papers for the usual price range.

Check the vehicle thoroughly for all of the following items:

- The body- new paint may indicate rust or a collision. Bubbles or ripples suggest rust underneath.

- The tires- uneven wear signals steering or suspension problems. Worn tires including the spare, are a future

CHECKING UNDER THE HOOD

- The engine- start it and listen for any unusual operating noises. Check all of the fluid levels, the belts, the hoses and service stickers. Check the color of the exhaust gas- blue signals major engine problems and black-grey indicates a fuel system problem.

- The control pedals- excessive wear may indicate stop and go driving (urban) or very high mileage.

- The controls and accessories- make sure they are all functioning properly.

- The doors and windows- should operate easily without squeaking and close tightly.

- The transmission- should engage smoothly without lurching or clunking.

Test drive the vehicle. It should continue straight (on level ground) when you release the steering. The brakes should work effectively (without pulling to the side) with normal pressure and the pedal should feel firm. The steering should not show any signs of looseness or shimmy.

If the vehicle passes this preliminary inspection, have the vehicle tested at a reputable diagnostic center or by your own trusted mechanic. A list of necessary repairs and their cost can then be added to or negotiated into the sale price. You will then be in a position to make an informed decision on the purchase.

Usually, you can expect an extra thousand dollars in repairs in the first year of ownership of a used vehicle.

Financing your Purchase

The least expensive way to buy a vehicle is with cash. You might put a fixed amount of money aside each month in a special savings account until you have accumulated the desired amount. For most people, some type of financing has to be arranged to buy a new or late-model vehicle. This can be obtained from banks, savings and loan associations, credit unions, finance companies, and often from the vehicle dealership.

You cannot finance the total purchase price; the limit is usually 80 percent- 20 percent is your minimum down payment. The larger the down payment, the less that needs to be financed; therefore, your purchase will cost you less. The lender will usually require collateral (something of value to secure the loan) in case the loan is not repaid. If the vehicle is offered as collateral, the lender retains the certificate of title until the loan is paid in full.

If you are a full-time student, the lender will require a responsible adult to co-sign the loan. Young adults without a sufficient credit rating may also need someone else to co-sign.

Shop around for your loan; interest and other charges vary. Get a written statement of the interest rate and other charges as well as the amount of your monthly payments and the length of the loan. Find out if it can be repaid without any penalty charges. Remember the higher the rate, the more you borrow and the longer it takes to repay are all factors that increase the total cost of the loan.

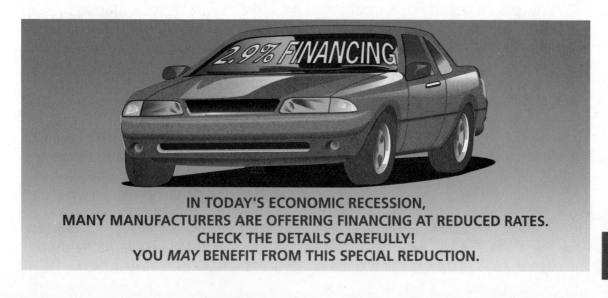

IN TODAY'S ECONOMIC RECESSION, MANY MANUFACTURERS ARE OFFERING FINANCING AT REDUCED RATES. CHECK THE DETAILS CAREFULLY! YOU *MAY* BENEFIT FROM THIS SPECIAL REDUCTION.

17

Insuring your Vehicle

All states require proof that an owner is capable of paying in case he/she injures a person or damages property in a collision. Some states permit the proprietor to put up a deposit of cash, a bond, or stocks of a fixed amount. Most drivers carry auto insurance. They pay a premium, or fee, to provide protection from financial losses which may arise from a collision or mishap in which they are involved. The insurance company issues a policy, or written contract, and a proof of insurance to the individual indicating how much and under what circumstances it will pay.

Enquire about the insurance required by your state financial responsibility laws.

WHERE TO ACQUIRE INSURANCE

There are several sources:

- Directly from an insurance company
- Agents who represent one company
- Agents who represent two or more companies
- Brokers who do business with many companies
- Auto clubs which may also issue insurance
- Employers, unions or fraternal organizations offering group plans

Whatever your choice, deal with someone who takes the time to answer your questions, who is willing to point out alternatives in coverage and explain the differences between them, and who has a good track record in the settlement of claims. Again you must shop around, ask friends and relatives, and check with consumer groups.

KINDS OF INSURANCE COVERAGE

Vehicle insurance is available in many forms to cover the possible situations that may arise.

LIABILITY INSURANCE, or responsibility insurance, protects you against any claims that may arise when you are held responsible for a mishap or collision. It comes in two forms: bodily injury liability (injuries to other people whether pedestrians or passengers) and property damage liability (repairing or replacing other people's property including public property). Both of these will also pay legal fees, court costs and lost wages up to the maximum of your insurance coverage. The minimum state requirements are insufficient as you will be held personally responsible for any claims that exceed your policy coverage.

COLLISION INSURANCE pays for repair or replacement of your vehicle, regardless of whether you are at fault, involved in a collision with an uninsured driver or the victim of a hit and run. (Uninsured motorist insurance is more complete coverage including your bodily injury) Because of the increasing cost of this

17

coverage, most insurance companies offer a deductible policy (the insured is required to pay the first $50 to $500). The higher this deductible; the lower the insurance premium will be.

COMPREHENSIVE INSURANCE protects you from losses due to vandalism, theft, fire, floods, or windstorms. Once again, a deductible affects the cost of this coverage.

MEDICAL PAYMENT INSURANCE is a specific policy covering medical, hospital, or funeral costs. It covers you, your passengers and your family in case of collisions causing injury or death.

NO FAULT INSURANCE has been adopted in many states. In this plan, you and your passengers receive payment for your adjusted claims directly from your own company regardless who is responsible. The advantages are faster settlement of claims and lower cost of insurance. This does not, however, prevent injured parties from suing for damages.

TOWING INSURANCE covers the cost of on-road repairs and the cost of having your vehicle towed.

Insurance is not a simple matter. Since each person's situation is unique, this means that you must arrange your coverage to meet your individual needs.

THE COST OF INSURANCE

Insurance companies use statistics to determine the cost of their insurance premiums. The following factors are also used in determining the cost:

- YOUR AGE- rates change as you get older. The youngest drivers pay the highest premiums.

- DRIVING RECORD- traffic violations, collisions, previous claims, etc. will increase your rates

- VEHICLE USAGE- if you drive to work, car pool, or use you vehicle for pleasure only; your premium will reduce accordingly. Higher mileage means higher rates.

- MARITAL STATUS- married persons pay lower premiums.

- GENDER- women drive less often and shorter distances than men and have fewer collisions. They therefore pay lower rates.

- YOUR VEHICLE- the more expensive the vehicle; the higher the premium will be. Sports models also cost more to insure.

- YOUR RESIDENCE- people residing in high density population areas pay higher rates.

- SPECIAL DISCOUNTS- some insurance companies offer discounts for air-bags, brake systems (ABS), alarm systems, having completed a driver education program, etc.

Despite the relative high cost of insurance coverage, make sure that you have adequate protection before driving your vehicle in the HTS.

17

Review

TERMS TO REMEMBER - WRITE A SHORT DEFINITION FOR EACH OF THE FOLLOWING :

- Status symbol
- Budget
- Rental
- Depreciation
- Warranty

- Consumer groups
- Test drive
- Vehicle options
- Diagnostic center
- Financing

- Interest
- Collateral
- Insurance premium
- Insurance policy
- Insurance claims

SUMMARY

Buying a vehicle is a major decision that requires serious consideration. Finances, transportation needs, the type of vehicle and the operating costs are all factors. Safety features should also be a major consideration. Take the time to examine all the details carefully as you will own the vehicle for a long time.

TEST A- ANSWER THE FOLLOWING QUESTIONS.

1. A) What are the different types of vehicles available on the market?
   B) What are the advantages and disadvantages of each of these?

2. A) How should you proceed to purchase a new vehicle?
   B) What are the steps in purchasing a used vehicle?

3. A) What sources are available to finance a vehicle?
   B) What should you check before deciding?

4. What should you check before deciding on your insurance coverage?

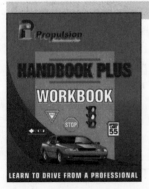

HANDBOOK PLUS WORKBOOK

*Check your comprehension and mastery of the contents of this chapter by completing the corresponding exercise that is found in the complement to the **HANDBOOK PLUS**:*

HANDBOOK PLUS WORKBOOK

Complete the exercise on Page 105 then check your responses by referring to the answer key on Page 109.
If necessary, review the chapter for each error and refer to your instructor for further guidance.

18

18 - A
Choosing
a Safe Route

18 - B
Preparing
the Vehicle

18 - C
Preparing
Yourself

18 - D
Planning
the Route

18- E
Review

Planning a Trip

One of the prime reasons for purchasing a vehicle is the freedom to drive where you want when you want. The ability to set your own timetable and to set out at a moments notice. The problem is that travelling on a trip, whether 20 miles or 500 miles, requires some special preparation.

The pre-driving checks and regular verifications that you perform assure the normal operation of your vehicle. High speed driving puts extra stress on all of the mechanical systems. The last thing you would want is a breakdown when you are far from home and at the mercy of unknown service technicians. Prepare your vehicle.

Extended high speed driving is also more stressful for the driver. Proper planning and foresight will avoid uncertainty and an unpleasant experience. Prepare yourself.

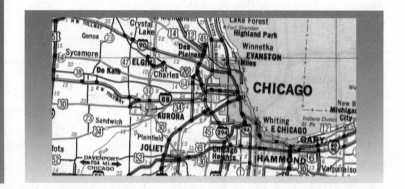

AFTER COMPLETING THIS CHAPTER, THE STUDENT MUST BE ABLE TO UNDERSTAND AND APPLY DESTINATION DRIVING TECHNIQUES WITH RESPECT TO:

- **the selection of a safe route.**
- **the preparation of the vehicle and him/her self.**
- **planning the trip.**

Choosing a Safe Route

Whenever you plan to drive a vehicle, you must consider where you are going and the safest possible route to use. A route that will present the least number of potential hazards thereby reducing the risk of a mis-adventure or having to cope with an unforeseen emergency situation.

Always work out the route in advance (use a map); planning the most direct route with the fewest maneuvers will usually diminish the risk. Take into account rush hour traffic, available freeways, one-way streets and problems associated with driving in an urban area. Listen to radio stations that broadcast road and weather reports.

Calculate the length of the trip in miles and calculate the average speed you can expect to travel on the type of roads that you have selected. How long should it take you to reach your destination if there are no unforeseen occurrences. Leave yourself sufficient time (with an extra margin) to reach your destination.

THROUGH STREETS VS. SIDE STREETS

In the city, engineers have designed major arteries to handle a larger volume of traffic. With this in mind, the streets are wider and usually have reserved lanes for left turns. Traffic signal lights control the major intersections. Though traffic is heavier, these streets are safer than side streets which are quieter but may present unforeseen hazards at any time.

Intersections on side streets are usually controlled by stop or yield signs and uncontrolled intersections may can be even riskier to cross.. The presence of parked vehicles may block your vision at the intersection and, at times, may make it difficult to recognize the intersection.

Side streets are residential areas and numerous other road users may be present. Children at play may enter the roadway, vehicles may back into the road, anyone of a myriad of road users may confront your path of travel.

ONE-WAY STREETS VS. TWO-WAY STREETS

One-way streets usually present less of a risk than two-way streets simply because of the absence of oncoming traffic that may turn across or swerve into your path of travel. The space available for traffic is also wider than on most two-way roads.

Traffic control devices on these streets are designed to regulate the flow of traffic. Though you must expect that some road users may not obey them (expect the unexpected), you are usually less at risk in a regulated environment. Manage space and select lane positions that require a minimum of adjustments (the lane of least resistance) and one-way streets can be a good choice.

FREEWAYS

Depending on the time of day and the density of the traffic on a particular freeway as well as the length of the journey planned, the controlled environment can offer less risk when utilized properly. Manage the entrance properly, drive in the correct lane while controlling space and then exit properly. This will permit you to use a freeway to get to your destination, possibly a little quicker, in complete safety.

PERSONAL CHOICE

Some drivers will choose to drive on a freeway whenever one is available; others avoid the freeway environment like the plaque.

Though you should be competent in all driving environments, you may feel more comfortable (and thus drive more at ease) on one type of road over another. This should also be a factor taken into consideration in your choice of a safe route to your destination.

Preparing the Vehicle

Your vehicle should always be in proper condition. Checks should be performed every time you drive. (See Chapter 6 - Preliminaries and Chapter 7 - Starting the Engine)

On a short trip, 50 miles or less, these will normally ensure a trouble-free excursion. However, before a longer journey, take the vehicle to your service station to be checked and serviced more completely.

This should include the following:
- Brakes- condition / adjustment
- Tires- condition / inflation (the spare)
- Fluid levels- battery, cooling system, power steering, brake fluid,engine , transmission,and differential
- Belts and hoses
- Front-end- steering and alignment
- Shock absorbers
- Exhaust system
- Lights and electrical system

When leaving, make sure that the fuel tank and windshield washer reservoir are full and you have plenty of windshield washer fluid in reserve. Check your emergency supplies and tool kit. (Chapter 13 - Adverse Conditions) Make sure that you have an extra set of keys on you at all times.

LOADING YOUR VEHICLE

Check the owner's manual for maximum load and recommended tire pressure; adjust the pressure to the specifications. Pack luggage carefully to distribute the weight as evenly as possible. Make sure the load is secure so that it will not move under hard braking or sudden maneuvers. (This is especially important in vans and hatchbacks as luggage is stored in the passenger compartment). Don't block your view to the rear or to the blind spots. Heavy articles should be at the bottom; emergency equipment and spare should be accessible.

Only light luggage should be stored in a car-top carrier and secured using straps. Check the tightness of these after one-half hour and again every time you stop. Be aware that the center of gravity/wind resistance of the vehicle changes with a roof-top carrier and adjust your driving.

TOWING A TRAILER

Towing requires major adjustments by the driver. Quick swerving maneuvers are not possible; stopping distances are increased. Acceleration is slower. Passing maneuvers take longer and need more space. Adjust following distance to a minimum of 4 seconds and scan further ahead. Control speed on downhills and assist the transmission on grades by shifting to the appropriate gear. Practice

reversing with an empty trailer until you are confident in your ability to park.

To tow a trailer consistently, the vehicle requires a tow package. (Suspension, shocks, radiator, differential, etc.) Check the engine oil and transmission fluid frequently. Use an appropriate trailer hitch and attach the safety chains. Install special side-view mirrors and a hook-up for the trailer lights. You may need extra emergency equipment for breakdowns. Check the trailer manual for additional information and the vehicle manual for the maximum towing load.

When packing, load heavy items at the bottom over the axle. Distribute the weight evenly from side to side and secure the load firmly. Check the trailer and vehicle are level when finished. After one-half hour of driving, stop and check the hitch connections, straps, etc. Repeat this verification each time you stop.

Preparing Yourself

Get plenty of rest prior to the journey. Plan your route and rest stops. Avoid rush hour and congested roadways. Be certain to bring extra money or credit cards to cover unforeseen expenses.

Never start out at the time when you would go to sleep. Your alertness is at it lowest at this time. If, while driving, you find yourself becoming fatigued, stop

and rest or change drivers. On long trips, travel with at least one companion who has a valid license and split the driving. Every two hours stop for a break. Make sure you have all necessary documents in a safe and easily accessible place. If you take medication, take along sufficient medicine to last the trip. Make sure your vehicle insurance and medical coverage is proper to the area you will be visiting.

Planning the Route

On short trips, work out the route in advance especially when traveling to places you have not driven to previously. Take into account rush hour traffic. Use a map to locate the route, highways, streets, etc. that you must use.

Contact road information services to verify the route you have chosen; have alternate routes already planned, just in case something unexpected develops. While driving, listen to a local radio station that carries road and weather reports. Leave yourself plenty of time for the journey.

For longer trips, consult your local auto club or tourist agency. They can supply maps (strip maps) as well as assist you to plan a route that will permit visiting interesting areas along the way, scenic routes or the shortest, quickest possible trip. Recommended service stations and hotels can also be supplied.

Plan your schedule with rest stops and overnight accommodations in advance. Reserve your facilities ahead of time; make sure you ask about rates and the availability of parking. If you are going to be late, call ahead and cancel if necessary. Don't speed up to make up for lost time or stay on the road longer as this will put you and your passengers in danger. Allow extra time for unexpected stops or delays. Calculate your budget for the entire journey and add an extra amount for unforeseen expenses.

Acquire the necessary maps that will direct you all the way to your destination. Familiarize yourself with these road maps. Get to know the legend (the map key that explains the symbols) that appears as an insert on the map. Study the distance scale and work out the distances to be traveled daily.

When travelling alone, never try to check a road map while driving; pull off the roadway to a rest area or onto the shoulder when this can be done safely.

While on the road, try to start out early each day, eat lightly to avoid drowsiness and allow time to stretch your legs at each stop. Keep your radio tuned to local stations that transmit regular road and weather bulletins (these are often posted on roadside signs). Often they will warn of unforeseen circumstances that you may be able to avoid by a slight detour.

An unplanned scenic stop to avoid being caught in rush hour traffic may get you to your final destination at about the same time without the aggravation. Keep alert. Adapt the SIPDE system to your driving environment and you will enjoy your journey without any mishaps.

Review

TERMS TO REMEMBER - WRITE A SHORT DEFINITION FOR EACH OF THE FOLLOWING :

- Maximum load
- Tire load
- Trailer
- Tow package

- Trailer hitch
- Safety chain
- Trailer axle
- Roof top carrier

- Auto club
- Map insert
- Map legend
- Map scale

SUMMARY

Choosing a safe route, even on short urban trips, will save frustration as well as diminish the risk. Planning a trip requires preparation to ensure an enjoyable, trouble-free journey.

Your vehicle, how to transport baggage, choosing the route, rest periods or alternate drivers, the finances, as well as the number of hours of driving must be considered carefully.

USING ROAD MAPS IS A BASIC SKILL THAT YOU SHOULD MASTER. ACQUIRE A LOCAL AND STATE ROAD MAP AND COMPLETE THESE EXERCISES.

A) On the local map, locate where you live. Determine the map co-ordinates for your home. (Map co-ordinates are located on two sides of the map. One side uses numbers and the other uses letters.) Place your finger on where you live and then move across the map horizontally to locate the letter co-ordinate. Repeat moving vertically to find the number. Put these two together (example D4) and these are the map co-ordinates for your home. Repeat this exercise for your school, the city hall and the local court house.

B) Find the map scale. (This informs you of distance in miles as related to this particular map) Measure the distance, using a ruler, as the "crow flies" from your home to the city hall. That is a straight line measurement. Compare this distance to the scale and convert it to miles.
How far is it? Repeat for your school and the local court house.

C) Plan the route that you would use to get from your home to school, the city hall and the court house. Be careful to include the possibility of one-way streets, recent construction, as well as the safest route possible. Notice that the driving distance is much longer than your previous measurement.
Calculate the amount of time required for this route. Allow for the speed limit and some extra time for unforeseen delays.

D) On the state map, find your community on the map index. It is listed alphabetically. Beside the name, you will find the map co-ordinates for your community. Locate your community on the map. Choose another community where a friend or relative lives outside your local area. Look it up on the index and locate it on the map. Are the names written in the same size type? The larger the type , the greater the population. Are the symbols used the same? Check the map insert for the legend as to the meaning of the different symbols.

E) Measure the distance between these two communities as the "crow flies" using the map scale. Check the map mileage chart. If both are listed, the driving distance will be listed.

F) Plan a route to travel from your home to the other community. Follow this route on the map. As you move from one place to another, the distance in miles will be printed over the roadway. Mark them down. When you reach your destination, add them up. This is your travelling distance. How long should this trip take?

G) As you move along your route, notice that all roadways do not have the same symbols. Check the legend to find the meaning of the different symbols. List the roads that you will use to travel to the other community. What speed limits will be posted on these roadways? What type of traffic can you expect? Plan rest stops.

H) As a class project, choose an out-of-state city or town. Plan a trip to this locale. Visit a local auto club to obtain a strip map to that location. Create a budget to travel and visit including overnight stops, gas, food, etc. Plan the route. Include some sight-seeing and the necessary rest stops. Compare notes.

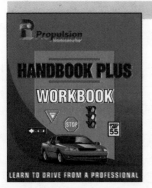

HANDBOOK PLUS WORKBOOK

*Check your comprehension and mastery of the contents of this chapter by completing the corresponding exercise that is found in the complement to the **HANDBOOK PLUS**:*

HANDBOOK PLUS WORKBOOK

Complete the exercise on Page 106 then check your responses by referring to the answer key on Page 109.
If necessary, review the chapter for each error and refer to your instructor for further guidance.

Student notes

_____
_____
_____
_____
_____
_____
_____
_____
_____
_____
_____
_____
_____
_____
_____
_____
_____
_____
_____
_____
_____
_____

# Glossary

ABS An anti-lock computerized brake system.

Absolute speed limit The maximum or minimum posted speed.

Acceleration Increase in speed.

Acceleration lane A highway merging lane to allow drivers to increase speed to blend with traffic.

Accelerator The pedal that controls the volume of air-fuel mixture entering the engine.

Administrative laws Laws that regulate licenses, vehicle registration, financial responsibility, vehicle standards and the general operation of the HTS.

Air bag A passive restraint device that inflates with air to cushion the occupants in the event of collision.

Alternator A device to produce electricity, when the engine is operating, to run electrical units and recharge the battery.

Antifreeze A chemical mixed with water to prevent freezing and corrosion in the cooling system.

Atmospheric conditions Weather and light conditions that affect your ability to see and drive.

Automatic transmission A system that shifts through the forward gears as the vehicle speed increases.

Axle The shaft connecting two opposite wheels on a vehicle.

BAC (blood alcohol concentration) The percentage of alcohol in a person's blood.

Back-up lights The white lights on the rear of a vehicle that are illuminated when the transmission is placed in reverse.

Banked curve The roadway slopes down toward the inside of the curve to help overcome inertia.

Basic speed limit The speed, below the absolute limit, that is adequate to the existing conditions.

Battery A unit that stores electricity in chemical form to permit starting your vehicle.

Bias-ply tires Tires with cord layers criss crossing under the exterior material.

Blind spots Areas outside the vehicle that are neither visible in the driver's forward field of vision nor in the rear-view mirrors.

Blow out A rapid loss of air pressure in a tire.

Blue book A price guide (red, black or blue) to the average value of used vehicles.

Brake fade A temporary brake failure due to overheating of the brake pads or shoes caused by hard continuous braking.

Brake pedal A foot control enabling the driver to reduce the vehicle speed.

Brake system An hydraulic and mechanical system to slow or stop a moving vehicle.

Braking distance The distance a vehicle travels from the time the driver applies the brake until it stops.

Carbon monoxide A colorless, odorless, tasteless and toxic gas produced as a byproduct of combustion.

Carburetor Mixes the fuel and air in the correct proportion to supply the engine.

Catalytic converter Reduces harmful exhaust emissions by means of a chemical reaction.

Center of gravity The point around which the weight of the vehicle is balanced.

Choke A device that restricts air flow and raises the idle speed when the engine is cold.

Clutch A driver operated mechanical device that permits dis-engaging the engine from the transmission (to shift or stop).

Collateral An object of value presented as security for a loan.

Collision A crash between any two objects.

Collision insurance Protection against damage to one's own vehicle in a crash.

Color perception Ability to distinguish color.

Comprehensive insurance Protection against damage or loss due to theft, vandalism, storms, or fire.

Compromising hazards Low risk involvement with a less serious hazard to avoid involvement with a more serious one.

Controlled intersection A regulated cross-road - signal lights, yield or stop signs.

Cooling system A system to remove excess heat and maintain engine operating temperature.

Countersteering Returning the steering wheel in the opposite direction after an initial steering motion.

Crankshaft The shaft that is turned by the piston movements and transmits power to the drive train.

Crosswalk A path marked on and crossing the roadway to guide pedestrians.

Crowned road A road that is higher in the middle than at the two sides.

C.V. Joint A connection in the drive shaft that permits drive angle changes (steering/suspension).

Cylinders Bored holes in the block that house the pistons.

Dashboard An illuminated panel with gauges, lights, and indicators that inform the driver.

Deceleration lane An extra lane at exits to allow drivers exiting the highway to reduce speed.

Deductible The sum the insured must pay before the insurance company pays in the event of a claim.

Defogger Electric wires to heat and clear the rear window.

Demerit point system A system to keep track of traffic violations by individual drivers and penalize them when they reach predetermined limits.

Depreciation The value a vehicle loses due to age and wear and tear.

Depth perception The three dimensional perception of distance.

Detour A deviation from the normal route due to construction.

Diagonal parking Parking spaces arranged at an angle to the curb or other boundary.

Differential A gear system that transmits rotation to the wheels while permitting them to turn at different speeds.

Dimmer switch A switch to select high or low beam headlights.

Disc brakes Brake units that slow/stop wheel rotation by squeezing a rotating disc.

Distributor An electrical unit controlling production/distribution of electrical surges to the spark plugs.

Downshift To manually shift from a higher gear to a lower gear.

Drive Belt A cogged, grooved or V belt that transmits rotation to other components.

Drive train The components that transfer the engine power to the drive wheels.

Drive wheels The wheels that receive the engine power to move the vehicle.

Driving while intoxicated (DWI) Operating a vehicle while the blood alcohol concentration (BAC) is above the legal limit.

Drum brakes Brake units that slow/stop wheel rotation by rubbing curved shoes (pads) against a drum.

Edge lines White lines painted on the pavement marking the limit of the roadway.

Electrical system A system to supply all the electrical needs of the vehicle.

Emergency brake The parking brake system.

Emergency flashers The hazard lights that activate all four turn signals at once to warn of danger or breakdown.

Emergency vehicle A police vehicle, fire department vehicle, ambulance, etc. which must be given the right-of-way by all road users when the siren or flashing lights are activated.

Entrance ramp A roadway leading to a freeway.

Exhaust manifold A collector pipe with passages through which exhaust gases leave the engine combustion chambers and enter the exhaust piping system.

Exhaust system Collects the burned gases from each cylinder, directs the harmful gases and heat through pipes and releases them behind the vehicle.

Exit ramp A roadway leaving a freeway.

Expressway A controlled-access, divided highway with more than one lane in each direction intended for high speed driving (freeway).

Fan belt A flexible rubber band driven by the crankshaft that powers the water pump and the alternator.

Fatigue Temporary physical or mental exhaustion due to lack of rest or sleep.

Field of vision The area that the eyes can perceive without moving the eyes or head; approximately 180 degrees.

Financial responsibility laws A law requiring proof of the ability to pay damages resulting from collisions before issuing registration/plates for a vehicle.

First aid Emergency treatment given to an injured person before medical professionals arrive.

Flywheel A metal disc attached to the crankshaft to balance engine rotation, transmit power to the drive train and is turned by the starter motor to crank the engine.

Following distance The space that a driver maintains from the preceding vehicle.

Force of impact The energy with which a moving vehicle collides with another object.

Friction The resistance to motion between two objects in contact.

Friction point The clutch position when the engine power begins to move the transmission.

Fuel system The system that stores fuel and supplies the correct fuel-air mixture to operate the engine.

Fuse A device designed to open a circuit when the current is excessive, to protect equipment in the circuit. A "burned" fuse must be replaced.

Gear A toothed wheel that meshes with others of varying sizes to transmit (the same, increased or decreased) rotation thus increasing speed/power.

Gear selector lever The driver control that permits choosing a gear on an automatic transmission.

Gearshift lever The driver control that permits choosing a gear position on a standard transmission.

Glow Plug A unit to preheat the combustion chamber on diesel engines.

Gravity The force that pulls objects toward the center of the earth.

Ground viewing habit Scanning near the pavement to determine the position of other vehicle's wheels and to notice any signs of movement that forewarn of potential vehicle movement.

Guide signs Signs that inform about location, services, or points of interest.

Hallucinogen A drug that affects the senses and distorts vision and perception.

Hand-over-hand steering A technique to turn the steering by crossing one hand over the other.

Hand signals Arm motions that warn others of your intention to slow, stop or turn.

Hazard lights A signaling device that activates all four turn signals to warn of danger or breakdowns.

Headlights White lights mounted on the front of the vehicle that should be illuminated when driving.

Headrest A restraint device attached to the top of the seat back to cushion the head in collisions.

High beams Brighter white lights on the front of the vehicle to see further than low beams.

Highway hypnosis Reduced attention to the driving task caused by long periods of high speed driving.

Hydraulic pressure Pressure exerted on a fluid is transmitted by the fluid.

Hydroplaning A layer of water between the tires and the road eliminating traction.

Idle The engine speed when operating without any pressure on the accelerator.

Ignition switch The switch to activate the electrical systems and start the engine.

Ignition system The electrical components that produce, control and distribute the spark that initiates combustion.

Implied consent law A legal requirement that all drivers submit to a blood alcohol concentration test when requested.

Inertia The tendency of an object in motion to stay in motion in a straight line and for an object at rest to remain at rest.

International signs Symbolic road signs used in many countries.

Intersection When two or more highways meet.

In-vehicle exam The DMV practical driving test.

Jaywalking The pedestrian practice of crossing a roadway without regard for rules or signals.

Jump starting Using another vehicle to boost a "dead" battery.

Junction See intersection

Kinetic energy The energy of motion.

Knowledge test A test on signs, signals, road markings and rules of the road at the DMV to acquire an instruction permit. (Written test)

Lane use signals Lights mounted above lanes to control the flow and direction of traffic.

Legend Key explaining the symbols and markings used on a map.

Liability insurance Protection from financial loss due to a collision when the insured party is responsible.

Low beams The normal headlight setting.

Lubrication system The components that supply oil to the moving parts to prevent damage/overheating.

Maintenance The checkups, service and repairs required to keep a vehicle in proper operating condition.

Margin of safety See safety cushion

Master cylinder Brake system unit where the fluid is stored and pressurized to activate the brakes.

Median strip A width of space that separates opposing lanes of traffic.

Medical payments insurance Insurance that covers the cost of hospitalization and treatments for injuries incurred during a collision.

Merging The gradual blending of traffic.

Minimizing hazards Reducing the risk of a collision from a hazard by adjusting speed, lane position or both.

Muffler Exhaust system device to minimize noise.

Multilane A road with two or more lanes in each direction.

Neutral A position in which the gears are not engaged and cannot transmit power.

Night vision The ability to see clearly, judge depth perception and recover from glare in the dark.

No fault insurance Insurance that pays claims to the insured regardless of responsibility.

Odometer A device that indicates the total distance a vehicle has been driven.

Oil filter Device in the lubrication system that removes dirt and particles from the oil.

Oil pressure gauge Light/indicator shows the pressure at which the oil is circulating through the engine.

Oil pump A device that forces oil to the moving parts.

Overdrive A gear that permits the vehicle to cruise efficiently at high speed.

Overdriving your headlights Driving at such a high speed at night that you would be unable to stop in the distance illuminated by the headlights.

Owner's manual Manufacturer's booklet providing detailed information about the vehicle, its operation and recommended maintenance.

Parking brake A mechanical unit that acts on the rear wheels to keep them from moving when parked. Also used to slow /stop if the hydraulic brake system fails.

Passive restraints Safety devices that act without requiring any action by the user. (Headrests, air bags, some safety belts)

Pedestrian An HTS user on foot.

Peripheral vision The portion of the field of vision outside the central conic vision of 3 degrees. Vision to the sides.

Perpendicular parking Parking at a 90° angle to the curb or boundary.

Piston A cylindrical-shaped component that moves up and down in the cylinders.

Power brakes A system that facilitates stopping the vehicle by increasing the pressure applied by the driver.

Power steering A system that facilitates steering by using hydraulic pressure supplied by a pump.

Power train The components that transmit the engine power to the drive wheels.

Premium The sum an individual pays the insurance company for insurance coverage - the policy fee.

Pumping the brake Applying pressure on the brake pedal, releasing the pressure sufficiently to allow the tires to roll and then re-applying the pressure.

Radial tires Tires with the plies straight across the tire parallel to each other encircled by a steel belt.

Radiator A heat exchange unit that stores and cools the engine coolant before it circulates in the engine.

Regulatory sign A sign that controls the flow of traffic at a given location.

Reverse A gear position that is used to back up.

Reversible lane A lane on which the direction of the traffic flow changes at specific times.

Revocation The cancellation of a driver's license for at least one year.

Right-of-way Traffic rules determine who should yield to other road users in given situations.

Risk The danger of involvement in a collision.

Road test See in-vehicle exam.

Safety belt A restraint device anchored to the vehicle designed to prevent occupants from striking the interior of the vehicle - seat belts.

Scanning The visual skill of searching the area around and ahead of the vehicle.

Separating hazards The technique of dealing with multiple hazards one at a time.

Shock absorbers Devices that limit and stop the bouncing action of the vehicle springs.

Shoulder The strip along the sides of a roadway, that may or may not be paved, intended for emergency usage only.

SIPDE system A five step driving strategy (scan, identify, predict, decide and execute) to process visual information and evade potential danger in an organized manner.

Space cushion A traffic free area around the vehicle that a driver should maintain to have room to maneuver.

Spark plug An ignition component that supplies the spark to initiate engine combustion.

Standard transmission A system in which the gears are shifted by the driver.

Stimulants Drugs that speed up the central nervous system.

Suspension The withdrawal of a driver's license for a period of 30 to 90 days due to traffic violations.

Suspension system The components that support the vehicle in a flexible manner absorbing road shocks.

Switchbacks Sharp turns on mountain roads, similar to a U-turn, that allow the road to climb a steep slope.

Tailgate Driving too closely behind another vehicle.

Temperature gauge An indicator light or gauge that indicates the engine operating temperature.

Thermostat A device that regulates engine temperature by controlling the flow of coolant to the radiator.

Threshold braking A braking technique in which the driver applies the brakes just short of locking up the wheels.

Title Legal proof of vehicle ownership - certificate of title.

Total stopping distance The total distance required to stop a vehicle.

Towing insurance Optional coverage that protects against the cost of on-the-road repairs and towing.

Traction The friction between the vehicle tires and the road surface.

Tread The raised pattern on the outer surface of a tire that contacts the road.

Tread wear indicator Bars that appear in tire treads when they are less than 1/16 of an inch deep.

Trip odometer An indicator that registers the mileage a vehicle since the last time it was reset to zero.

Turnabout A turning maneuver to travel in the opposite direction.

Turn signal Lights activated by the driver to warn of his/her intentions. Also hand signals.

Two second rule Technique for calculating and maintaining a minimum following distance under ideal driving conditions.

Uncontrolled intersection An intersection that has no signs or signals regulating it.

Uninsured motorist insurance Protection from financial loss due to a collision caused by a driver who does not have insurance coverage.

Universal joint Connectors that permit a change of angle while transmitting power - parts of the power train.

U-turn A turnabout (without reversing) maneuver performed by turning left.

Vapor lock Fuel vaporizes in the fuel lines and the fuel system cannot pump it into the carburetor or injectors.

Velocitization The improper sensation of vehicle speed. After high speed driving, the sensation of moving more slowly than the vehicle actually is.

Visual acuity The ability to see details up close and from afar.

Visual eye lead time The time and distance that vision precedes the vehicle.

Visual Tracking Aiming and steering in the desired path of travel of the vehicle.

Warning lights and gauges Dashboard indicators to inform the driver of the condition of the vehicle systems and warn when problems occur.

Warning signs Traffic signs that warn of danger ahead.

Warranty A written guaranty from the manufacturer to repair or replace defective components for a limited time or mileage.

Water pump A device that circulates the engine coolant under pressure.

Wheel alignment Mechanical adjustment of the steering components to vehicle specifications.

Yield To give another road user the right-of-way.

A

ABS, 10.6
Absolute speed limit, 2.4
Acceleration, 7.7 - 7.11
Acceleration lane, 12.12 - 12.14
Accelerator, 5.6, 7.2 - 7.3, 7.7, stuck , 14.2
Accessory position, 5.5
Administrative laws, 3.1 - 3.8
Adverse conditions, 13.1 - 13.20
Aging and driving, 4.2
Air bags, usage 11.3 - 11.4, 17.3
Air filter, 15.8 - 15.9
Alcohol, 4.5 - 4.7
Alternator, 15.7, gauge, 5.3, 15.7
Amber traffic signal, 2.22 - 2.23
Angle parking, see diagonal
Animals, 1.3, rural driving 12.10 insects in the vehicle 14.14,
Antifreeze, 13.16, 15.4 - 15.5
Antipollution devices, 15.10
APE system, 7.2
Assess, 7.2
Automatic transmission, 15.11 enter traffic 7.5 - 7.6, usage 5.7 - 5.8
Automobile insurance, proof of 3.3, types of 17.8 - 17.9

B

BAC, 4.6 - 4.7
Backup lights, 5.8
Banked curves, 9.6 - 9.7
Basic speed limit, 2.4, 3.4
Battery, 15.7, 15.12
Belts, 15.4 - 15.5, 15.7
Bicycles, 1.3 -1.4, 12.5
Blind spot, position of 6.5 - 6.6
Blind zone, 6.2
Blow out, 14.2
Blue book, 17.5
Boosting a vehicle, 15.12
Brake system, 16.7 - 16.9, failure 14.7, lights 5.3, pedal 5.6, winter 13.14
Braking, control 7.7 - 7.11, techniques 10.5, time, distance 10.2 - 10.4
Buses, 1.4 - 1.5
Buying a vehicle, 17.1 - 17.9

C

Carbon monoxide, 4.11, 12.3
Car loan, 17.7
Carburetor, 15.8 - 15.9
Catalytic converter, 15.10
Center of gravity, 9.4
Certificate of title, 3.3
Changing lanes, 12.4, expressway 12.13 passing 12.10 - 12.11,
Changing a tire, 16.4
Child restraints, 11.4 - 11.6
Choke, 15.9
Chronic illness, 4.4
City driving, 12.1
Clutch, component15.11, pedal 5.7, usage 7.9 - 7.11
Cockpit drill, 5.2, 6.5
Collateral, 17.7

Collision, avoid 3.7, force of 9.8, head-on 14.12, in case of 3.9, insurance 17.8, rear-end 14.12, restraint 11.2, side 14.12
Color perception, 4.11
Comfort system, 5.5
Communicating, 3.6, basic rules 12.2, horn 5.5, turn signal 5.5
Comprehensive insurance, 17.9
Compromise hazards, 8.6
Construction signs,2.2, 2.15
Controlled braking, 10.5
Coolant, 13.16, 15.4 - 15.5
Cooling system, 15.4 - 15.5, winter 13.16
Countersteering, off-road recovery 14.9, three point turns 12.16 - 12.18 skids 14.10 - 14.11
Crankcase, 15.5 - 15.6
Crowned road, 9.7
Curves, driving 9.6 - 9.7, signs 2.9

D

Danger zone, 8.5, 10.4
Dash lighting, 5.3, rheostat 5.4
Dead battery, 15.12
Deceleration, see braking
Deceleration lane, 12.14
Decide, 8.4
Deductible, 17.9
Defogger, 5.5
Demerit Point System, 3.4
Department of motor vehicles, 3.2
Depreciation, 17.4 - 17.5
Depressants, 4.4
Depth perception, 4.8 - 4.9
Deserts, 13.6
Diagonal parking, 12.19 - 12.20
Differential, 13.19, 15.11
Dimmer switch, 5.5
Disc brake, 16.7
Distributor, 15.7
Door locks, winter 13.16
Downshifting, 7.11, for hills 9.4, 13.4
Driver's license, 1.5, obtain 3.2 - 3.3
Driving while intoxicated, 3.6, 4.7
Drugs, 4.2 - 4.7

E

Electrical system, 15.7, winter 13.15 - 16
Electrical wires, 14.14
Emergency equipment, 13.16 - 13.17
Emergency vehicles, 1.5, 3.7 - 3.9, 14.13
Emotions, 4.5
Energy of motion, see Kinetic
Engine, 15.2 - 15.3
Entering traffic, diagonal park 12.20, perpendicular park 12.23, side of road 7.5 - 7.7
Entrance ramp, 12.12, 12.13 - 12.14
Evasive maneuvers, 14.12, 14.19
Execute, 7.2, 8.4
Exhaust system, 15.10
Exit ramp, 12.14
Exiting a vehicle, 7.15
Expressway, 12.1, 12.12 - 12.14

F

Fan belt, 15.4 - 15.5
Fatigue, 4.2 - 4.3
Field of vision,4.10
Financial responsibility, 3.3, 17.8 - 17.9
Fire, 14.8
Fluid levels, 15.3
Fog, 13.14 - 13.15
Following distance, factors 10.4
Force of impact, 9.8
Friction, 9.2 - 9.3
Friction point, entering traffic 7.7
Fuel gauge, 15.8 - 15.9
Fuel injection, 15.8
Fuel system, 15.8 - 15.9, gauge 5.3, winter 13.16

G

Gas pump, 15.9
Gauges, 5.2 - 5.3
Gears, 5.8 - 5.9
Gearshift, 5.9
Glare, dash 5.4 - 5.5, 13.10, 13.12 oncoming 13.14, protection 13.11, vehicles behind 13.12
Glow Plug, 7.2, 15.8
Gravel, 13.2, approach to 13.3, driving on 13.3 - 13.4
Gravity, 9.3 - 9.4
Guide signs, 2.2, 2.13 - 2.14

H

Hallucinogens, 4.4
Hand brake, see parking brake
Hand-over-hand steering, 7.4
Hand position on steering, 7.4
Hand signals, 2.26
Hazards, signs 2.8 - 2.12
Hazard lights, switch 5.3
Headlights, daytime 13.9, failure at night 14.3, switch 5.4 - 5.5
Head restraints, adjustment 6.4
Heating system, 5.4 - 5.5
High-beam indicator, 5.3 - 5.4
High-beam headlights 5.3, dim 13.13, night 13.10
Highways, signs 2.13
Highway transportation system (HTS), adapting 8.6, understanding 1.1 -1.4
Hills, 13.4, gravity 9.3 - 9.4, parking 12.25, signs 2.12 starting off 7.6 - 7.7
Hood, flies open 14.4
Hydroplaning, 13.7 - 13.8

I

Identify, 8.3
Ignition switch, 5.5, 15.7
Ignition system, 15.7 - 15.8
Implied consent law, 3.5
Inertia, 9.6 - 9.7
Information signs, 2.13 - 2.14
Instruction permit, 3.2 - 3.3
Instrument panel, 5.2 - 5.6
Insurance, 17.8 - 17.9
Interior lights, 13.10, 13.12
International signs, 2.16
Intersections, rules 3.7 - 3.9, signs 2.7, 2.11
In-vehicle test, 3.3

J

Jaywalking, 1.3
Jump starting a vehicle, 15.12
Junctions, see intersections

K

Kinetic energy, 9.5
Knowledge test, 3.2

L

Lane-use, freeways 12.13
    lines 2.17 - 2.20 , reduction signs 2.10,
    signs 2.5, 2.10, signals 2.24
Laws of physics, 9.1 - 9.8
Leaving traffic, 7.13 - 7.14
Left turn, lanes 2.18 - 2.20
Liability insurance, 17.8
License plates, 3.2
Locks, doors 6.3, service 16.10
Lubrication system, 15.5 - 15.6

M

MADD, 4.8
Maintenance, 15.4 - 15.10, 16.4 - 16.10
Medical payment insurance, 17.9
Mental condition, 4.2 - 4.3
Minimize hazards, 8.6
Mirrors, adjustment 6.5, glare 13.12
Momentum, see Kinetic energy
Motorcycles, 1.4, 12.5
Mountains, 13.5
Muffler, 15.10

N

Natural laws, see laws of physics
Neutral gear, 5.8 - 5.9
Night driving, 13.10 - 13.14
No-fault insurance, 17.9

O

Obstacles, avoiding 14.9, signs 2.11
Odometer, 5.3
Off-road recovery, 14.9
Oil, 15.5 - 15.6
Oil pressure gauge, 5.3, 15.5 - 15.6
One-way streets, signs 2.4
Overdriving your headlights, 13.11
Overheating, 14.6
Over-the-counter drugs, 4.3 - 4.4

P

Panic, 14.1 - 14.2
Parking, diag. 12.1, parallel 12.23 - 25,
    perpendicular 12.21 - 12.23
    markings 2.21, on hill 12.25, signs 2.6
Parking brake, component 16.7,
    lever 5.7, winter 13.19
Passing, advance no passing 2.3, 2.11,
    night 13.12 - 13.14, lines 2.17 - 2.20,
    rural 12.10 - 12.11, rules 3.6
Passive restraints, 11.3
Pavement markings, 2.23 - 2.24
    pedestrians 1.2, intersections 12.5
    right-of-way 3.7 - 3.9, signs 2.5 - 2.6
Pedestrian signals, 2.23 - 2.24
Perception distance, 10.3
Perception time, 10.3
Peripheral, 4.10, tunnel vision 4.11
Perpendicular parking, 5.21
Physical condition, 4.2 - 4.4
Planning a trip, 18.1 - 18.6

Posted speed limit, 2.4
Potholes, 13.2 - 13.3
Power brakes, 16.7, failure 14.7
Power steering, 16.6, failure 14.5
Power train, 15.11
Predict, 8.3 - 8.4
Prepare, 7.2
Pre-driving protocol, 6.3
Premium (insurance), 17.8 - 17.9
Prescription drugs, 4.3 - 4.4
Prohibitory signs, 2.6
Pumping the brakes, 10.5

R

Radiator, 15.4
Radiator cap, 15.4
Railroad crossing, signs 2.3, 2.11,
Rain, 13.6 - 13.8
Reaction distance, 10.3
Reaction time, 10.2
Rear-end collision, 14.12
Rear-view mirror, 6.5, glare 13.10
Registration, 3.3
Regulatory signs, 2.2, 2.3 - 2.7
Reversing, 7.12 - 7.13
Right-of-way, 3.7 - 3.9, 12.3
Roadside services, signs 2.14
Road surface, adverse 13.2 - 13.9,
    traction 9.3
Route markers, 2.13
Rules of the road, 3.6 - 3.9
Rural driving, 12.1, 12.10 - 12.11

S

SADD, 4.8
Safety belts, facts 11.6, light/buzzer 5.3,
    usage 11.1 - 11.3
Scan, 8.2, intersections 12.5
School bus, signs 2.8, stop for 3.8
Seat adjustment, 6.4
Selector lever, 5.8
Separate hazards, 8.6
Shifting technique, 7.8 - 7.11
    downshifting, 7.11, 13.4 - 13.5
Shock absorbers, 16.5
Signal lights, 2.22 - 2.24
SIPDE system, 8.2 - 8.6, strategy 10.4
Skids, 14.10 - 14.11
Smog, 13.14 - 13.15
Snow, 13.15 - 13.20
Space, from parked vehicles,, 12.2
    managing 8.4 - 8.5, stopped 12.3
Spark plug, 15.7
Speed limit, 2.4
Speedometer, 5.3
Springs, 16.5
Stall, engine 14.5, in winter 13.20,
    on railroad tracks 14.5
Standard transmission 15.11, basics 5.9,
    entering traffic 7.7, usage 7.8 - 7.11
Starting a vehicle 7.2 - 7.3, cold 7.3,
    flooded 7.3, glow plug 7.2, 15.8,
Steering control, 5.6, 7.4
Steering system 5.6, components 16.6,
    failure 14.6
Stimulants, 4.4
Stopping distance, 10.1 - 10.4, 12.3

Sun glare, visors, 13.15
Survival kit, 13.17
Suspension system, 16.5
Swerving, 12.2
Switchbacks, 13.5

T

Tachometer, 5.3
Tailgate, 8.5, 12.2
Taillights, 5.4
Temperature gauge (light), 5.3,
    system 15.4 - 15.5
Three point turn, on road 12.18
    Back into driveway 12.15 - 12.16,
    drive into driveway 12.17
Threshold braking, 10.5
Tires, construction 16.2 - 16.4,
    traction 9.2 - 9.3, winter 13.16
Towing insurance 17.9
Traction, 9.2 - 9.3, aids in winter 13.20
Trailer, 18.4
Tread, 16.2 - 16.4
Tune-up, 15.7 - 15.8, winter 13.15 - 16
Turnabout, 12.15 - 12.18
Turns, left turns 2.6, 2.18, 2.20
    maneuvers, right turn 12.6 - 12.7,
    left turn 12.7 - 12.9
Turn signal, hand 2.26, lever 5.5,
    lights 5.3, pre-driving checks 6.2,
    rules 3.6
Two second rule, SIPDE 8.5,
    techniques 12.2

U

Uninsured motorist insurance, 17.8
Uphill, 7.11, 9.3 - 9.4, 13.4
Urban driving 12.1, 12.9
Used vehicle, 17.4 - 17.6
U-turn, 12.15

V

Vapor lock, 13.5
Vehicle failure, 14.2 - 14.8
Vehicle registration, 3.2
Velocitization, expressway 12.13,
    leaving an expressway 12.14
Ventilation, 6.5
Violations, violators 3.4 - 3.6
Visibility, 13.9 - 13.14
Vision, 4.7 - 4.9, fog 13.14 - 13.15,
    night vision 13.8 - 13.12
Visual eye lead time, SIPDE 8.2

W

Warning signs, 2.2, 2.8 - 2.12
Warranty, 17.4
Water 13.6 - 13.8, immersion 14.14
Wet brakes, 13.7
Wind, 13.8 - 13.9
Windshield, adverse conditions 13.1,
    dirty 13.10, pre-driving check 6.2,
    winter 13.16, wiper failure 14.4,
    wiper/washer control 5.5
    Winter accessories 13.16 - 13.17

Y

Yellow signal, 2.22 - 2.23
Yield, 2.3, rules 3.6 - 3.9